BILL SNYDER

They Said It Couldn't Be Done

*An Inside Look At The Man, The Coach And
The Greatest Turnaround In College Football History*

By Mark Janssen *with* Bill Snyder

KCI SPORTS VENTURES, LLC
CHAMPAIGN, IL

CREDITS

ISBN: 0-9758769-6-1

Published By:
KCI Sports, LLC
2005 Emerald Drive
Champaign, IL 61822

Publisher: Peter J. Clark
Managing Editor: Molly Voorheis
Developmental Editor: Thomas Mocadlo
Photo Editor: Kristofor Hanson
Cover Design: Terry Neutz Hayden
Book Layout and Design: Terry Neutz Hayden
Sales & Marketing: Bret D. Kroencke, Janet Perkins
Media & Promotions: Tim Young, Matt Ashmore, Rich Bristow

Front Cover Photos: Courtesy of Kansas State Sports Information Office and John LeBarge

Insert Photos: Courtesy of the Bill Snyder family, Chris Hanewinckel, George Olendorf and the Kansas State Sports Information Office.

Printed and bound by Worzalla Publishing, Stevens Point, WI

DEDICATION

To my family. They are my life and I love them more than one would ever imagine possible. I love you, Sharon. I love you, Sean and Wanda. I love you, Shannon. I love you, Meredith and Bryan. I love you, Ross. I love you, Whitney. I love you, Katherine. I love you, Tate. I love you, Matthew. I love you, Sydney. I love you, Alexis. I love you, Gavin. I love you, Kadin.

And in loving memory of my mother, father, grandmother, and grandfather, whose love, caring and diligence guided my life.

— BILL SNYDER

In memory of my father; with love for my mother; with love and pride in Peg; Travis, Christy and Avery; Kelly and Presley.

— MARK JANSSEN

ACKNOWLEDGEMENTS

The authors wish to offer a very special thank you to the following for their assistance in the production of this book:

Kansas State University Sports Information Director Garry Bowman, George Olendorf, Bob Ross, *The Manhattan Mercury*, Eric Barton, Hayden Fry, General Richard B. Myers, Joan Friederich, Sean Snyder, Tom Ross, Jim Colbert, Bob Krause, Jon Wefald, Jack Vanier, Ernie Barrett and Pat Roberts.

FOREWORD

It was another fall day and another football game, this time between Kansas State and the University of Oklahoma. In spite of another dismal season, there were several thousand students in the stands. No one expected us to win. But when we finally scored late in the fourth quarter in another lopsided loss, a mere touchdown was enough for celebration and a trip to Aggieville for a brew.

That was in the early 1960s, and we students at the time took solace in the fact we had great basketball teams. But that fact didn't quite offset our dashed hopes, season after season, as our football team worked its way to the first Division IA team to log 500 losses.

Then in the mid-1980s something remarkable happened. Dr. Jon Wefald was chosen as our university president. One of his first and most brilliant decisions was to hire Bill Snyder to coach our hapless Wildcats. And the rest, as they say, is history. No doubt the close relationship and friendship between Dr. Wefald, the team owner, and the coach was key in the success that followed.

Universities are diverse communities and have many moving parts. Excellence demands all the parts of the organization work well. Organizations can survive not being their best or losing more than they win on occasion, but it's absolutely unacceptable to be the worst over a long stretch of time. Repeated failure, even in one part of an organization, doesn't engender pride; and that is a slippery slope to mediocrity, and often not just in the sports department.

The importance of athletics is open to debate at institutions where the emphasis is necessarily on academics. But in my view, Coach Snyder's contribution at Kansas State went far beyond the successes on the green turf of Bill Snyder Family Stadium. By any measure, in the Snyder era all the important trend lines were up-academic successes, enrollment, alumni support, and monetary contributions to the university. Clearly this wasn't all Coach Snyder's doing, but he was a major force in bringing back pride in our institution, cohesion in our university community, and a winning attitude. These are powerful forces.

Coach Snyder also showed a great respect for the young men he coached, respect for the game, and an understanding of where the game of football fits in the game of life. His Midwest values stood him in good stead. Like many Wildcats I'm sure, I had a sense of pride just seeing his demeanor on the sideline, winning or losing. He always showed great discipline and remained calm even in the most stressful situations. He never stopped mentoring or coaching. The many young lives he touched and helped shape on and off the field will no doubt be one of his most important legacies.

As a military officer I studied leadership during my entire 40 plus year career. Coach Snyder has, as we say, lots of leadership molecules, and it was only his great leadership skills that brought our football program out of its predicament. He had the fundamentals down cold: from a vision, goals, hard work, and discipline come success, and from success comes pride. Changing the culture and instilling a winning attitude were not easy and required great perseverance and confidence, confidence in himself, his assistants, and the young men he worked with year after year. It also required the confidence of the university leadership. This remarkable effort continued to build on itself until you have the vibrant environment you feel the minute you set foot on the Kansas State campus today.

Whenever coaching legends are talked about, Coach Snyder's name will come up often. He showed us all what is possible through great leadership and a great value system, and he has left a legacy at Kansas State University that has gone far beyond the football field. This good and decent man changed the course of history at a major university and instilled a pride and winning attitude that all past, present and future Wildcats will cherish for a long, long time!

— Richard B. Myers
General, USAF, Ret.

FOREWORD

Without question, Bill Snyder is one of the most highly successful football coaches in America. A Hall of Fame coach? Without question. All he has to do is wait the five years to become eligible.

I remember talking to Kansas State's athletic director when I was head coach at Iowa and telling him, "If you talk to Bill Snyder, you'll hire Bill Snyder."

That's the way it was with me when I first hired him at North Texas State. I had received this playbook from a young assistant at Austin College, and just marveled at how complete it was. He had diagrams of pass patterns and reasons behind each play. I remember thinking, "This guy is good."

I've sent 26 assistants to head coaching positions in both college and professional football, and Bill Snyder is right at the top of that list. First, the man is such a gentleman. But he also possesses a passion for what he is doing and a love for the players he is coaching. He is so intelligent, but in addition to that, he's a perfectionist with everything that he does. He is a great communicator, a tremendous recruiter and a wonderful teacher.

Even though Kansas State University was at the bottom of the barrel in college football, there was no doubt in my mind that Bill would turn that program around. Now, did I think he would turn it around to the degree that he did? I don't know of anyone who believed it was possible to do what Bill did, to the degree he did, for the period of time he did it.

This book is a fitting tribute to a rare person: a man who is a workin' dude and a winner. I hope young coaches read this story and find inspiration in a man who did it the right way and was as successful as they come.

— Hayden Fry,
Former head coach, University of Iowa

CONTENTS

"Occasionally, a coach comes along and does the impossible. Coach Bill Snyder did exactly that at Kansas State University. In 1976, I took over a downtrodden Florida State University program and the only team we could beat was Kansas State. After Bill Snyder arrived, FSU, and nobody else, wanted a piece of them. Coach Snyder has retired, but he leaves a legacy and protégés to keep the spirit of Bill Snyder alive."

— **BOBBY BOWDEN**, *Head Coach, Florida State University*

"Bill Snyder is an obvious Hall of Fame coach. His accomplishments speak louder than words. But more importantly, he is a Hall of Fame person. It was an honor to coach with him, and against him."

— **DAN McCARNEY**, *Head Coach, Iowa State University*

"I don't think anybody in America has done a better job taking a program that was down and building it up to a program of national prominence. I can't think of anybody who has even equaled what he has done, let alone bettered what he has done."

— **DeLOSS DODDS**, *Athletic Director, University of Texas (former KSU AD)*

"Bill is a guy I admire very much, both as a person and as a football coach. I hope we have young people who are coming into it with the same type of commitment to what college football is all about and not necessarily how much money they are going to make."

— **JOE PATERNO**, *Head Coach, Penn State University*

"Starting at Kansas State with Coach Snyder at a young age gave me the foundation I needed and developed me as a coach. I am very thankful for that."

— **BOB STOOPS**, *Head Coach, University of Oklahoma*

"Coach Snyder has set a standard of excellence in college coaching that serves as a model for all of us. He has impacted the lives of many people, including mine."

— **MARK MANGINO**, *Head Coach, University of Kansas*

"Bill Snyder won where it was impossible to win, but that's underselling the accomplishment. Bill Snyder's success changed a university's culture and the way Kansas State viewed itself not unlike Oklahoma under Bud Wilkinson and Alabama under Bear Bryant."

— **BLAIR KERKHOFF**, *Kansas City Star*

"He's not the coach of the year, he's not the coach of the decade, he's the coach of the century!"

— **BARRY SWITZER**, *former Head Coach, University of Oklahoma*

INTRODUCTION

I'm not very complicated. I am what you see, I believe.

— BILL SNYDER

Bill Snyder has been thrown plenty of penalty flags in life, but each time, he's turned them into first-downs, if not touchdowns. He grew up in a single-parent family but lived according to his mother's expectations. He turned a nearly straight-F first-semester at the University of Missouri into solid B's the next three years at William Jewell College. He climbed the ladder from prep football coach to coach of the greatest turnaround in college football history at Kansas State University.

In each area of life, he refused to accept a no-can-do attitude. Instead, with each challenge, his sole mission was to find a solution to the next task. He conquered a series of personal life-altering moments and won; he took over Kansas State's football program and did the seemingly impossible in elevating it to elite status.

He's a man of 66 years but to this day he has a sincere appreciation for the movie *Pinocchio*. A pattern of life? Perhaps.

In *Pinnochio*, a woodcarving chap named Geppetto crafts a puppet, Pinocchio, out of a slab of wood, with passion, persistence and consistency. Snyder plays the role of Geppetto; the Kansas State University football program was his Pinocchio. From no more than a hunk of driftwood evolved a creation in Wildcatland that few believed possible.

Okay, let's be honest. It was an accomplishment no one believed possible. No, not even the ever-optimistic K-State President Jon Wefald, who said, "History didn't have to happen the way it did. We should thank our blessings it turned out like it did. It doesn't hurt to be a little lucky."

Check it out if you like, but upon Snyder's arrival at Kansas State prior to the 1989 season, the Wildcat 93-year football record was a miserable 299-510-40. No program at the time— none, nada, zippo—had a poorer won-loss record in NCAA Division I history than Kansas State.

So why? Why would this 49-year-old highly successful offensive coordinator from the University of Iowa risk his football reputation by accepting the challenge in a location dubbed "Futility U." by *Sports Illustrated*?

"A diminutive IQ," quips Snyder.

But seriously, why?

Interrupting the question, Snyder, 17 seasons removed from first saying "I do" to the Kansas State University program, explained:

"I believed in the people. Yes, the program was down, but I guess I asked myself the question, 'Why couldn't Kansas State win? Why did the past have to dictate the future?' As far as having 500 losses and all the history that went with Kansas State football, I wasn't concerned with that."

Snyder's legendary accomplishments in his 17 years with the Wildcats have given hope to athletic teams across the country, to entrepreneurs with even a spark of an idea that might lead to riches and fame.

Yes, dreams can come true.

Snyder's blueprint for success—a simplistic concoction designed by a less-than-model student at Lafayette High School in St. Joseph, Missouri, and certainly not by your 5-star player on the playing field at nearby William Jewell College—allowed the realization of a personal vision. How did Snyder achieve such greatness?

"If you're asking me to point to one thing, I would say perseverance," Snyder said. "In this profession, if a problem hasn't knocked on your door today, then hang on because it's coming. Especially in those early days, there were a lot of knocks on the door. There was just a bombardment of issues and concerns that we could not put a hold on. You had to have the perseverance to hang on."

Hang on, and have the innate ability to focus morning, noon and night. An ability, Snyder says, he developed over time by going from six hours of focus, to eight, to 12, to 15-plus hours a day.

"Today they call that multi-tasking," Snyder said. "But I believe all head football coaches, if they want to be successful, need to have the ability to do that."

At Kansas State University, it's a focus, an attention to detail, a work ethic that was the only way "The Miracle In Manhattan" could be accomplished.

Rick Baker, President of the Cotton Bowl, said, "Coach Snyder will always be the standard for turning around a football program. The job he did at Kansas State will be the measuring stick for all other programs across the country."

When Snyder left the comfort of being an assistant at the University of Iowa for the unknown at Kansas State, he knew it would be a life-changing moment. Little did Kansas State University know that it too would undergo a change that would alter the status of football on campus forever.

The ever positive Champions Tour golfer and KSU alumnus, Jim Colbert, had warned Snyder early in his stay at Kansas State that after his early success of five, seven, and five wins in 1990 through 1992, it might be wise to get out while the gettin' was good.

The former Wildcat golfer said, "We weren't close friends at that time, but I was just trying to be his friend and told him that he had already done the impossible and that the program would never get much better than it was at that time. I think all he did was smile, and say, 'okay.'"

The next year, Kansas State became a nine-game winner and advanced to the Copper Bowl in Tucson, Arizona.

As Colbert remembers, "I had just gotten back to the hotel lobby from playing golf and had my 'Jim Colbert' golf bag sitting in front of me. Now, I'm not sure if Snyder would have remembered me otherwise, but as the team's walking out to the buses, here comes Coach.

"He never broke stride, barely looking over at me. All he said was, 'And you said it couldn't be done.'"

Chapter One
The Early Years

As a child growing up, I was energetic, eager, caught up in sports of every kind. I was somewhat shy, but considerate of people. That's always been a trait that my mother taught me. I was a good worker in areas where I wanted to be a good worker.

— Coach Bill Snyder

Focus?

Discipline?

No, what the definition of Bill Snyder is today are bits of the English language that had little to do with the first 18-plus years of Billy Dean Snyder's life.

With the exception of references to Snyder on the football field, basketball court, baseball diamond or swimming pool lanes, focus, discipline, and attention to detail were words that were rarely used to describe Bill Snyder.

"Knowing him as a kid," laughed Dick Sipe, a childhood friend, "never, never, never would I have thought he would become the person he's become."

Born to Tom and Marionetta on October 7, 1939, in St. Joseph, Missouri, Bill Snyder moved with his parents to Chicago as an infant, where his dad worked as a salesman for the Certain-Teed Roofing Company. The family moved to Kansas City for a short period, and then briefly returned to St. Joseph, where they lived with Grandma and Grandpa Snyder.

The Snyder home, located on King Hill Avenue, was five blocks from the stockyards and two blocks from the fire department.

"I remember my grandfather and I would walk to the firehouse where he knew some of the firemen, and I would go up in the loft area and then slide down the pole," Snyder reminisced.

The next move would be to Salina, Kansas, where the family would reside at a duplex on the west end of Crawford Street until Bill was in the first grade. Admiringly, Snyder recalls his as a tough-love family.

"I got in a fist fight once and came home crying," Snyder reflected. "My father said, 'You go back out there and don't come back until you stand up to him.' So I did, and got beat up again. But at least I didn't get a spanking."

There was the day that Bill snuck off without permission to the city swimming pool. When captured, he was ushered to his home where his dinner was waiting: "I can still hear my mother saying, 'You eat and then go downstairs to see your father.' I knew I'd receive a spanking, so I ate everything I could get my hands on. I wasn't a big eater, but that night I ate and ate and ate and did so slowly," Snyder said with a laugh. "I was even eating ketchup with a spoon."

His parents divorced when he was seven, so Snyder has few memories of his father, but said his mother always spoke well of him.

Tom Snyder later landed in Omaha, Nebraska, where, according to his son, he started running with a "faster crowd … good people, but a faster crowd."

In 1967, at the age of 47, he was killed when he lost control of the car he was driving and hit a bridge. The coroner's report was uncertain as to whether he died from the accident or perhaps a heart attack preceding the crash.

Bill Snyder, 28 at the time and coaching in the prep ranks in California, learned of the news via a telephone call from his mother.

"My father's death was painful, but it wasn't like I had an on-going relationship with him," said Snyder, who did return from the west coast to attend the funeral. "I went to see him when he lived in Omaha, but those were short visits, mainly just going out to dinner clubs with him and his wife. He enjoyed sports, but we didn't go to ball games, and he never came to any of my games when I was in high school."

Bill and his mother moved from Salina to St. Joseph, a railroading and meat-packing community located 50-some miles north of Kansas City. With its western limits resting alongside the banks of the Missouri River, it was a community of nearly 70,000 and known as the locale where gunslinger Jesse James was killed.

For Snyder, St. Joseph was where persistence and perfectionism were nurtured, with his mother, plus her father, Grandpa George Owens, doing most of the mentoring.

"She was a stickler for having everything in its proper place and doing things right," Snyder said of his mother. "Our apartment wasn't much, but it was always clean. I wasn't the neatest kid in the world, but when it was time, I'd clean up my area because it was also her area."

Mother and son lived their life in a one-room residence, part of a large house located at 508 North Rubidaux Street that was built around the 1850s and modernized into multiple apartments by the mid-1940s.

The Snyder's second-story room, which included a bathroom and a tiny kitchenette, served as the living room/bedroom for both, with Marionetta sleeping on a roll-away, and her son on a Murphy bed. Only when the bed was pulled out of the wall would Bill's room come to life. The single partition was decorated with St. Louis and New York baseball pennants and baseball cards. During the winter, a multi-angled coat-hanger served as a basketball goal through which Snyder shot taped-up socks.

In a matter of fact tone, Snyder said, "When I put my bed up, my bedroom disappeared."

Marionetta, who died at the age of 77 in 1997, was a tiny lady, no more than 4-11 and never seeing 100 pounds. However, her only son vividly remembers, "She was stout when she wanted to be. There were times when she would stand in front of the door when I was trying to leave and I knew it wasn't happening. I wasn't getting through that door."

Marionetta had the reputation of being a classy, well-manicured woman, who worked as a clerk and a buyer at the highly respected Townsend and Wall Company, in its time a high-end department store in downtown St. Joe.

"She worked hard. If my work ethic came from anyone, it came from my mother," Snyder said.

In a single-parent home, funds were tight, and without a car, Marionetta walked to work each day from that one-room home on the corner of 5th and Rubidoux. Of his mother never having a driver's license, Snyder said, "When I was 16 and could drive, I gave her one lesson. Apparently that was enough for her. She looked at me and said, 'I will walk.'"

The Snyders lived on the minimum, but that was fine. They shared an attitude that "if you didn't have it, you didn't miss it. I never felt short-changed. I thought we were doing fine. I was never embarrassed by how we lived. I was proud of it."

Snyder recalls with fondness the simplicity of his life. The Sunday chicken dinners served around the dining room table of the Owens', often followed by a lazy car ride that would end up at Ozenberger's for ice cream.

He remembers being the tinsel hanger for the Christmas tree, and buying his mother packages of five-cent hair pins as gifts. His annual handmade Christmas card to his mother would include coupons redeemable for completion of chores, such as doing the dishes or cleaning the apartment.

He remembers the first TV in the house, a 13-inch rabbit-eared black-and-white set purchased in 1957, or as Snyder recalls, "The year that Kansas and Wilt Chamberlain played North Carolina in the NCAA Tournament."

Snyder enjoyed watching shows like *Howdy Doody, Roy Rogers,* and, of course, *Superman.* In all honesty, though, he preferred to be outside throwing a ball against a wall than watching television or listening to a game on the radio.

From his mother, Snyder said, "I learned how to present myself, how to work hard and for long hours. She was a competitive woman, but in such a mild way.

"My grandfather was a pretty strong guy as well. He didn't interfere often, but when he said you needed to do something, it was understood that it needed to be done," Snyder reflected. "He was an honest individual. Blatantly honest, and a very caring man."

Snyder said his grandfather never finished high school, but was a most intelligent man, especially when it came to common sense.

"He could make sense out of almost anything," Snyder said. "It didn't take him 500 words to define what he wanted to say. He was to the point, and said things with humor."

At the age of 101, that humor was still present as Owens was quizzed about his age by a visiting reporter.

"Doesn't really make much difference at this age, does it?" he replied. And as an accompanying photographer asked Owens to move to a better background for a picture, he quipped, "Who cares about the background, I'm pretty enough."

Snyder said his grandfather was a very religious man, to the point that during his final years people from the King Hill Baptist Church, where he attended, would ask him to pray for them.

"His friends strongly believed that he had the power to talk to God and get things to happen a little quicker," said Snyder, who himself attended Sunday school at Trinity Methodist Church when he was growing up.

Of his grandfather's death, Snyder said, "I honestly believe he just thought it was time. His two children and his wife had died before him, and I honestly think he just said, 'It's time to go and be with them. I've done all I can do.'"

Both Snyder's mother and grandfather had an uncanny knack of teaching values without attempting to be "too fatherly or motherly."

A railroader by trade, Grandfather Owens also dabbled in the used car business, giving the 12-year-old Snyder his first job, washing cars for 25 cents per auto.

Just weeks prior to Owens' death on September 19, 1996, he described his grand-son as being "a little bull-headed" as a youth, but caring enough as an adult to trav-el on a weekly basis to the Heartland Hospital in St. Joseph "just to say hi to me. He called me all the time from Pittsburgh, Philadelphia—there's no telling where he might call from, but he always seemed to have 1,001 things on his mind," said Owens.

Growing up, Snyder first attended Hall Elementary School, but later moved to nearby Washington Elementary School where he became a teammate of Sonny Younger on an 8th grade basketball team.

Both Younger and Snyder were fine athletes. The twosome would help lead their team to the city recreational title, plus team up on the premier Goetz Junior fast-pitch softball team that won the Missouri state title.

No matter the sport, Younger recalled, "Bill was a kid who would compete. He would stick his nose in there and play hard. Always fair, but hard, and he would compete to win."

Compete to win he did. From every activity offered at the YMCA, Snyder's home away from home, to the two- and three-day Monopoly games and marble matches that dominated the neighborhood, Snyder would accept nothing short of victory.

"Our marble games were like gambling," Snyder chuckled. "Every marble you knocked out of the circle, you kept. I had cans full of those things."

The YMCA would offer tournaments where youngsters would receive points for placing first, second or third in a particular competition. The individual with the most points would then be allowed to attend summer camp. More summers than not, the point system was the way Snyder punched his ticket for camp. If he didn't attain enough points through competition, he would go door-to-door selling soap to earn his way to Camp Hillyard.

"That was the only way I was ever going to go to camp, so I took it seriously," Snyder said. "I learned at an early age, if you want something badly enough, and you are willing to work hard, you can accomplish your goals."

Everything Snyder did, he took seriously and worked hard at, from playing tackle football on the brick street in front of his home to racking up big numbers with his baseball card collection.

Living two-plus miles from the elementary school, Marionetta gave her son 35 cents bus fare each morning. He was to walk three blocks to catch the bus to school, which was a nickel each way, and use the remaining 25 cents for his lunch.

"I saved my coins," Snyder said. "I would put my bicycle out of sight to the side of the porch and ride it to school. I don't remember how I would get out of school, but when lunch time came I would go to a nearby grocery store and buy those bubblegum trading cards with my bus and lunch money."

Eventually, Marionetta caught on to what her son was doing. Snyder recalled, "My bicycle was put on hold. My mother always had a consequence, and I appreciated that."

Chapter Two
A Hoodlum Priest

I loved sports, but academics I probably didn't give much of a chance. I was focused on athletics and competitive-type things. I liked woodworking, but that was about the only class I did put an effort in. In sports, I enjoyed them all, but I wasn't good enough to have any kind of ego issues. I enjoyed the game for the game itself.

— Coach Bill Snyder

While Snyder denies the label, his buddies said he was considered a prep star for the Irish of Lafayette High School.

"Man oh man, was he a natural," said buddy Dick Sipe. "He just played everything so effortlessly. Guys like me would be tripping and falling, but he not only did everything, he did everything so well. He didn't seem to have to work. The talent was just there."

Teammate Sonny Younger added, "He was so versatile. Just a natural."

Another childhood pal, Bob Ross, remembers his Irish teammate for being ambidextrous: "He was left-handed, but he could do all the same things with his right hand."

In football, Snyder earned all-city and all-Pony Express Conference honors as a spinner-back, starting on the varsity as a sophomore in Lafayette's single-wing offense coached by Jerry Hampton.

"He would come across on a reverse and throw that left-handed pass," Hampton said of the 88-reverse play. "When I got there, they were already using a single-wing, but if not, I would have had Bill as my quarterback in a Wing-T."

Hampton called Snyder a "tremendous leader," but added, "You would have liked him to be a little more disciplined. Everybody liked him. He had that confidence that if he had called a play, everyone would have thought it was the right play."

Snyder was never better than when playing cross-town rival Benton High School in a 19-6 win in his junior season.

"I had two long runs, plus threw a touchdown pass," Snyder said. "I remember I was so excited and just jabbered away in the huddle until one of the seniors told me to "shut up, the game's not over."

Was Snyder an athlete with 4.5 40-speed? "You might want to reverse those numbers," Snyder confessed.

In whatever the sport of season, friends remember an early hint of the focus that he later displayed as a coach.

Rival Central High School athlete George Olendorf remembers his first unofficial meeting with Snyder at a city tourney staged at the City Auditorium.

Having played in the first game of a double-header, Olendorf was leaving the auditorium when he looked back courtside: "I saw Bill Snyder bringing the ball down the court. I was amazed at how he was surveying the court. His concentration. You could see it in his eyes. It was something I hadn't seen before. I never forgot it."

The favorite shot for the 5-11 Snyder was a sweeping hook shot coming across the lane, perfected during his middle-school years on the Washington Elementary School playground when playing against older and bigger kids.

Swimming was Snyder's best sport, but he also took part in all the events track and field had to offer, and was a first baseman, centerfielder and pitcher on the diamond, once attending a tryout camp of the Kansas City Athletics.

"Good glove, no hit," said Snyder of his left-handed throwing, but right-handed hitting abilities. "The tryout was a short-lived experience."

Best friend George Jones said, "Oh, he was a quality baseball player. I'll never forget one time a runner was coming down the first base line and Bill caught the ball and reached behind his back to make the tag. He was such a natural. I don't think many kids would have had the awareness to do that, but Bill just did it naturally."

As gifted as Snyder was athletically, he was equally crafty. It wasn't unusual for Snyder and pals to sneak into the YWCA for basketball play on Sundays when the YMCA was closed. And when they were run out of that gym, there was always the nearby church that had a small gymnasium where play would resume until caught again.

Snyder also demonstrated his slyness at the St. Joseph City Auditorium where professional wrestling bouts took place. Snyder remembers finding a back door he could slide through so he wouldn't have to pay for his ticket. It was on one of those nights, after the bouts, that Snyder experienced a life-altering moment.

"I was back in one of the hallways where the wrestlers went to dress after their match. Through this crack in one of the doors, I saw the two guys I had just seen beating the tar out of one another straddling the same wooden bench with a bottle of liquor between them," Snyder said, reliving the moment. "That broke my heart. Until that moment, I always thought those matches were real."

As for showing that same ingenuity for reading, writing and arithmetic—now that was a different story. B grades were celebrated, C's and D's were the rule.

"I often said if there were entrance exams to get into college in those days, I wouldn't have been considered," Snyder said.

Of course, it might have helped if Snyder would have gone to school on a consistent basis instead of having a serious case of 'who cares' about academics. It wasn't unusual for Snyder to leave for school about the same time his mother left for work, but after a wave good-bye, Bill would make a u-turn and head back to the apartment.

Comparing Snyder's days at Lafayette to today, former assistant principal Basil Hoehn smiles and chuckles as he says, "I'd say there's been a turnaround in Bill's life." A total turnaround?

"Well, I wasn't going to say that, but yes, a total turnaround," laughed Hoehn, who said that multiple times he hosted Snyder in Lafayette High's in-house suspension.

But Hoehn did add, "Bill always responded favorably to a negative situation. If he was wrong, he knew it and admitted it. He didn't flaunt not going to school, he just didn't like going. He wasn't into education."

So, Hoehn would call Marionetta, and then would go to the Snyders' apartment, knock on the door and announce, "Mr. Snyder, you have 15 minutes to be in the building."

"I had all the respect in the world for that man," said Snyder, not denying a word of the story. "He had a consequence for my actions. In his case, it was staying after school, which meant taking athletics away from me. That was the quickest way to get my attention. He was a good man, a fair man."

Hampton, who was just a 24-year-old head coach at the time, liked to call his star footballer "the hoodlum priest."

"He wasn't a worthless guy," Hampton said. "He had a great sense of humor, but just didn't seem to know the importance of the classroom."

In looking at Snyder as a head coach later in life, Hampton said, "One thing is for sure. His players won't be able to put anything over on him. He's been there, done that. He knows all the tricks. He really was a hoodlum priest."

No one argues that many of Snyder's non-athletic minutes of the day weren't planned. He would wake up and do whatever came along. And it's not as though Snyder was a bad kid, who was constantly dodging the long arm of the law, but as Bob Ross remembers, "Like the rest of us, we weren't real motivated to be the best we could be. We all had a beer now and then, and did some things we shouldn't have, but none of us were bad guys."

Still, Marionetta, who didn't continue her education past high school, did as well as she could in cracking the whip when absolutely necessary.

"We would talk about the importance of academics at home in the evenings, but it was usually a pretty one-sided conversation," Snyder said. "I wasn't doing much to uphold my end of the bargain."

As he turned 16, Snyder received a nearly new yellow Mercury convertible from his father.

With his mother frowning at the gift from day one, and her son showing the lack of maturity to handle such a ride, Snyder recalls, "My mother called my father and said, 'You come get this car and I'm not asking you.' My father had no choice but to come get the car. My mother did right."

By working for his grandfather and teaching swimming lessons, Snyder saved enough money to purchase his second car, a 1946 black Chevrolet. Fifty bucks was the cost for his "pride and joy" vehicle.

Of Snyder's purchase off his own car lot, Grandfather Owens chuckled, "He got the ones I was glad to get rid of. He had several of them, and wherever they died, that's where he left them. Bill's not a mechanic. He could gas it, turn the key and that's about it!"

Ross tells of borrowing Snyder's car once to go from the swimming pool down to L.R. Violett's barber shop.

"Bill tossed me the keys, and said, 'Careful, the brakes aren't that hot,'" Ross said. "Well, I at least thought it had brakes, but God's truth, it had no brakes at all. To stop his car, I had to hit the curb and keep bouncing off it until the car stopped. But Bill had been driving that thing all over the country without brakes. Not even an emergency brake," Ross said.

Yes, this Billy Dean Snyder was the whole package. Friday night hero to, according to Coach Hampton, the most popular boy in school who chummed with a large group of classmates, including Judy Frederick, whom he would later marry.

Snyder denies the ladies man reputation by saying, "I didn't have girlfriends, but I had friends who were girls."

"He was so irresponsible. Oh my gosh!" said Frederick-Snyder, who now lives in Greenville, Texas. "To become as totally focused as he is today, it's really kind of funny."

As Younger said, in those days, it wasn't cool to be much of a ladies man. "We'd go down to Teen Town for dances, but most of the guys would stand around on the sideline while the girls would dance with each other, or dance with the guys who were a little, how do I want to say this, uncool."

Laughing, he said, "Let's see, there was a group of us who were cool by just standing around watching the uncool guys dance."

The stories get better with years, but Sipe laughs as he says, "Bill will laugh about some of the stories when we get together, but I think he would just as soon put some of them to rest."

While not the model citizen of St. Joseph, Snyder does remember his roots with fondness and loyalty.

Several weeks after his daughter Meredith was severely injured in a car accident in Dallas, Snyder kept a commitment to his home town to help kick off a fund-raising drive for a locker room in Lafayette High.

"Bill is very humanistic," Hoehn said. "He does a wonderful job of telling of his past in hopes that it doesn't happen to other young people."

Snyder also served as a pallbearer at the funeral of Skip Tillman, who in the mid-1950s was Lafayette High's first black letterman in football.

"I know some are surprised Bill turned out the way he did, but I'm not one of them," said Roland Tillman, Skip's younger brother. "If Bill ever committed to anything, you knew he would do it. If he said he was gong to make a watch, I knew he would do it and it would be a darn good one."

But instead of being a watch-maker, Snyder became a football coach. And a darn good one.

Chapter Three
The Coach Patterson Factor

What I did at Missouri was very painful for me. I had let my mother down, which is something I never wanted to do. She had invested so much into my education. She had saved, and she had gone without.

— Coach Bill Snyder

To today's recruiting gurus, Snyder was probably a 2-star recruit, if that. He had no scholarship offers out of Lafayette High and was in limbo with where life was going to take him. A St. Joseph banker who had contacts with the Missouri Tiger football program called the Dan Devine coaching staff, with the end result being an invitation for Snyder to try out for the freshman team that numbered over 100 players.

Al Onofrio, who would later become the Tigers' head coach, was the freshman coach, and had Snyder inked in at—"This is the truth," Snyder says—10th team quarterback.

"That's not 10th team overall, that was 10th team among the freshmen," Snyder emphasized. "They played a T-formation, and I had never played anything but single-wing all my life. I had never had a hand under center."

Snyder said he's not sure if Onofrio ever said boo to him and that he was nothing more to the coaching staff than "that guy over there."

Not once did Snyder step on the field for a game, and he says his only claim to fame was beating out Ron Taylor, who was 11th team QB. Taylor, however, later became a three-year starter for Mizzou.

Snyder had to deal with more than just the challenges on the field. He explains, "I took 15 hours, and certainly didn't pass them all in my only semester at Missouri."

Could he have returned for a second semester?

"I don't know. I didn't stay around long enough to find out," he said. Grades were bad, football was bad, so for Snyder, "it didn't make any sense to stay and waste any more of my mother's money."

Leaving Missouri would be a turning point in Snyder's life because he had let his mother and grandfather down.

"I felt ashamed because I knew it was her hard-earned money that went to that semester of school," Snyder said. "My mother and grandfather were good about it. They didn't feel as badly about me as I did."

Snyder promised to make it up to them. Not financially, but he said he would continue to pursue his education and finish in four years. And he did. Calling himself a "slow learner," Snyder finally realized that if he wanted to continue to be active in sports, he had to be a decent student, too.

That was an important moment for Snyder, as was his introduction to William Jewell coach Norris Patterson, which came via his former high school coach, Jerry Hampton, who had played at William Jewell in 1952 and 1953.

"I just told Coach Patterson that Bill might be a good player for his single-wing, but he had to turn his life around academically," Hampton said. "It was amazing how someone without much discipline finally got the message."

Coach Patterson would become a mentor to Snyder, who to this day refers to him as either Doctor or Coach, depending on the setting.

"I appreciated the fact that while he didn't know me from anyone, he showed an interest, and was willing to take a chance after I had failed to do what I needed to do at Missouri."

It's why Snyder said he was thrilled to be inducted, along with Patterson, into the Missouri Sports Hall of Fame class of 2006.

"That was really an honor for me. He was such a mentoring individual. He was a great role model. He was always matter of fact in what he said, but had the knack of being encouraging when telling you the truth."

Patterson wasn't about to give Snyder a free ride, but he did encourage him to get his grades right at St. Joseph Junior College (now Missouri Western) and prove that he wanted to be a student-athlete for the first time in his life. Emphasis was placed on the "student" part of that label.

"I looked at his grades out of Missouri and just laughed," reflected Patterson, prior to his death in 2002. "To be truthful, I never gave him much of a chance of accepting that challenge."

The F's from Missouri turned to B's and C's in junior college, which paved the way for Snyder to join Patterson at William Jewell College in nearby Liberty, Missouri, where he would receive a B.A. in physical education and Spanish in 1963.

For Snyder, it was a time where, in his words, "I was just out on a limb. Here was a second chance and the realization of what an education meant. After I got pointed in the right direction, I was an okay student. It just took a while to get my competitive juices flowing academically."

While any teacher Snyder ever had in high school would have said he'd be wasting his time in college, Snyder enjoyed the challenge.

From day one, if someone told Snyder he couldn't do something, he made certain to find a way to complete the task, a trait he carried with him into coaching.

"There was never a doubt in my mind that I could get the grades because I knew that's what I had to do to be able to coach," Snyder said. "My life was centered around sports. I don't think there was ever a time in my life where I thought I would do anything but coach at some level. It just seemed to me: Play the game for as long as you can, and then go coach it."

Snyder, a slender 5-foot-11, 163 pounds, enrolled at William Jewell in the fall of 1960 and became a defensive back for the Cardinals, seeing occasional spot duty on offense when a halfback-pass was needed.

Snyder said he was basically a player who was in the right place at the right time, but to be honest, not too much more than that.

"I was pretty non-descript," Snyder said of his own abilities. "Nobody was throwing the ball back in those days, so I could sleep half the game as a defensive back and it would be okay."

While not a superstar athlete, Snyder was the type of player Coach Patterson had an appreciation for in that he knew the game and made the smallest detail important. While teaching plenty of X's and O's, Patterson also reinforced to Snyder the art of meeting people, which he had already learned from his mother.

Hampton tells the story of being with a friend on his way to enroll at Central Missouri State. The two made a quick stop to the William Jewell campus to see cousins, but were soon introduced to Coach Patterson.

"The man made us feel that he had been waiting for us all year long," Hampton said. "He seemed so interested in us, so caring. He's the main reason that I got into coaching."

Today, Snyder carries that same caring personality. He has a warmth and sincerity that makes a 30-second "hello, how are you" handshake with a total stranger into the highlight of that individual's day, week, or month. He has an innate ability to make the young feel mature and give the aging a spark of youthfulness.

Now, don't get the idea that young Mr. Snyder became a sit-in-the-first-row classroom nerd. To a certain degree, he kept that same Billy Dean ornery personality that he spent the first 18 years of his life perfecting.

At William Jewell, Snyder joined the Phi Gamma Delta fraternity where he lived for his first two years. Later, he moved across the street to a basement apartment that he shared with Olendorf, his old rival from Central High School, with whom he had become friends through competitive swimming.

"Awful! It was awful," Olendorf said of their bachelor pad. "I think we split $75 in rent."

Olendorf remembers Snyder as a dandy defensive back and highly competitive, no matter the activity. Olendorf recalls their softball games at Goetz Field in St. Joe. "Bill played first and I was the catcher," Olendorf said. "He threw that ball so damn hard it hurt my hand. Hurt to the point I really got mad at him. But every inning, he'd do the same thing. He would fire that softball as hard as he could.

"Finally I shouted at him, 'Bill, do you think there's a scout in the stands?'" Olendorf reflected. "I got so mad I'd sit at the other end of the bench from him. Between the lines, Bill was really one helluva competitor."

The friends lost touch with one another over the next 20-some years, until Olendorf was watching the 1986 Rose Bowl game. During the telecast, cameras zoomed in on the press box where Snyder was at work as the offensive coordinator of the Iowa Hawkeyes.

"I went, 'For God's sake! That's where he is,'" Olendorf said. "We've stayed in contact ever since."

Olendorf later dropped Snyder a congratulatory note after he had accepted the K-State coaching position. Today, Olendorf still treasures Snyder's response:

Received your note and apologize for this late response. Nothing is more important to me than hearing from friends like yourself, who care enough to write or call. It was great to hear from you.

This is certainly a monumental task here. The opportunity is unique and challenging, and one that I am enthused about. Leaving Iowa was not an easy task either. I have spent 10 of the finest years of my life there, and leave behind many fond memories and friends.

I hope all is well with you and that you enjoy a pleasant holiday season.

Thanks for being special.

Warm personal regards,

Bill

In the mid-1990s, Snyder returned to Liberty to give William Jewell's Achievement Day speech. "It was like a college president was talking," Patterson marveled. The influence Coach Patterson had on young Bill Snyder came to the forefront nearly forty-plus years later. The William Jewell coach had a slogan that he coached by, which was borrowed from Michelangelo. Written on Patterson's playbook were these words:

Little things are trifles;

Trifles make perfection;

Perfection's no trifle

Those same three lines were used by Snyder as a portion of his philosophy in turning around the K-State program.

RIGHT LEADER, RIGHT TIME

Having always thought we could win in football at Kansas State, I knew it would take leadership and support from the administration for it to happen, and it all came together in 1989 under Coach Snyder.

I used to joke with Coach about my philosophy of having won in the '50s under Bill Meek, and again in the '70s under Vince Gibson. His comment: "Sure hope we don't have to wait another 20 years."

"Wait" was not in Coach Snyder's plan.

Naturally, he made some demands in accepting the job, but those demands were realistic and because of the leadership and enthusiasm of (KSU president) Dr. Wefald, new facilities became a reality, as did the challenge to be competitive in the Big 8 and later the Big 12.

It took time, patience and a lot of long hours and dedication, but the reward for success was magnificent.

During his short 17 years at K-State, Bill Snyder captivated and motivated the people of the State of Kansas by setting an example for his players and K-Staters everywhere. He was a leader, and he demonstrated the discipline necessary to have his players ready for every contest.

Coach Snyder is a friend. A very good friend, and a true gentleman in every sense of the word.

He proved he was a champion, and he brought great success to Kansas State University!

— Ernie Barrett
Former KSU Athletic Director
Current KSU Director of Development

Chapter Four
He's Now Coach Snyder

With William Jewell being a liberal arts school, you had to take two years of Spanish. I learned how to write it, and how to read it, but was anything but conversational in it. Spanish ended up being my minor, and in my first teaching job I was teaching four classes in Spanish. I had classes for four, six, seven and 10 students.

— Coach Bill Snyder

Check out the northeast corner of Missouri where Highways 13 and 6 intersect. That's Gallatin. "Population, oh, about 1,000 at that time," said Snyder.

The 1962 school enrollment totaled about 100 for grades K-12. Snyder served as assistant coach for football, basketball and track (as well as bus driver), in addition to teaching a full load of classes—all for an annual salary of $3,600.

"I thought I had died and gone to heaven," Snyder said. "I was a coach and they were paying me $3,600."

But of those Spanish classes, Snyder said, "With anything I tried, I wanted to be good at it. I wanted to be a good Spanish teacher, but I had to do everything in my power as far as homework to try to stay one step in front of the students. I mean, I'd get sick to my stomach I was so anxious about it."

After one year at Gallatin, Coach Patterson hooked Snyder up with Joe Dixon, the athletics director at Eastern New Mexico University in Portales, New Mexico.

"You talk about a place being flat," Snyder said. "Portales is one of those places you can see everywhere from."

As a natural progression, Snyder was a graduate assistant in the physical education department, while working on a master's degree in physiology and physical education. Snyder breezed through the curriculum in a year and a summer, earning grades he had seldom seen—A's. Down playing the achievement, he joked, "I think it was one of those programs where you got either an A or an F."

With master's in hand, Snyder kept moving on, this time landing in the Coachella Valley, about two driving hours east of Los Angeles, where he taught at Indio High School, a school of about 1,800.

He would serve as head swimming coach, plus assist with football and basketball and teach physical education and Spanish. But this time the foreign language was going to be taught in a community where there was a population of Mexican-American green-card workers, who had come across the border for agricultural work.

"We had a major communication problem," Snyder said. "I went home that first night and did some serious soul-searching."

Snyder had two options. The first was to tell the principal he couldn't teach the class and risk losing his job. The second was to come up with a solution. With 37 students in the class, and more than half of those speaking only Spanish, Snyder came up with the idea of having the Spanish-speaking students teach the English-speaking students Spanish, and vice-versa.

"Basically, I just monitored their interaction for one semester," Snyder said.

Yes, he was a solution man, on and off the field. It was during this time that Snyder married Judy Frederick, his Lafayette High School friend, whom he had only started to date about three months prior to leaving for California.

"It was fine with my parents because they had known Bill for years," Frederick-Snyder said. "I admired Bill because I knew there was not a team, whether football or swimming, that he could not turn around. I really admired him for that."

She added, "I can remember as a young wife sitting in the stands and getting into more than one verbal confrontation with fans who were bad-mouthing my husband. I learned real fast that you weren't going to win that battle, and started sitting in front of the band so I couldn't hear them."

The Snyders, Bill 25 and Judy 24, would celebrate the birth of their three children—Sean, Shannon and Meredith—during the next 10 years in California. Judy remembers the early years as happy times, filled with side-trips to San Diego and Las Vegas. Was Snyder a good father?

"Probably not because I was away from home a lot," Snyder admitted.

Throughout Snyder's prep coaching days, he was just as much into swimming as he was football. He coached club swim teams, plus wrote articles for publications such as *Swimming Technique* and *Scholastic Coach*, with most of the articles focusing on the physiology of the sport.

Snyder next furthered his coaching career by going to USC in 1966 at a position that would today be known as a graduate assistant. Snyder figured he could get up close and personal with legendary USC coach John McKay, plus work on his doctorate in physiology.

While not included in many of the staff meetings, when given a chance, Snyder played the role of a sponge, learning everything he could about Trojan football.

"I was probably more of a nuisance than anything else," Snyder said. "I never knew what I was going to be asked to do from day to day. Many days it was nothing."

While thinking he knew his way around, Snyder quickly found out how naive he was about the USC environment heading into the season opener.

Prior to the first game, Snyder asked quarterback coach Craig Fertig about the game-day routine. Fertig—"who was in charge of keeping me out of the way"—told Snyder to just go through the tunnel into the Coliseum and that the locker room would be on the right.

With USC practices staged only on campus, Snyder had never been to the Coliseum, which is located about three blocks from the practice field. On the day of the first game, Snyder ran into some problems.

"I went over early to the practice field and started looking for this 'tunnel' that takes you underground to the Coliseum," Snyder said. "I kept looking and looking for an entrance into a tunnel, and now it's getting closer to game time and I'm having no luck finding this 'tunnel.'

"Finally, I just raced by foot over to a ticket gate at the Coliseum about four blocks away, but I assure you, nobody knew who Bill Snyder was. I had to plead for someone to go to the locker room and find Coach Fertig to send word that it was okay to let me into the stadium."

Much to Fertig's amusement, only then did Snyder find out the lore of "the tunnel" at the Coliseum.

Snyder's sideline task was to chart plays off of a television monitor. While thinking he was a factor in each USC win, he admitted, "Not once were my charts ever asked for."

Snyder's season ended much like it started. With the Trojans in the Rose Bowl against Purdue, Snyder remembers McKay looked over to one of his real assistants and said, "Make sure what's-his-name gets a couple of tickets."

Snyder liked McKay's swagger, which he toyed with copying.

"I found out real quick, this is not for me," Snyder said. "I had no swagger; I had no reason to have a swagger."

But the time on the field was well spent learning about USC's I-formation and the power sweeps.

"I was always amazed at how he could see it all happen in a practice environment," Snyder said of McKay. "He could stand behind the offense and see it all. Most people see just little portions."

Snyder returned to Indio High School in 1967 and 1968 as the head coach with the traits he utilized at Kansas State 30 years later already part of his repertoire at the age of 28.

"I went back there thinking I was John McKay and I was not John McKay," Snyder laughed. "I planned to out-work everyone, and I flat wore out my own coaches."

Entering the season, his coaches would meet in the morning, in the afternoon, and into the late hours of the night.

"It was nonsense, but I went to each coach telling him how to coach his position," Snyder said. "I think it almost got to the point of them saying, 'Okay, if you want to coach my players, then go ahead. I'm leaving.'"

It was around this time that Snyder began honing his unusual eating habits. He's never been a hearty breakfast man. His lunches? An apple or banana, maybe a handful of carrot or celery sticks to nibble on during his glides to and from meetings or his dates with a film projector. Rarely arriving at his home before 11 p.m., he would fix what he called "a substantial meal.'"

Defined?

"When I was young in coaching, I found a steamer that was the neatest thing in the world. All you had to do was pour water in it, dump the vegetables in, plug it in, wait eight minutes, and there was your meal. You would dump the water out, wash your fork, and you'd be ready for the next day."

But why not stop and take time out for lunch?

"You would be amazed how much you can accomplish over a noon hour when everyone else is gone." Pausing and smiling, he added, "As my wife says, a lot of people live to eat, I eat to live."

Indio had the total Trojan package, as Snyder installed the I-formation, the USC defense, and of course, "I was John McKay."

Snyder was so into making the most of every waking moment he sought out a hypnotist. He recalled a swimmer from Ohio State, Kenneth Copeland, who had gone from a 160-pound diver to a 5-foot-6, 350-pounder, who, according to Snyder, "didn't have an ounce of muscle on him."

Copeland had gone to a hypnotist to lose weight, which gave Snyder the idea of being put in a hypnotic state so he could work non-stop without sleep.

The hypnotist, somewhat surprised at Snyder's request, simply said, "We don't do that. We don't tamper with a person's health."

"Those were not some of my smarter days," Snyder admits.

They were days, however, when Snyder was already looking ahead to coaching at the college level. In fact, he decided that if he learned to fly a plane, he would have a recruiting advantage.

Snyder specifically remembers it being his "ninth hour" of training in a dual-controlled plane. On this particular Saturday morning, as Snyder recounts the scene, "The instructor started climbing and all of a sudden we're going straight up. I mean straight up! I don't know what I was thinking, but it wasn't good. All of a sudden, we lost power, and then basically stopped in mid-air. About that time I was saying some things I shouldn't have been saying, but then he moved the stick forward, regained power, and pulled it out to where we were level again. He said, 'That's a stall. Now I want you to do it.' I said, 'Wrong! What we're going to do is put this plane on the ground right now. This lesson is over.'" Snyder said, "I never went back. That scared the daylights out of me."

In yet another air incident, Snyder was being flown by Copeland to Las Vegas to hear some of the mega-stars of the mid-1960s. On one of those flights, Copeland's plane, as Snyder remembers, "...was not low on fuel, but out of fuel." Copeland would land the plane on a ribbon of highway in the heart of the desert west of Vegas. The two caught a ride into Las Vegas, and had someone pull the plane into the airport.

After a two-year stay at Indio, an opening at one of the area's bigger schools materialized and Snyder made the move to Foothill High School in Santa Ana,

California. From 1969 to 1971 he served as an assistant to Ed Bain, before becoming head coach from 1971 through 1973, posting a record of 32-10-3.

Throughout this period Snyder was a coaching clinic junkie. If Don Coryell of San Diego State or Tommy Protho of UCLA spoke, this young California prep coach was there to greet them at the door.

Snyder would leap into the collegiate world of coaching in 1974 and 1975, moving to Austin College in Sherman, Texas, located an hour north of Dallas. A former William Jewell teammate, Vance Morris, was already on the Austin coaching staff and had notified Snyder that there was a head swimming job and assistant football combination available at the NAIA school.

"I had never been in the state of Texas in my life, but to me, it was leap-frogging to a higher level," said Snyder.

He put his $19,000, 1,300-square-foot home, with a swimming pool, on the market and sold it for $35,000 the day the family was leaving town. Two years later, the same home sold for $200,000.

Snyder spent only two years at the private Southern Baptist institution. He served as offensive coordinator for Larry Kramer, who Snyder defined as a "great guy who didn't make things any more complicated than they needed to be."

Whether it was Snyder's swim team, Kramer's football team, or Bob Mason's basketball team, Austin College played college sports the way they were meant to be played.

"There were no scholarships and everyone coached and played the game for nothing more than the love of the game," said Snyder. "Everyone was there for the right reason, but I did not understand that until I was gone."

Chapter Five
Hayden, Here I Come

I was a guy who was always looking for more to do. I'd finish my work, then look for more. There was never an end. At times, it was just work for work's sake.

— Coach Bill Snyder

Even before Hayden Fry and Bill Snyder met clipboard-to-clipboard, Fry had an inkling that this young whipper-snapper from Austin College was unique, with a bit of ingenuity that most coaches in their mid-30s did not have.

"He wrote me a letter and sent a playbook," Fry said. "He said he was interested and could do a good job for me. I was impressed with his confidence at that age."

Fry studied Snyder's set of passing plays and called to invite him up to North Texas State, in Denton, Texas, for an interview.

Snyder's patterns were very sound. Fry could see that consideration had gone into how each play could attack different secondary coverages. Though they were just pass plays, each had a purpose behind it. Snyder referred to the plays as "some of my cock-eyed philosophies. I guess in an arrogant way, I thought I was ahead of the times, but the bottom line was, I wasn't."

Known for giving tough interviews, Fry sent Snyder to the blackboard with chalk in hand.

"I gave him a pretty good test," laughed Fry, "but I found Bill to be very accurate in everything that he did."

Fry offered Snyder the job of defensive back/wide receivers coach for less than $20,000. Snyder accepted.

As the Snyders were leaving the interview, they saw hundreds of cars around the North Texas State basketball arena. To celebrate being a part of the NTS family, the couple decided to attend what they thought was going to be a basketball game. As they reached the ticket window, they found that tickets cost $20 or $25.

"We thought, 'This is crazy. This is big-time athletics,'" Snyder said. "But we were feeling better about life than we should have, so we bought tickets and started to find our seats."

Inside the arena, they saw that the playing floor was covered with chairs. Turning to an usher, they were told they were at a Willie Nelson concert.

"Now, we were Californians. We were new on this block," Snyder chuckled. "We didn't even know who Willie Nelson was, so we got our money back and went home. We missed the opportunity to see Willie Nelson!"

To this day, it's a topic of friendly needling from Bill Brashier, with whom Snyder coached at North Texas State and Iowa.

Once on the Fry coaching staff, Snyder went about being, well, Bill Snyder. He was going to do everything in his power to try to impress his new boss.

"He was a workaholic," Fry said of his new coach. "He was the first guy in the office and the last guy to leave the building. He was a goin'-Jessie.

"I never gave my coaches time tables. I would tell them to do what was needed to be done to accomplish our goals," Fry said. "But, from time to time, I'd tell the coaches to make sure they got out of the office by midnight or to go play nine holes of golf. But with Bill, it would just go in one ear and out the other."

With Judy and the kids back in Sherman trying to sell the house, Snyder stayed in a dorm room. Alone, and with nothing better to do, he decided to splice together all the offensive plays from the previous season onto separate reels. Play, by play, by play, by play.

Now remember, these were the days of 16-millimeter film.

"I stayed up three nights in a row. Probably 72 hours without sleeping a wink before I finally ran out of gas," Snyder said, giving his head a how-stupid shake.

But in Fry's words, Snyder was intelligent, sensitive and reliable. He said Snyder always had time to listen to other ideas, and was concerned about each of his players. "He was just right on top of everything," Fry said.

The two worked magic for the Mean Green from 1976 through 1978, winning 7, 10 and 9 games for the winningest three-year stretch in the history of the school.

Offensively, Snyder marveled at Fry's knack for play-calling, and his timing for running a trick play.

"He just had a feel for it. This day and age, you go off of scripted charts. But not back then. He did it by feel," Snyder said. "I would think, 'He's not going to do that, is he?' And then I would say, 'How in the heck did that happen?' He did things that shouldn't have worked, but they did. He just had a feel."

Bill and Judy separated in 1978, and then divorced in 1979, in the midst of Snyder making his next coaching move to the University of Iowa. Fry had just become the head coach and had invited his entire five-man North Texas State coaching staff to join him.

"It was the hardest decision I ever made," Snyder said. "That was a period of time, that in all likelihood, if I went to Iowa, I would have to leave my children. It was a painful decision, but if I'd stayed I would have been out of a job."

Snyder followed Fry to Iowa, where in a 10-year period, the Hawkeyes would attend eight straight bowl games. In the last five of those seasons, Iowa would rank first in passing efficiency and third in passing yardage in the nation.

"I think this says it all," Fry said. "Bill was with me 10 years at Iowa and in five of those years (Chuck Long in 1983, '84 and '85; Chuck Hartlieb in 1987 and '88) he coached the first-team All-Big Ten quarterback. Now, what does that say about Bill Snyder's coaching ability?"

Going from a soft laugh to a hearty one, Fry reflected on the only time that he ever corrected Snyder on the field. "We were in a practice and Chuck Long was completing every single pass that he threw. Now, this was a guy who was All-Big Ten a couple times and runner-up in the Heisman Trophy voting to Bo Jackson.

"We were in a passing drill, and every single pass was caught. Some wobbled and some might not have been between the numbers, but every single pass was caught," Fry said. "But each time, Coach Snyder would go over and correct Chuck on something. He was over-striding, he didn't get his thumb down. Just little things.

"I walked over to Coach Snyder and said, 'Just let the kid throw the ball one time and not correct him,'" Fry continued. "I'll tell you what. The blood vessels in Bill's neck bulged, his lip started to quiver, his face turned red. I had to turn my head because I was laughing. But that tells you what a perfectionist he was."

It was also Snyder's study in physiology at work.

"I was always really into the science of body movement and how I could apply that to coaching and how to teach players to execute at their position more effectively," Snyder said. "How to change direction in the most efficient manner of getting from one spot to another; the most efficient way to get a proper trajectory of a pass for the maximum distance or maximum velocity utilizing the entirety of the body in a throwing motion; the proper position of the feet for the most appropriate push-off and stride; the proper rotation movement for hips and shoulders. I was always looking for ways our players could improve."

All of this is part of the reason that when Snyder was hired at KSU, Fry predicted, "I think he'll do the job much quicker than anyone anticipates in regards to taking Kansas State to respectability."

Snyder says he would just as soon be called "teacher" Snyder than "coach" Snyder, but added, "it just doesn't sound right. It doesn't fit."

But he adds, "Coaching is teaching. I don't know anyone in the profession who sees it any differently. Teaching is so many things. It is teaching the fundamentals of football and knowledge of the game. It is teaching life lessons of values, principles and leadership. You are constantly teaching. If there's any other reason you're getting into coaching, you're getting into it for the wrong reason."

For sure, Snyder was in coaching for the right reason.

Long laughed as he said, "He's the only coach I've ever seen who can smile and get on you at the same time. He had that ability to smile, but chew you out at the same time, and do it very effectively."

As player and coach, Long said the two would have hardly considered each other friends, but that was fine.

"I was not one of those guys who wanted to be buddy-buddy with a coach. I wanted him to teach me. I wanted him to be hard on me, if needed," Long said. Laughing, he added, "And he was. He never went out of his way to sugar-coat anything. I wanted him to be my coach, and not be concerned if he liked me or not."

Now single, Snyder said of his Iowa work days, "I couldn't squeeze any more out of them. It was just a task of trying to learn how to be more efficient in doing what you were doing. There always seemed to be something else you could do."

Giving a semi-chuckle, Snyder said, "Other people probably do it far better and in less time than it took me. That doesn't speak very highly of my intelligence. It just takes me longer to do things."

That included recruiting, with Long being a perfect example.

Long came from a small school in Illinois with a football team that threw the ball only two or three times per game. To get a feel for his abilities as a drop-back passer, Snyder studied every single inch of film from Long's senior season. While rival recruiters didn't have that patience, Snyder saw the proper techniques, and in an interview setting, he heard the intelligence.

"Bill recruited just as hard as he coached," Fry recalled. "He did a great job with the kids, but also the moms and the dads. If the family had a dog named Spot, Bill would remember it and bring the dog a bone."

On the field, Fry called the plays, but always had an open ear to Snyder, who took up residency in the press box.

"I can't tell you how valuable he was," Fry said. "He was just so smart."

Smart? Yes. Focused on football? Without a doubt. So much so that Snyder says his Iowa City home included only bedroom furniture for himself and for the kids when they visited during the summer. The living room?

"It didn't have a bit of furniture in it," Snyder said. "It served as the recreation room when the kids visited."

The kitchen? Seldom used. That's because most of Snyder's meals, when he ate, were in the kitchen of a restaurant called The Pumpernickel, where he discussed the issues of the day with owner and cook Ron Ameche until closing time, and beyond.

As word of Snyder's coaching talent began to spread, a number of schools inquired about his interest in becoming their head football coach. For the most part, his interest rested only in making the Hawkeyes the best possible team in the Big Ten Conference.

At Iowa, Snyder's offensive teams set or tied 43 out of 45 individual offensive records. The Hawkeyes' 10-year record while Snyder was on the coaching staff was 77-49-4 with eight trips to bowl games.

"I have always believed that it's best just to be where you are. If something is supposed to happen, it will," Snyder said of his patience in landing a head coaching position. "It wasn't that I didn't think about being a head coach, but I wasn't one of those guys who was networking himself all the time and chasing a dream that way. I was getting great satisfaction out of doing what I was doing."

Then, in mid-November of 1988, Snyder's office telephone rang. Kansas State was on the other end, offering an opportunity to interview for the head coaching job of the Wildcats.

Snyder, who had married Sharon Payne, the principal of Wright Elementary School in Des Moines, Iowa, in 1986, went to Fry for advice.

Laughing, Fry said, "I told him it was a pitiful program!"

Turning serious, Fry said that in the two games Iowa had just played against K-State—a 38-13 win in 1987 and a 45-10 win in 1988—the Wildcats had played hard from start to finish.

"I challenged him pretty good, explaining how the program was really down, but that if anyone could get the job done, Coach Snyder was the one," Fry said.

Chapter Six
Intro to Futility U.

We were in the Big Ten Conference and really didn't pay too much attention to what was going on around us. The only thing I knew of Kansas State was the recent history of having played them in each of the previous two years. Aside from that, Kansas State was a non-entity on my radar screen.

— Coach Bill Snyder

Snyder says he knew a bit of the Kansas State tradition, or lack thereof, prior to coming in for an official interview. But could he have possibly known? Really known?

With a head coaching offer on the table from KSU, Snyder would become familiar with many details of Wildcat football prior to his arrival in late November of 1988.

Kansas State had played 93 years of football. Sixty-eight of those were losing years. The leather-helmeted men of Coach Lynn "Pappy" Waldorf won a Big 6 Conference title in 1934, but that was the only football trophy ever earned by the school.

In all those decades of trying, only <u>once</u>, the Independence Bowl in 1982, did Kansas State even qualify for postseason play. And of course, they lost that game to Wisconsin, 14-3. In the 54 years prior to Snyder's arrival, the school cheered only four winning teams—Bill Meek's 6-3-1 1953 and 7-3 1954 squads; Vince Gibson's 6-5 1970 team; and Jim Dickey's 6-5-1 unit of 1982 .

The jokes came so frequently the Wildcat faithful became numb, and even told them on themselves:

Did you hear about the guy who called the athletic director and asked him what time the game would start? His reply: "When can you get here?"

How about the guy who parked in downtown Manhattan on a Saturday morning and left two K-State football tickets on the windshield. When he returned, there were four.

When legendary track coach Ward Haylett took the football position in 1942, he said, "It was thrust upon me."

He would soon hire Henley Haymaker as his freshman coach. Haymaker was the head of the KSU botany department. For players, Haylett said, "We took who showed up. There was no money to recruit."

In 1945, K-State would hire Lud Fiser, who was coaching at Manhattan High School. Fiser lasted one year, as did Hobbs Adams after him, and Sam Francis after Adams. In 1955, K-State athletic director Moon Mullins elevated 34-year-old Bus Mertes from offensive coordinator to head coach at a salary of $10,500.

Without much of a recruiting budget, Mertes went with "65 percent Kansas boys." They played in archaic facilities, including the on-campus Memorial Stadium, which had bench seats for only 20,000, but which turned out to be more than adequate for the number of fans turning out for the games. Mertes' teams won four, three, three, three and two games during his five years on the job, leaving him to say, "If you win, you're going to be accused of cheating; if you lose, you're going to get fired. Take your choice."

Mertes was fired by athletic director Bebe Lee.

Enter Doug Weaver, a Michigan State graduate hired off the Missouri Tiger coaching staff. A line coach, Weaver was just 29 years of age. The head coaching job was his first. Weaver coached from 1960 through 1966. Seven fall seasons scoring a total of eight—yes, eight—victories with a best season of 3-7 in 1964. These were seven years when the Wildcats did not score a single touchdown against arch-rival University of Kansas, losing games 41-0, 34-0, 38-0, 34-0, 7-0 and 34-0, before a 3-3 tie in 1966.

Upon his dismissal, Weaver directed this Bible verse to the administration through the media: "Do not be deceived. God is not mocked, for whatever a man sows, that he will also reap."

Vince Gibson, a defensive guru from Tennessee, was next. He stormed onto the Wildcat scene with a tornado-like force and a southern drawl, shouting phrases like, "We Gonna Win!" and "We Got Pride!"

Years later, Gibson laughed as he thought about his accepting the Wildcat job at the age of 32. "Like a dummy, I took the first head job offered. I was young and cranked up. I believed I could whip the world."

Gibson, in fact, did realize success, defeating each Big 8 Conference rival during his eight years on campus, and in 1969 earned Coach of the Year honors for going just 5-5.

With a white-shoed quarterback named Lynn Dickey and an explosive 5-foot-5 mighty-mite of a back named Mack Herron, Gibson seemed poised to turn around the K-State program. Gibson-coached teams played in a newly constructed 34,500-seat KSU Stadium and the Wildcat athletes lived in their own dormitory. For the first time in ages, fans began to hope.

The team went 5-5 in 1969 and 6-5 in 1970. In 1970, they started 6-1 and needed only one more win in the final month of the season to earn a spot in the Liberty Bowl.

That win never came, but a three-year probation for recruiting violations did.

Laughing years after the fact, Gibson said, "My one major mistake was Pepper Rodgers (coach at Kansas). It was a personal thing. We hated each other!"

Sensing that the Wildcat community had become divided with him at the helm, Gibson resigned after the 1974 4-7 season, leaving a coaching record of 33-52-0. At the time he was the school's second winningest coach behind Mike Ahearn, who won 39 games from 1905 to 1910.

The Wildcats then went with one of their own in Ellis Rainsberger, an academic All-American and former offensive lineman, who was returning to dig his alma mater out of the football doldrums. In three years, Rainsberger's Wildcats went 0-21 in Big 8 play.

But it gets worse. That league record, and overall mark of 6-27-0, came during a time when scholarships were handed out like Halloween candy.

"We had an internal problem in counting," Rainsberger explained when the school was hit by its second three-year probation within a decade.

The count was off by 33 scholarships!

With President Duane Acker taking the place of James McCain, Rainsberger would say, "The new President gave his new athletic board the challenge of keeping football where it belonged."

Next? Jim Dickey.

A defensive genius, Dickey came from North Carolina where he had coached Lawrence Taylor. Dickey inherited a mess, but possessed that familiar coaching attitude.

"We've all got egos. There was a feeling deep down that I could do something where others had failed," said Dickey, who was taking his first head coaching job.

Dickey was saddled by the probation, facilities that were falling apart, financial woes, and a severe lack of administrative support.

"It was non-existent," Dickey said of the support offered by Acker.

Dickey floundered, with seasons of three or four wins in his first three years. Then in 1981, he decided to red-shirt nine senior starters. The hope was to even the playing field and not have Wildcat teenagers playing against 22- and 23-year-old fifth-year seniors at Nebraska.

The next year, Kansas State went 6-5-1 and received a bid to the Independence Bowl.

The success was short-lived. The Wildcats won just three games in 1983, and three more in 1984. Dickey was fired after losses to Wichita State, 16-10, and Northern Iowa, 10-6, just two games into the 1985 season.

Turning to a hot-shot offensive-type, K-State hired Stan Parrish from Marshall University, a I-AA school. The Wildcats would go 2-9, 0-10-1 and 0-11, which included a 1-19-1 Big 8 record, in Parrish's three seasons.

Enter Bill Snyder.

Welcome to a program on a 13-game losing streak; say howdy to a franchise that had not won in 27 games (the 'Cats tied Kansas 17-17 in 1987). Hello to a club that had scored less than 10 points nine times in its previous 21 Big 8 games, and had allowed at least 34 points in 14 of those same games. When Snyder arrived, K-State had gone 1-36-1 in its last 38 games of the 1980s.

"Arguably, Kansas State was the worst football program in America," said the ever-positive KSU President Jon Wefald.

All of this to better define the accomplishments of Snyder.

K-State had tried offensive guys and those with defensive expertise; coaches who went by the letter of the NCAA law and those who were more liberal in their interpretation; coaches in their first head-coach position and those with years of experience.

The one commonality was nothing worked.

What Haylett said in the 1940s could have been repeated in the 1950s by Meek and Mertes, in the 1970s by Gibson and Rainsberger, and in the 1980s by Dickey and Parrish:

"If I had quality, I never had the depth; if I had the depth, the quality wasn't good enough."

The Kansas geography also contributed to the team's failure. Even into the early 1980s, Dickey was saying that it was difficult to land the quality black athlete in Manhattan.

Couple the lack of bright lights and the distance from a major airport with the losing tradition, and the words of sports psychologist Thomas Edwards hit home: "Nothing hurts recruiting like a reputation of being a loser and the lack of a black cultural environment."

So the Kansas State story went.

Until November 30, 1988.

Chapter Seven
The Search For Coach Snyder

I saw Steve Miller, KSU's Athletic Director as being very open and very enthusiastic. He pretty much told it like it was. (Chuckling) At least most of it like it was.

— Coach Bill Snyder

Today, the stories surrounding the search for a replacement for Stan Parrish are comical. The name Bill Snyder was nowhere to be found for six weeks after the early-season resignation of Parrish.

KSU President Jon Wefald said, "In 1988, there were not too many coaches thirsty for this job. Several that we approached showed a monumental indifference."

Here are a couple of names that were on the Wildcats' "A" list, with then-athletic director Steve Miller's assessment of their interest in the head coach's job:

Jack Bicknell of Boston College: "… graciously, but firmly, said, 'I don't think so.' He wouldn't even allow us to visit him," Miller said. "But 'Cowboy' Jack Bicknell was fascinating on paper."

Mike Price of Weber State: "… was a favorite, but he was a graduate of Washington State, a school that was looking for a head coach at the same time."

Miller did not want to offer the job to someone and have it turned down.

"That would have added to the disaster we already had here," Miller said.

John Fox of Pittsburgh, who would later go on to NFL head coaching success, also came in for a look-see during the season, but never appeared before the search committee.

"He came in for a visit, but it was very difficult for him to conceal his dismay with our football program," said associate athletic director Jim Epps.

By Miller's count, 18 different individuals received at least an off-campus face-to-face discussion.

Among those, three were brought onto campus for official visits with the search committee: Bill Thornton of TCU, former Wildcat legend Ron Dickerson of Temple, and Milan Vooletich of Navy. All three interviews went okay, according to Miller, but he added, "We were waiting to really be touched in some way, and that wasn't happening."

The search team also visited Frank Solich of Nebraska, Charlie Bailey of Memphis State, Larry Coker of Oklahoma, plus a host of others.

Miller was incredulous about some of the candidates who threw their hat in the ring for the position. "I met some guys in the profession and just said, 'Holy Christ! This is a Who's Who of those with an IQ of 10 and under.' It was startling to me the types of people who were getting solid recommendations."

Saying it was the honest to goodness truth, Miller said he met with coaches who wanted to know how academic non-qualifiers could get into school? Or how accessible would the party life be to football players?

One coach dropped to his knees in prayer during the interview, asking guidance from God. One coach even wanted to put a dome over the top of KSU Stadium.

Seriously.

"I told that coach that we didn't even have enough money for meals, how could we dome the stadium?" Miller said. Breaking into laughter, he continued, "I'm telling the truth. His idea was to get a bunch of parachutes and have the home economics department sew them together, and then stretch them across the stadium.

"I said, 'Won't we need a pole to support the parachutes? Won't that pole have to be at the 50-yard line?' I remember breaking into laughter, but he was dead serious."

Another coach thought a way to save money would be to take a train to all road games, and have a study hall on the train.

"I just said there aren't tracks leading out of Manhattan to every city where we play," Miller said.

Some of this stuff was, and still is, hysterical, but it's also the truth.

Finally, Miller called a time-out, and told Epps, "We're starting over." Kansas State had just played Iowa in a home-and-home set, in Iowa City in 1987 and in Manhattan in 1988.

"I was sitting in this very office and happened to still have an Iowa media guide lying around," said Epps. "I started reading about Iowa's coordinators and what caught my attention were all of the offensive records that had been set during Bill's tutelage.

"I thought, 'What the hell, we've already called 50 others. Why not one more?'" Epps said.

Worn out by an exhaustive search filled with "No thank you's" or "Are you kidding?" replies, the call to Bill Snyder was a semi-last ditch effort.

Recalling the initial phone call to Snyder, Epps broke into a reflective chuckle.

"Surprisingly, he said he would be interested, but that he was busy working, and could he call me at home that night?"

That call was placed, and immediately separated Snyder from all of the other candidates. Epps found Snyder's interests to be unusual: the university culture, academic programs, relationship with faculty, support from the central administration, the Manhattan community.

Little was asked about the football facility, what the salaries would be, or what the weight room was like.

Prior to visiting Kansas State, Fry and Snyder talked, but never was there any chatter about the thought that it was an impossible task. All he asked Fry before the K-State interview was, 'What do I need to know?'"

Fry told Snyder to find out about the backing he had from the president and the athletic director: "Do they truly want a good football team, and what are they willing to do in terms of facilities and salaries for coaches? He had a real good checklist when he went down there.

"I remember when I came to Iowa. I would put our president on the spot in public whenever I had a chance. At booster meetings, I would ask him, 'Do you truly want a good football program to match the excellence we have in academics?'" Fry said. Laughing, he added, "What could the man say?"

On November 20, 1988, Miller and assistant athletic director Chris Peterson traveled to Snyder's home in Iowa City.

"Immediately," Miller said, when asked how soon he knew that this guy Snyder was the answer. "He was totally, I mean totally, different than all of the others. He was much more methodical, intuitive, held his cards closer to his vest, and talked an octave or two lower than the others. That's why I refer to him as 'Just Plain Bill.'"

Miller went through the spiel that he had with all the other coaches. Cheating would not be permitted. ("We didn't have the money to cheat.") Facilities were not good, his student-athletes would be held accountable, etc.

Miller only promised an unwavering support from his office and that of President Wefald.

"I remember he looked me right in the eye and said, 'I think I can do this,'" said the KSU president of his first meeting with Snyder. "He had a look of determination, and then it was later that we learned all about his work ethic and unbelievable attention to detail."

Bob Krause, KSU's vice-president for institutional advancement, added, "You could tell he had a passion and was relentless. You could tell he was a man who could move mountains."

During his first visit to K-State, Snyder separated himself from his host committee and made his way to the Wildcat campus as an inquisitive bystander. He talked to students and stopped faculty members just to get a feel for the climate of the school. He asked about the educational system, the classroom environment, anything he could think of to talk about while he was still an anonymous visitor.

"I was taken by how friendly the campus was," Snyder said. "Normally, people are in such a hurry that they don't have time, but they stopped, talked and were really friendly."

Miller said K-State, with athletics being about $4 million in the red at the time, would do what it could to spruce up the place, but it had to be within reason.

With that understanding on the table, Miller said, "After that, I told him I would answer 'Yes' to every thing that he wanted. When he started asking questions, I would just say yes, yes, yes."

"As long as you're not cheating, lying or stealing, I'm going to answer yes," Miller said.

"How could he say no?"

When Snyder was presented to the search committee, to the person, Snyder was the coach of choice.

The committee appreciated that Snyder could relate not only to K-State's circumstance, but also that his personality and temperament paralleled the people already on campus. Snyder had lived in a small town, he had taken a school that had been a loser and made it into a winner, he was not afraid of hard work and he had glowing recommendations.

Miller's favorite came from Michigan head coach Bo Schembechler, who said, "Hire him! Get him the flip out of the conference." (Or something similar, just a little more R-rated.)

The Wildcats were impressed with Snyder, and Snyder with K-State, starting with its president.

"He seemed friendly and down to earth," Snyder said of his first meeting. "You put people into certain categories based on the position they hold. You have a concept of what a president of a university should be like, but Jon wasn't that way."

At breakfast, President Wefald started chattering of heights, weights and star-status of returning Wildcats.

Chuckling, Snyder said, "I had no idea if he was accurate, but what was important was that you didn't expect that type of interest from a college president."

So sure was Miller that Snyder was the man that he cancelled an interview with Bailey of Memphis State, and offered the job to Snyder on November 26.

It was a five-year deal calling for $85,000 the first year, which Snyder bargained to $90,000. There was also the guarantee that he would have $120,000 more than the former coach to hire a coaching staff.

Snyder's main charge to the university? "If you give us a chance to win by continually supporting us, if you give me that chance, we can win."

Laughing, Miller said he had the obvious question: "How soon can we win?"

And he remembered the reply from Snyder.

"A foundation must be built and there is absolutely no quick-fix way. It would take several years," Miller said of Snyder's reply. "He didn't say five years, just that the process would require time."

The promise of commitment was made, and on Monday, November 28, Snyder said, "I'll take it."

As lackluster as it sounds, Snyder took the job for a variety of reasons. He liked his home visit with Miller and the friendliness of the campus. He liked Wefald's interest in the team and the stability of donors like Jack Vanier and Howard Sherwood.

"There wasn't one moment or one statement that made the difference," Snyder said. "It was the accumulation of people."

Plus, as the old saying goes, "The timing was right. If I was going to be a head coach, I needed to get off dead-center and do it."

Snyder took the job, but only with the understanding that he could coach in the Peach Bowl, where Iowa would meet North Carolina State on December 31.

"I am a strong believer in loyalty, and I had that loyalty to the University of Iowa, to Coach Fry, to our players, and to our fans," he said.

On November 30, Snyder was introduced as the Wildcats' head football coach.

On his hiring, Snyder quipped, "I had several people offer their suggestions and several offer their condolences."

Likely out of hope, Miller said on that hiring day, "We've hired the best architect in America. We have hired a person who is going to build this program into something we can all be proud of. Anyone who believes that this cannot change just doesn't understand history, and just doesn't understand what greatness can do. There are people who can have impact and make change."

At his initial press conference, Snyder referred to himself as a coach with a good work ethic, a coach who was precise, dedicated, loyal, and a coach who cares about people and the school.

He didn't lie.

Snyder would not sign his contract for months. To him, "a handshake was good enough. I trusted people, and I wanted people to trust me."

An agent? No way. Not then, not now.

"I'm not saying agents are bad guys, but I just never felt I needed one," Snyder said. "I always wanted my dialogue with my university to be face to face based on trust and not through an intermediary."

Seventeen years later, Miller looks at the hire by saying, "Bill Snyder was a special guy in a special circumstance. Could he have been a success at a USC? Maybe. But Bill Snyder was the perfect fit for Kansas State in this geographical setting and this political setting.

"I firmly believe great leaders are great leaders because of the convergence of circumstances that allows the leadership capacity to be outstanding," Miller said. "Bill had total control, the perfect focus, the perfect unwavering attitude and did a job I'm not sure anyone else in America could have done."

Snyder wouldn't have taken the job had he not truly believed there was an opportunity for success. "Life's too short for that," he said. "I think I felt what any football coach feels when he takes any head coaching job: 'I can get this done.' We're all naive to a lot of things to where something drives us to say, 'Yeah, we can accomplish something.'"

Seventeen years later, Miller says, "Bill Snyder was as good for Kansas State as Kansas State was for Bill Snyder. Not every roadshow plays in every single town, but this was a match made in heaven."

This Coach Was 'Different'

The first time I met Bill was in the Bramlage Coliseum Legends Room when I was serving on the search committee to find a new football coach. It's hard to put into words, but a person just felt comfortable with him.

One coach we brought in from Texas could only talk about Texas. We had a feeling he had never been north of the Red River. Another coach was just dull as paint.

But from the first day, Bill was as honest as a man can be. He said it was going to take time, our fans were going to have to be patient, and that he would need a lot of help, with quite a bit of that being financial. I remember saying to him, it wasn't a blank promise, but I said, "We'll get you what you need." (Chuckling) Little did I know what that would end up being.

Bill was just different than any coach I had met. He was always in a tie, always quiet, always a gentleman, not a "We Gonna Win!" guy. He wasn't a rah-rah guy, just very matter-of-fact in everything he did.

I've always told him that if he didn't try to tell me how to run a ranch, I wouldn't tell him how to coach. But this year I finally told him, "Now when you come to the (Dr. Richard) Spencer Scholarship Fish Fry, I don't want to see you in a tie." He didn't listen to me for 17 years, but after he retired, he didn't bring a neck tie to this last one. I said, "You're finally listening to me."

In 1989, we would have all been tickled to death with four or five wins. No one ever dreamed that we would come so close to playing for a national championship. Had someone said we would win four Big 12 North titles and one overall championship, I wouldn't have laughed at them, I would have just told them they were crazy and felt sorry for them.

I think Bill accomplished what he did through his dedication to his job. People talk about how he handles every detail, but it's more than that. It's a dedication unlike any I've ever seen.

The man has just done a marvelous job for Kansas State University. He's far exceeded everyone's dreams.

— Jack Vanier
Close personal friend
(The KSU football complex carries the name of Jack and Donna Vanier)

Chapter Eight
Where Do You Start?

The up side was that you were already flat on your back. If you took a breath, you were a little better off than where you started. You weren't going to go any lower than you were at the time.

— Coach Bill Snyder

Tom Ross, owner of a lumber company in Des Moines and a favorite friend of Snyder's, remembers a phone call from Snyder shortly after the initial Kansas State press conference.

Normally, the two would talk on a weekly basis, but Ross remembers Snyder calling to say, "Tom, we won't be talking for a while because there are a ton of things to do here."

With the Wildcats, the difference was not going to come with a peculiar Purple offense or a weird White defense. It first had to do with the muscles between the ears, instead of those of the biceps and triceps.

From day one, the new Kansas State coach said, "Our No. 1 priority was dealing in attitude development. We had to develop an attitude of respect for each other, an attitude of confidence, and an attitude of improvement each day."

To help change that attitude, every facet of the Wildcat program had to be remodeled.

First, Snyder had to introduce himself.

"I wasn't going to be a guy they had ever heard too much about. They weren't going to find my name in any record book," Snyder said.

But what the new coach did have was a bit of built-in respect from the fact that Iowa had played Kansas State in each of the last two years and had defeated the Wildcats.

Snyder's first meeting was with the 22 out-going seniors. He heard stories of players being embarrassed to wear their letter jackets on campus and a host of other tales of woe concerning this stinker of a program.

"It was like a kindergarten class. They would raise their hand, and I would call on them. They truly wanted to express themselves," Snyder said. "I'll never forget one player raising his hand and saying, 'Coach, in our game with Iowa last year, we had one thing in common. We only trailed 17-10 at the half, but do you know the thing we had in common? You knew Iowa was going to win, and Kansas State knew that Iowa was going to win.'"

Iowa did win 45-10.

Snyder later looked into class attendance and grades. With each year, he found the team grade point average dropped. The humiliation they were experiencing on the field was having an impact on their academics.

This attitude was not new to Snyder. He had seen the same thing in Iowa City where the Hawkeyes had endured 17 straight losing seasons prior to the arrival of Fry and Snyder.

Heck, in 1974, the Hawkeyes pulled a Kansas State-type year, going winless for the entire season.

"The players at Iowa didn't understand what was important in winning. They didn't know how to stop losing, they didn't know how not to beat themselves, they were beaten back by losing," Snyder reflected. "These young men at Kansas State were the same, but to a greater degree. They were good young people who wanted to succeed, but just weren't sure how to go about it."

As Snyder said, some of these players arrived on campus 6-4 in height, but had been beaten down to 6-foot because of their attitude about losing. Somewhere along the line, each one of them had to step back and say, "Enough is enough. I can't accept it any more."

One of those players who had already said enough is enough was Michael Smith, who as a freshman in 1988 caught eight passes for 77 yards.

"I had already flown home to New Orleans, right after the Colorado game (November 19, 1988). I flew straight home. I was done. I was gone!" Smith said. "I had made arrangements to take my finals early, and had already talked Frank (Hernandez, another freshman KSU receiver) into joining me at Tulane."

Smith was a walk-on to the Stan Parrish program, and just four games into his Wildcat career, his coach resigned effective at the end of the season.

"The rest of that season had the prisoners running the prison," Smith said

On Christmas Day, Snyder called Smith at his New Orleans home and asked him to reconsider his decision. Snyder was offering a scholarship.

"I've told people that I didn't look at any of the old video, but I did cheat a little," Snyder recalled. "I wanted a general idea of what we had around here, and I saw this No. 88 making some catches, and I didn't see anybody any better on the team."

"That call really surprised me," Smith said. "I had never met the man. I had never heard of the man, and he was offering me a scholarship."

Of the early discussions with Coach Snyder, Smith said no promises were made, no mention of winning a Big 8 title, but that "he was going to have us do a lot of stuff we might not think we're capable of doing. He just wanted us to improve every day as a person, as a player and as a student. If we would commit to that, we would see change."

And for the 5-9, 160-pound Smith, he finally had a coach who believed in him.

"Being a smaller guy, I've always been told I couldn't do this and couldn't do that, but all I ever wanted to do was play football," Smith said. "Coach Snyder was giving me that opportunity. I was raised with the understanding you had to prove yourself every day, and that's what coach was asking each of us to do."

Others, however, fell by the wayside.

Most of those who decided to tough it out relished the change. One was Brooks Barta, a redshirt-freshman in 1988.

"We had just gone through the (Stan) Parrish thing and the discipline certainly wasn't what I expected from a Division I program," Barta said.

"That changed the day Coach Snyder walked in. He was clearly organized, had a vision and an expectation." That was demonstrated with the first conditioning practice where a visible toughness was demanded.

"If we put our hands on our knees, our group would be disciplined. There were up-downs to pay. If anyone was caught loafing, that group would be disciplined," Barta said. "There was a big emphasis on team building. Those were tough sessions. It was an hour of having a high heart rate. I think the idea was to find out who really wanted to be there."

Snyder stressed to his new club that their future was ahead of them. They would not be judged by whether or not they had started the year before.

Workouts would be tougher than ever before and self-limitations would not be accepted. "I believe they are capable of far more than what they've done in the past," said the new coach.

Quarterback Paul Watson remembers Snyder promising to turn the program around, but he couldn't do it himself. The players had to do their share.

In Snyder's system, you had to do it day by day by day.

Snyder told the players their priorities should be their faith, their family, and to be the best person they could be, the best student they could be, and the best football player they could be—in that order.

"The idea was if each one of us found a way to make that daily improvement, then individually we would grow, which means collectively we would be growing," Snyder said. "If each person was putting his chips in that day, the pot would grow immensely because everyone was contributing on a daily basis."

While difficult, the sales job Snyder had to do in 1988 was easier than in today's society of instant self gratification.

Seventeen years ago, said Snyder, "That wasn't necessarily the trademark of young people. We had young guys hungry to win. They were saying, 'What do you want us to do, and we'll do it.' They didn't know what it was going to take, because they had never been successful. But there was an attitude of whatever it is that you want us to do, we will do."

Workouts were difficult and new rules enforced. Caps were not allowed in the Vanier Football Complex; earrings were not permitted; class attendance was mandatory; being on time a must. Some 'Cats couldn't cut it. To them it wasn't worth the effort. Snyder didn't view those individuals as bad guys or guys with poor character. To them, it just wasn't worth the price, which was okay to admit.

If rules were violated, the 8-8-8 rule was put into effect. At 6 a.m. on Sunday, players would be required to run eight laps around the football field, run the stadium stairs (one step at a time) eight times, and go the length of the field doing up-downs eight times.

Other rules came in meetings. Both feet on the floor at all times, eyes on the clinician, and in recognition of the speaker, one clap upon the introduction and one clap after the presentation. (This later became two claps.) The goal was to establish discipline and team unity.

"It was a way of showing how we cared and were going to do everything in our power to help them live their lives in a positive way," Snyder said.

To Bob Krause, the vice-president of institutional advancement, this attention to detail was a microcosm of what was about to come.

"A lot of people are focused, and a lot of people pay attention to detail. But very few individuals can put a vision together, seeing not only the big picture, but all of the small details as well, and in rapid transition. Snyder had that ability in the blink of an eye."

The attitude and perception of the Kansas State fans also needed attention, but that, Snyder knew, would probably only come with winning.

In the Purple Pride years of 1969 and 1970, K-State averaged 33,987 and 38,002 fans respectively in a stadium that seated 42,000, including portable bleacher seats.

Since that time, average home attendance had plummeted to 18,949 in 1986, and was still at just 20,975 in Parrish's last season in 1988. And that was at the start of the game. By mid-third quarter, a head count of no more than 12,000 was the rule in more games than not.

Out of a KSU enrollment base of nearly 19,000, only 2,600 students coughed up the four or five bucks a game that tickets cost in those days.

As concerned as Snyder was about tackles, guards, and running backs, the lack of Sunflower State support equally troubled the newly-named coach.

"It'll take a state-wide effort. It can't happen conventionally. The fans must come out before the team begins to win. Whatever our fans want—six, seven, eight wins—they can't wait for that," Snyder challenged. "If they wait, I don't know if it can happen. The way it happens, or the best chance of it happening, is if we can put people in the stands.

"This is the only program in the country to lose 500 games, and I get to coach it," Snyder said. "I think that 10 years down the road, we can be winning four, five, six games a year, and every once in a while get to a bowl game."

Chapter Nine
New This, New That

Nothing is more important in changing an attitude of a team than honesty. I've never been a believer in saying, 'Everything is good.' I believe in being positive, but I believe more in being honest. Young people know when you're being straight with them, and more importantly, they know when you're not. If you don't tell them like it is, there will be a time when the truth is uncovered and all of a sudden you have lost the trust and respect of your team.

— Coach Bill Snyder

Iowa with its corn and Kansas with its wheat are states of similar geographic size, alike in population and conservative Midwest personality.

Iowa had its three schools—University of Iowa, Iowa State University and Drake University. Kansas had its trio—University of Kansas, Kansas State University and Wichita State University.

So it was reasonable to think what worked in Iowa City just might be the answer in Manhattan.

After all, Iowa City was a community of around 50,000, just slightly bigger than the Little Apple. Iowa City had Cedar Rapids and Des Moines within a two-hour drive; Manhattan had Topeka and Kansas City.

The traditions were identical as well. As *Iowa City Press-Citizen* sports editor Al Grady penned, "I think people had come to accept a bad football program here. But there was always enormous support for basketball."

Ditto for Kansas State.

The challenge awaiting Snyder at K-State would be much the same as when he and Hayden Fry first arrived at Iowa.

"Bill had to build a new tradition and a new image," Fry said of KSU's new coach. "When we came to Iowa, every visual image of the past, and losing, had to go."

Epps remembers walking Snyder around some of the KSU facilities, with a bravado of what the Wildcats had to offer.

Snyder politely encouraged him, along with Miller, to go to Iowa City and view their facilities. Snyder wanted to model some things after the Hawkeyes' program.

Miller and Epps did visit the Iowa facilities, and after a few minutes, "We just looked at each other like, 'Oh my God! What have we done?' We quickly learned how the other half lived in college football," Epps laughed. "What we were offering Bill wasn't much by Iowa's standards."

Work would soon start on refurbishing the Wildcats' locker room, with the offices of assistant coaches being next, then the training room and equipment room.

It wasn't too many months later that construction stopped.

"I remember calling Steve, and saying, 'The hammering has stopped. Why?'" Snyder said.

The reply was that monies were not available to pay the contractors. They had pulled off the job.

Snyder's next comment stunned Miller, and to Snyder's relief, didn't become a reality.

"I told Steve that I would write him a check. I was thinking it was going to take $100,000 to get them back on the job," Snyder said. "I wasn't bluffing. I didn't have it, but I was going to cash in everything I had to get them back on the job."

Miller told Snyder that something would be worked out, and eventually it was, without the money from the coach.

Did Snyder's wife know of her husband's offer of generosity?

Smiling, Snyder said, "No, not at the time."

This was the first advertisement of Snyder's immediate loyalty to his school of less than 100 days.

That loyalty, that commitment, never wavered throughout his career. During the most recent expansion project, K-State found itself $500,000 short of what was needed to begin construction. Meeting in Dallas, with KSU's decision makers, Snyder again offered the monies so the project could be put into motion, but President Wefald refused the offer.

Several of Snyder's initial changes to the KSU program came without great expense, and were ideas borrowed from the Iowa philosophy.

Prior to spring practice, a green tarp was draped along the chain link fence that surrounded the facility to the southwest of KSU Stadium. From the first day, putting the team in the best possible environment for learning was stressed. To Snyder, cars buzzing down College Avenue to the west of the practice field would only serve as a distraction.

Practices were closed to everyone but athletic department officials.

"At USC I remember all the 'suits' that came to our practices and how Coach McKay felt obligated to talk to them," Snyder said of the Trojans' boosters. "Players would be saying, 'Hey, there's so and so.' 'Hey, look who's here.' We attracted some pretty unique people at USC, and even at my young age as a coach, I always looked at that as being a distraction."

Plus, Snyder admits, with coaches there is always a paranoia about who could be watching a practice session, providing information on what the team was working on.

One of Snyder's first conversations with equipment manager Jim "Shorty" Kleinau was to get samples for a new uniform. Iowa had taken on the Pittsburgh Steelers look and Snyder wanted Kleinau to work off the look of the Dallas Cowboys.

"The Cowboys had proclaimed themselves America's team, and had a clean, modern look, yet not too modern," said Kleinau. "Coach wanted a look that the country could identify with. A look and a logo that would sustain itself over time. Once we got to winning, people would identify the look with Kansas State football. He didn't want three different looks over the next eight years."

Snyder liked the silver in Dallas' uniform, which would be a change from the purple and white. And he wanted no part of the purple-over-purple uniform that Stan Parrish had introduced.

"That one wasn't going to make it," Snyder said.

It was a time when Kansas State was making the move from Russell uniforms to all Nike apparel.

The first task was to find a purple deep enough to, well, almost not be purple.

Parrish had used a lighter shade, but Nike developed what Kleinau calls "Snyder

Purple" or what Nike termed "Dark Orchid."

At the time, purple had a bad connotation. All the teams around the country wearing purple were pretty bad football teams. Texas Christian, Northwestern, Kansas State. While Snyder knew K-State couldn't do away with purple, he was going to tinker with the shade as much as possible.

If you want to bring a hearty hoot from Kleinau, ask him about a meeting with Snyder and Terry Swartz, the Nike sales representative.

Snyder wanted a deeper purple, and Swartz kept saying the current purple was as deep as they could go. Laughing, Kleinau recalls Snyder telling Swartz "If we can put a man on the moon, then you can make a darker color of purple."

Snyder also changed Kansas State's travel look. On any flight or when attending any significant team function, the Wildcat travel party wore navy blazers. It was a look of uniformity that created a business-like atmosphere. Snyder is known for wearing suits to the office, whether it be January, July or November.

"It's a way of saying, 'I'm going to do my part,'" said Snyder. "It demonstrates a professional presence and sets an example for the players in the program. To the players, it's likely that everyone they have known in their life that wore a suit held some type of position of authority."

"I promise you," said Brent Venables, an early-1990s linebacker for the Wildcats, "when I got my blazer for the first time, I felt I was somebody."

If not a snazzy new uniform, maybe a new logo was the answer to the Wildcat woes.

"I know a lot of K-Staters didn't want to mess with that little guy waving the flag, but I wanted something that would identify Kansas State football," said Snyder, referring to the Willie the Wildcat waving a KSU pennant that is still used today by the Alumni Association. "I never intended for the logo we would come up with to go outside of the football program."

The talents of local illustrator Tom Bookwalter, who in December had just moved to Manhattan from Waterloo, Iowa, were called upon to develop a logo for football. Knowing that Bookwalter had done work for Hayden Fry and basketball coach Lute Olson at Iowa, Snyder asked for something that was simple, yet contemporary, and he didn't want "KSU" any place on the logo. He wanted it to stand alone.

"Like with many coaches taking over a losing program, the first thing you think about is we can't be the way we were," Snyder said. "We wanted a new front to our program."

Of the first eight to ten sketches, Bookwalter said with a laugh, "Bill looked at them and said, 'Try again.'"

He did, and his next attempt struck gold. Today the logo is known as the Powercat and it truly is one of the most recognized logos in athletics. Bookwalter hand-painted the logo on a K-State helmet and took it to Snyder.

"He looked and looked at it and then finally said, 'You've hit a nerve here. Let me check it with the team.'"

While the team accepted it, long-time K-Staters fond of Willie the Wildcat did not.

"I remember some pretty rude comments about the new Powercat, like, 'I hate it!'" laughed Bookwalter. Bookwalter remembers Snyder telling him that if you turned the Iowa logo upside down it looked like Barney Rubble of the *Flintstones*. "He said not to worry about it. We'd work through it."

The Powercat logo became an instant success story, and today, despite Snyder's original intent to simply create a new symbol for the football team, it is the most identifying mark of Kansas State University.

Bookwalter, an assistant professor in KSU's visual communications department, still owns the Powercat logo, but has given a copyright assignment to the university and receives a quarterly royalty check based on wholesale sales from K-State.

"I've done illustrations for Fortune 500-type companies, but I don't think anything ever turned out to be this popular," Bookwalter said. "It's one of the best marks in sports."

As for Snyder, his only return has been the satisfaction of having a logo that is flown from Manhattan to tent-cities in Iraq.

In every possible manner, it was out with the old, in with the new. Whether it was replacing a grungy shag carpet, tattered wallpaper, or simply giving the players a couple new t-shirts.

"We were used to having nothing," said Barta. "A nicer t-shirt was special to us. Give us a decent pair of shorts or team sweats, and our eyes would light up. We had an image of a second-class program, and it was hard for players not to feel anything but second class, if that."

Quentin Neujahr, a member of Snyder's first recruiting class, had a similar story. The sweats the team members were issued were incorrectly printed with a "3" before each number.

"They were printed '367' or '386,' but since we were K-State, we had no leverage to go back to the printer and make them do them over," Neujahr said. "They probably knew they weren't going to get paid, anyway."

Snyder didn't want frills, but did preach consistency.

For the first four seasons, Kansas State's press guide had nothing more than a Powercat helmet or two decorating the cover. In two of the four years, there was a splash of a yellow star-like figure.

"At that time we were stressing consistency with our football team," Snyder said. "To me, that was another way to stress the importance of consistency. It was another way of identifying what we expected. Don't go bounce off the walls just because it's a new season. I've always thought repetition was a great teacher."

Snyder also ruffled some feathers when he opted to remove the 1982 Independence Bowl trophy from the football complex lobby.

"There were mixed feelings about that," Snyder admitted. "It represented some tremendous effort on the part of a lot of people. It was representative of Jim Dickey and Kansas State's first bowl game, and I understood that.

"On the other side of the coin, it was a runner-up trophy in a two-man race," Snyder said. "If we were going to start from scratch, we needed to remove all those things that had a connotation of not being as good as we can be."

The trophy was given to Kleinau for safe keeping in the Wildcats' equipment room.

In talking change, the 17-year debate on scheduling must also be mentioned. Money games at Tennessee, Clemson and Ohio State were replaced by games against the so-called directional schools or I-AA opponents.

Of 19 non-conference games on the books for the 1990 through 1994 seasons when Snyder arrived, only eight were played.

Perhaps Snyder did know what he was doing. The only two schools who refused to negate contracts were Arizona State and Washington. Snyder debuted at Sun Devil Stadium on September 9, 1989, and lost 31-0.

In 1991, the Wildcats were smacked by a No. 4 Washington team, 56-3.

Laughing, Fry said, "Bill got that scheduling thing from me, but took it even further."

Fry said he always scheduled one game he knew his team would win, another game where he had a 50-50 chance of winning, and a third game where Iowa would have to play very well to defeat the opponent.

"You can't schedule wins, but at that time we needed to try to schedule teams we had a chance to defeat," Snyder said. "In the Big 8, we knew we were going to have seven very tough games. Before the season started, we were already going to play seven teams that were better than us. Far better than us."

"With those money games, all we were going to do was get people hurt, destroy all continuity and damage the attitude and confidence of our team," Snyder said. "We couldn't continue putting ourselves in a position where we were limiting our opportunities to achieve success."

Even into the late-1990s when K-State was winning division titles, that scheduling philosophy never wavered.

Once K-State joined the Big 12, the team would face eight rugged Saturdays of football.

"Just because we were on top of the world a few of those years didn't mean we would stay there," Snyder reasoned. "It just didn't make sense to jeopardize ourselves for those eight games by playing the elite teams in the country early. Our goal was to achieve continuity and gain momentum early in the year. It allowed us in most seasons to reach many of our 16 Goals of Success, which we may not have reached had we overscheduled."

Plus, Snyder always preached, "Win your games, and you'll get to where you want to go."

He explained, "The fact that we didn't play for the national championship in 1998 had to do with only one thing. We didn't win the game for the Big 12 championship that we had to win. It had nothing to do with who we played in the first game of the season. It had to do with how we fared in the last game of the season against Texas A&M."

Most importantly, Snyder said with a slight chuckle, "It was in my contract that I had complete control over the schedule, so it wasn't something you could blame the athletic department for."

It was Snyder's program. Whether it was a new logo or scheduling the teams the Wildcats would play, there was no doubt these were the decisions of one man.

Chapter Ten
Recruiting A Staff

Before I took the job, I had formulated a list of people that I knew, or knew of, and had a semi-pecking order at every coaching position. I just started at the top of each list, and was lucky enough to get a majority of my number one choices.

— Coach Bill Snyder

Del Miller was Snyder's first hire to the 1989 Kansas State coaching staff.

Miller, who was Iowa's recruiting coordinator and helped Snyder with the quarterbacks and wide receivers, vividly remembers the hire. The Hawkeyes had played the Wildcats in each of the last two years, winning 38-13 in Iowa City in 1987, and blistering the Wildcats 45-10 at KSU Stadium in 1988.

"We played at KSU and I remember telling Fred Mims (assistant athletic director at Iowa), 'You know I'm not job looking, but if I ever think about coming to a place like Kansas State, you kick me right in the butt.'

"When I told Bill that I would come I called Fred and just said, 'I'm grabbing my ankles. I'm going to Kansas State.'"

Knowing of the Snyder hire, Iowa coach Hayden Fry called a staff meeting to try to confirm that all of his coaches were staying with him, and not going with Snyder. Miller recalls Fry going around the room and telling each coach what his responsibilities would be the following year. Miller was going to be moved to tight ends coach and continue to serve as recruiting coordinator.

Miller reflected, "Hayden went around the room and said, 'Now, I don't need an answer now, but soon.' He then proceeded to go back around the room and wanted to know what each coach was going to do."

That night, Snyder called Miller to offer him a job. He wasn't exactly sure what his position would be, but he was promised more money than he was currently making, so Miller jumped at the opportunity.

"Del was a good person and always professional about what he did," Snyder said. "He had been in on every meeting I ever had with the players, so he knew how I worked."

Of Snyder, Miller said, "I had known him for 10 years, but he's a hard guy to get close to. Ours was a business relationship. But I knew nobody who could stay as focused to a task for such a long period of time as Bill could. I mean nobody! He's one of a kind, and that made me believe he could get the job done at Kansas State."

Miller, the Wildcats' first offensive coordinator and recruiting coordinator, was the only member of Fry's Iowa staff that Snyder took.

That was out of loyalty to Coach Fry, but also, "I knew it was a lateral move at best for the Iowa coaches," Snyder said. "In a way, it would have been insulting to them because Kansas State wasn't near the program that Iowa had going."

Snyder did, however, lean toward assistants who had Iowa ties.

Bob Stoops was hired as the secondary coach. A former All-American defensive back at Iowa, Stoops was the team's MVP in 1982, plus a member of the Big Ten title team in 1981. He had coached at Kent State in 1988, after serving two years as a volunteer assistant at Iowa in 1986 and 1987, and three seasons as a graduate assistant prior to that.

"He came from a football family and was in it for the long haul. I always liked the way he would compete," Snyder said. "But it was a tough choice for Bobby because I think he looked at Kansas State as maybe one of those dead-end programs."

Stoops said otherwise.

"I looked at it as an incredible opportunity. I've said it many times that I was so naive. I had held a fulltime assistant job for only nine months, and I was 28 years old. But I had such a belief in Coach Snyder because of the way we had won at Iowa. I just didn't see any way that we wouldn't win again at Kansas State. We had gone to Rose Bowls and to other bowl games for eight years in a row. I guess it never entered my mind we wouldn't be successful at Kansas State."

Laughing, Stoops added, "Plus being in the Big Ten, we really didn't pay too much attention to other conferences. I don't think I had any idea that Kansas State was as down as it was."

Nick Quartaro joined Snyder as tight ends coach, assistant recruiting coordinator and special teams coach. He was Iowa's place-kicker in 1975, and had spent the 1978 season at Iowa as a graduate assistant. Quartaro was making the move from

Drake, where he had served as head coach from 1986-1988. Other coaching stops had been at Northwestern and Hobart College in Geneva, New York.

"I'm sure Coach Snyder knew, but as assistants, I'm not sure if any of us knew how gigantic of a task it would be," Quartaro said. "All those man-hours we put in were a must to put the program on the path to success."

Tom Grogan was Del Miller's right-hand man serving as assistant quarterback coach and assistant recruiting coordinator. Grogan spent five years at Iowa as the Hawkeyes' backup quarterback, graduating in 1984. His claim to fame was being the only college athlete to ever participate in the NCAA Final Four for basketball and the Rose Bowl in football. Grogan's move to Kansas State came after a four-year stint in the human resources department of the Black and Veatch Architecture firm in Kansas City, which was his home town.

Prepping at Turner High in Kansas City, Grogan said, "Out of high school I didn't even consider Kansas State, knowing how far down the program was. Now, I was about to coach a K-State program that had the longest losing streak in college football. I was trying to figure out how we were going to get kids to come there.

"But I respected Bill a lot, and he's the reason I wanted to get back into coaching. It didn't take much of a selling job," said Grogan.

"Tommy was an all-around excellent young guy," Snyder said. "He had been in the system, so he knew what we were gong to do. He was always an extremely intelligent quarterback, who always had you in the right formation and knew the entirety of the offense."

The rest of Snyder's initial staff would come outside of the Iowa coaching tree:

Bob Cope, defensive coordinator / linebackers coach, came from University of Pacific where he had served as head coach the previous six years. While at North Texas State, Snyder had met Cope, an assistant on the Baylor staff. Snyder liked the idea that Cope knew the prep coaches in the state of Texas.

Charlie Coe would coach the running backs. A 1973 Kansas State graduate, Coe played football and baseball for the Wildcats, and was coming from Missouri, where he had coached the four previous seasons.

John Latina, offensive line coach, came to K-State from Temple where he had been an assistant for the previous six seasons, after beginning his coaching career at Pittsburgh and Virginia Tech.

Mike Nelson, defensive line coach, was a product of the San Diego State coaching staff where he had served the previous two years, with prior coaching stops at Dayton, Southern Illinois, Virginia and Ball State.

Kevin Ramsey, linebackers coach, was a graduate of Indiana State. He was the only holdover from the 1988 Stan Parrish coaching staff.

Former Wildcat Dana Dimel served Snyder's first coaching staff as a graduate assistant.

"At the time, each one of these individuals was improving himself by coming to Kansas State," Snyder said. "Some were without a job, and this job was better than no job. With others, it was accepting a title (coordinator) that they did not have at their previous school."

At one time or another during their coaching stay at K-State, Latina, Quartaro, Miller and Stoops all held positions of associate or assistant head coach. Co-offensive coordinator status was held by Miller, Latina, Dimel, Ron Hudson, Mark Mangino, Paul Dunn and Greg Peterson. On defense, Cope, Stoops, Jim Leavitt, Mike Stoops, Phil Bennett, Bret Bielema and Bob Elliott all served as coordinators.

By the end of his 17 years with the Wildcats, 34 different men had served Snyder as assistants. As is common in the sports arena, coaching staffs are in constant flux, and Snyder's was no different.

In 1990, Coe and Nelson left, opening the way for Dimel to become a fulltime coach, and for Jim Leavitt to join the Wildcats from the University of Iowa, where he had served as linebackers coach.

In 1991, John Hendrick came to KSU from LSU, and Ben Griffith from the arena football ranks, while Ramsey and Cope left. With the departure of Grogan in 1992, Mike Stoops came onto the scene after playing and coaching at Iowa for 11 years. In 1993, Nelson Barnes joined the staff from Western Illinois when Hendrick left.

In 1994, Rod Humenuik came to KSU from the NFL ranks, Latimore returned to his alma mater after coaching at Missouri, Manny Matsakis joined the Wildcats from the Hofstra program, and Mark Mangino was elevated from recruiting coordinator to a position coach. The additions took the places of Barnes, Griffith, Latina and Quartaro.

The new additions marveled at their leader.

"He is meticulous. Nothing is too small to take for granted," said Humenuik, who had been coaching in the professional ranks. "A lot of coaches have a plan for every hour, but he has a plan for every minute. His determination is relentless."

"The stamp that Bill Snyder put on my coaching career was persistence," Mangino said. "Being persistent in what you believe in, sticking by your guns, and when things are bad, finding a way to make them better. Nothing was impossible with Bill Snyder."

Hudson from Ohio State, Peterson from graduate assistant status, and Larry Kramer from Emporia State joined the Wildcats in 1995, filling the spots vacated by Humenuik, Matsakis and Miller. Ironically, it was Kramer who had first hired Snyder at Austin College two decades earlier.

"Bill is one of the most intelligent men I've ever been around," Peterson said. "His attention to detail and his organizational skills on a day-to-day basis were just astonishing. With this program, Bill was involved from A to Z."

Cope returned to K-State in 1996 when Bob Stoops went to Florida. Brent Venables stepped up from being a graduate assistant when Leavitt left for South Florida.

In 1997, Jon Fabris joined the staff from Notre Dame where he had served as a graduate assistant, and Michael Smith was upped from graduate assistant to fulltime coach. Leaving the program were Dimel and Cope, who would be claimed by cancer in the summer of 1997.

Smith, a former All-Big 8 receiver for K-State, had been released from Calgary in the Canadian Football League in 1994, and was working as a desk manager at the Olathe (Kansas) Holiday Inn. He was also driving back and forth to Manhattan trying to finish up his degree.

"I'll never forget it," Smith said. "Coach hired me as a graduate assistant on March 17 and my daughter (Kylie) was born two days later.

"He just sat me down and said I want you to be with me through this until I quit," Smith said. "He said he would work me to death, but if I was willing, it would pay off."

Smith became a fulltime assistant two years later, and true to Snyder's word, the former Wildcat wide receiver was with his head coach until he retired following the 2005 season.

"He is as loyal as they come," Smith said.

Paul Dunn from Vanderbilt joined K-State in 1998, when Kramer left the program.

In 1999, Bennett joined the Wildcats from the Oklahoma staff, Bob Fello from James Madison, Jim Gush from Garden City Community College, and Matt Miller was elevated from graduate assistant status.

They filled the spots left by Mangino, Venables and Mike Stoops, who joined Bob Stoops at the University of Oklahoma. Fabris also left Wildcatland.

"As a player, you knew of his attention to detail, but as a coach, it was even more evident," said Matt Miller, who had quarterbacked the Wildcats in 1995. "A lot of coaches talk that talk, but very few walk it like Coach Snyder. He understood what it took to be a champion."

There were no changes on the K-State coaching staff in 2000 and 2001 which, along with 2005, would be the only years that would happen in the 17-year Snyder era.

In 2002, Bob Elliott came to K-State from Iowa State, Bret Bielema from Iowa, and Del Miller returned to the Wildcat staff after stops at Southwest Missouri State as head coach and Oklahoma State as offensive coordinator. Leaving the 'Cats were Bennett, to become the head coach at SMU, plus Gush and Fello, who followed Bennett.

2003 changes had Joe Bob Clements and Bob Stanley being promoted from GA status with the loss of Dunn and Hudson. In 2004, enter Chris Cosh from South Carolina when Bielema went to Wisconsin.

From 1989 to 2005, Snyder's way never wavered, nor did his work-ethic.

Elliott served as a graduate assistant at Iowa in 1976, returned to the Hawkeyes as secondary coach from 1987-98, and later joined Snyder at K-State in 2002.

"I knew he was a different bird, so to speak, but those stories you hear about how he works aren't embellished," Elliott said. "I don't think anyone can believe how hard he works until you see it. There is no one like him in college football. I would bet maybe one percent of the people in this country can concentrate like he can."

In fact, Elliott's not so sure that assistants are even needed under Snyder.

"He calls the offensive plays, basically runs the special teams, and keeps us accountable on defense," Elliott said. "But along with being a great coach for players, he's also a great coach of coaches."

That's true with X's and O's, but also dealing with the personal issues some of his staff faced.

When Michael Smith divorced between the 2001 and 2002 seasons, he called his parents first. Snyder, who was a reader in Smith's wedding, was the next to know.

"He was just amazing with me," Smith said. "He just told me it was the toughest thing I was ever going to go through, but that each day would get better."

Pausing to collect himself, Smith continued, "I remember him saying, 'Michael, you take care of those girls (Kylie and Kenzie).' My father had told me the same thing, but it was reassuring to hear it from Coach.

"The man has been my mentor in life," Smith said.

And had Snyder not been a football coach, Elliott says, "I think he would be a great general. A General Schwarzkopf type."

Bill, The Human Being

"Bill's on the phone," my wife said to me.

Over the years, Bill and I had talked almost every week, so a call from Bill was not out of the ordinary.

However, the topic of the conversation was. He called to say that he had decided to retire as the head football coach at Kansas State University, and he wanted to let me know before it was announced publicly.

While the message came as a surprise, the fact that Bill called to tell me personally was not. Throughout his life, he has never put himself first. He has sincerely concentrated on caring and helping those around him in every possible way.

The public saw the coach; his family, players, staff and friends knew the person.

The principles and values he learned early in life—love, honesty, respect, honor, loyalty, dedication, attention to detail, duty, hard work, and purpose—have guided him and given him strength through both the difficult and joyous times.

Some will say that the most significant accomplishment of Bill's life was the phenomenal success of the football program he built at Kansas State.

They would be wrong.

The significance of this extraordinary man's life is manifested in his love for his family, his profound leadership qualities, and in the legacy of the lessons he taught.

The record shows that Bill Snyder is one of football's all-time greatest coaches, but he is an even greater human being.

— Tom Ross
Personal friend from Iowa

Chapter Eleven
The 16 Wildcat Commandments

The human mind is an amazing thing, and we know so little about it. At times I labor under the assumption that everybody's mind is like mine. And then I think, 'Oh, I hope not. God bless them if that's the case.' But I'm filled with thoughts 24 hours a day. I go to sleep with a notepad by my bed, and I wake up and my mind is still racing.

— Coach Bill Snyder

Bill Snyder was serving as a head coach for the first time. And while thinking the move up from coordinator to head coach would be no more than just another step, he quickly found otherwise.

"My first call back to Iowa was to say, 'Coach (Fry), I want to apologize. No one knows what it's like to sit in this chair until you've sat in this chair,'" Snyder said.

Fry's response? "He laughed."

"There's no way anybody can tell you," Snyder said of preparing to be a head coach. "There's no reason why you should know, and no way you would know."

Serving as the foundation for Snyder's program from day one were the Wildcats' "Goals For Success."

The walls of the KSU locker room were always strangely bare, particularly for a sport known for slogans and chants. Instead, the primary decoration that graced the Wildcats' off-field home was a plaque listing the Wildcats' 16 Commandments.

"I remember those early meetings when Coach was going over the goals for the first time," Brooks Barta said. "He could talk for hours on each one of them. I think the first night we got through maybe four or five of them, and it didn't change through the years. He could talk forever on them."

To Snyder, this is not coaching football, but coaching life's lessons.

As a coach, Snyder said, "I think I am charged by families to be a father, a mentor and a teacher to young people. These are lessons of life that will also make you a better player on the field."

Here are Snyder's definitions of the 16 Wildcat Commandments:

Commitment: We wanted a feeling of commitment from everybody involved in our program, from our players, to our coaches, to our administration and our fans. We wanted everyone committed to a common cause. It's so easy to say, 'I'm going to do this or do that,' but there had to be a commonality of commitment. It had to be a case where one player would look the next one in the eye and know that that individual had the same commitment that he did to create a collective success as a team.

Unity—Come Together As Never Before: There had to be a unity of 120 guys drawing closer together. Again, it was a commonality of purpose and caring about one another and our team. "As never before," simply meant however unified we've been, we can become even closer.

Be Tough: I think the game of football exudes a toughness on the field, but there is also a mental toughness and a toughness in making the hard decision. It takes a certain toughness to stay focused during the course of a long meeting, during the course of two-a-day practices, or on a Saturday afternoon. There has to be the ability to get through and extend that breaking point where you become distracted from the task at hand. The first day you may only get through warm-ups, the fourth day you may make it through the first hour of practice, the second week you may make it through the entire practice with a focus, and consequently, you will then make it through the entirety of a ballgame where you can play with the toughness and focus that it takes to play effectively.

Great Effort: We stressed that each of our players had complete control over each of these goals. Great effort is something every player on our team had total self-control over.

Never Give Up: This is the persistence part of it that every athlete should learn. It's never over until it's over. Don't give in. Continue to fight with the understanding you still have a chance. Don't give up in the classroom, don't give up on the practice field, don't give up during the course of a game and don't give up in life.

Refuse To Allow Failing To Become A Habit: We may fail today, but our determination to succeed the following day should be as prominent as ever with the attitude that success will happen.

Expect To Win: There are times when there is an indication that this game is going to be a difficult one. We might not win this game. I want our team to always expect to win if they have done all the things necessary during the course of the week to be successful, and if they play that way consistently on game day. If you have done this, then you should expect to win. If you say you expect to win, but have not done the necessary things on Monday, Tuesday and Wednesday, then it's likely not going to happen. But if you do collectively prepare to win—players and coaches—there is every reason to believe that it can culminate in success.

Leadership: We are continually encouraging our youngsters to be good examples for each other. Helping lead others into successful situations will only help our football team. On a football team, you only want two groups—leaders and followers. What you don't want is a third group pulling players out of those two circles.

Improve Every Day: We tell every athlete that we want him to have a goal to be a better person, a better student, and a better player every single day. Do something each day to help you improve in each of those areas as well as with faith and family. In the early years, players would be asked after each practice if, and how, he improved that day.

Self-Discipline—Do It Right And Don't Accept Less: This simply means that whatever it is that you're doing, do it the way you're supposed to do it, and do it that way every single time. It's a discipline of making yourself as good as you can absolutely be. This applies to you as a student, as a person, and as a player.

Eliminate Mistakes—Don't Beat Yourself: It was obvious when I first came to Kansas State that these young men had beaten themselves down and were almost committed to making errors that caused an ineffectiveness, resulting in our losing football games. One of the first things stressed was simply eliminating the types of mistakes that we had total control over. In the beginning, we were going to judge our football team not by what the scoreboard said, but by the amount of improvement we were making day to day. These were things we could see on tape after each practice. Then on Saturday, we would judge ourselves on how we improved fundamentally as individuals and collectively.

No Self-Limitations—Expect More Of Yourself: Everyone has expectations of other people. The left guard has expectations of the center, the quarterback, and the coach. We must expect a great deal out of ourselves. Expect more out of ourselves than anyone else. That gives us license to expect more from others. As a coach, if I'm gong to have great expectations for a player to work hard and be focused, then I need to set that example in my life. If we're all involved in these common goals, then we will eventually put ourselves in a position to achieve success collectively.

Consistency: All of the things we are charged to do as coaches and players—being on time, being at practice, being at meetings—we need to be consistent about. If we do it the right way over and over again, we're developing positive habits. Those positive habits allow you to do things consistently right on Saturdays.

Responsibility: There has to be accountability with each of our players, coaches and staff members. The responsibility comes with holding yourself accountable to achieve the things that you have total control over. I have never asked a player to do something he had no control over. Sometimes it's not easy, but the fact is, it's something completely within their command. There's an accountability to follow through with responsibility.

Unselfishness: Team sports require unselfishness. In this day of instant self-gratification, that is not an easy task.

Enthusiasm: 'Don't leave home without it.' I would ask our coaches to create an attitude of enthusiasm within their players prior to each practice. Each day, coaches turn in an agenda for their group meeting with the first and last topic being 'motivation.'

Chapter Twelve
Recruiting

We initially made the decision in 1988-1989 to not attempt to recruit the blue chip athletes outside of the state of Kansas. It was apparent that to do so would have been a drain on man hours and finances with little return. To spend time, effort and money to finish second in recruiting just wouldn't be efficient for us and at the time there were not very many reasons for the out-of-state blue chippers to come to our program.

— Coach Bill Snyder

No one defined the cast of characters that Bill Snyder inherited at Kansas State back in 1989 better than Ekwensi Griffith, who somehow found his way from the Big Apple of New York City to the Little Apple of Manhattan, Kansas, the year before Snyder's arrival.

"When I came to Kansas State, they were taking anyone," said the Brooklyn, New York, native. "I was 5-10, 250 pounds and slow as molasses. I had to call schools, they didn't call me."

It didn't take long to make introductions when Snyder met with his first football team prior to winter conditioning. While the NCAA limit was 95 scholarships at the time, Snyder was greeted by just 47 scholarship players.

"Our recruiting message was relatively simple that first year," Snyder said. "There was a tremendous opportunity to jump in and play relatively quickly. It depended on their abilities, but the opportunity was certainly available."

As Snyder remembers, the College Football Association numbered approximately 60 schools in 1989. When the CFA officials met that winter, Snyder finagled his way onto the agenda. He asked for some leniency in recruiting numbers for schools like K-State, so they could more quickly even the playing field with scholarship numbers.

"They didn't vote no, they voted heck no," Snyder said. "I think the vote was 61-1, and you know who the one was. They felt bad, but not badly enough for our plight."

Without question, Snyder said K-State was in the basement of the NCAA Division I football arena when it came to the number of scholarship players, and in the lower five percent, if not one percent, in perception.

Remember the recent history Snyder was inheriting—13 losses in a row, 27 consecutive non-winning Saturdays and only one bowl game in the history of the school.

"We knew we couldn't recruit the best of the best, so we did our best to recruit out of that second group, or even third group, to try to make us a little better," Snyder said.

By focusing on players that rival schools didn't consider highly ranked, Kansas State was able to exceed the amount of attention given to those players by other schools who were focused on the highest profile talent. The players K-State was recruiting felt certain that they were of the highest priority to the Wildcats, and not fall-back recruits as they were with other schools.

The first recruiting class included Reggie Blackwell out of St. Louis. Some schools questioned Blackwell's abilities as a defensive end because he had only one eye, but at K-State he played with great heart and effectiveness.

Blackwell was joined in the recruiting class by another defensive end, Ramon Davenport. The two linemen tipped the scales at weights of 205 and 215, respectively.

Jaime Mendez joined the Wildcats, but only because he was from Youngstown, Ohio, the hometown of assistant coach Bob Stoops. Mendez would go on to earn All-America honors in 1993 as a free safety.

Quentin Neujahr signed as a 230-pound offensive tackle and Brad Seib a 210-pound tight end. Seib came from the western Kansas community of Hoisington, which had a population of a couple thousand, but that was a metropolis compared to Neujahr's home of Suprise, Nebraska.

According to Snyder, "Not too many schools were going to go to the effort to fly into Omaha or Lincoln, drive hundreds of miles to a town like Suprise with a population of 76. Those were things we had to do, and we found Quentin to have the qualities we were looking for." Good thing they did as Neujahr would become an All-Big 8 center in 1993 and enjoy a six-year NFL career with Cleveland, Baltimore and Jacksonville.

Making life even more difficult was the fact that Snyder didn't recruit with any grandiose promises. His only testimony was that the goal would be improvement with each and every day.

"I remember Snyder coming into our home and talking about discipline and restrictions for off-campus living," said Tulsa native Kevin Lockett, a member of the 1992 recruiting class who still holds the Wildcat receiving records. "My parents were loving every minute of it, but as an 18-year-old boy, it was not the stuff I wanted to hear. But Coach was true to his word, which is why it was such an easy decision for Aaron (Lockett's brother, who came in 1997) to come to Kansas State."

Brooks Barta, a 6-0, 195-pound, linebacker recruited in the Parrish era, was another player that few felt could successfully compete in Big 8 football. By his sophomore year, Barta was a captain and would become a three-year starter.

"We were looking for guys like Brooks," Snyder said. "He was one of those mild-mannered guys who led by example. Even older players respected him because of how he worked and how he played. He played hard on the field and was a wonderful young man. He was one of several guys we had in those early years that we could build a program around."

As K-State stepped into the arena of respectability, and then into Top 25 status, the Snyder staff gravitated to recruiting a higher-caliber athlete. Still, it was that mid-talent guy by Big 8/Big 12 standards, that elevated the Wildcats into the 9, 10 and 11-win level and 11 consecutive bowl games.

"There became a time where we could have gone after the five-star-type youngster and stayed in the race longer, but all that would have done is invest more money and effort for someone we still probably weren't going to get, instead of investing time on a young man who fit our system and who we had a better chance of getting," Snyder said.

An example would be Vince Young, who led the Texas Longhorns to the 2005 national championship. Word on the internet had it down to the Longhorns and Wildcats, but with one problem. Young would never visit Manhattan.

"We were on several lists, but I think for the most part Vince had his No. 1 choice, and we were just there to keep Texas on its toes," Snyder said.

The Wildcats would prowl the prep ranks in Texas and Florida, letting the heavyweight programs battle over the Top 100 players, while K-State would slip in and do the best it could with that next 100, who were good players, according to Snyder.

In Florida, guys like Eric Hickson were lightly recruited by the Division I powers in their home state. "There wasn't a Florida school that recruited Eric, but he was a young man who fit our needs and became a tremendous running back for us,"

Snyder said. "We were fortunate to have so many young men like Eric both at Kansas State and Iowa."

Today, Hickson ranks third in all-time rushing, behind only Darren Sproles and Ell Roberson.

Snyder recognized early that Kansas State was not a household name in recruiting. If he hadn't already recognized this fact, the realization hit home on a recruiting trip to the state of Utah in the early 1990s.

Arriving at the home of a prospect in blizzard conditions, he found multiple television trucks poised for a story.

"I quickly found out that I wasn't the story," Snyder laughed. "I went to the door, but was asked if I could wait in my car. Bill McCartney, the head coach from Colorado, was making a visit.

"As I went back to my car, there wasn't a television camera pointed my way. They had no idea who I was," Snyder said.

After taking his turn with the recruit, Snyder returned to Manhattan where he learned that the recruit had committed to Colorado before Snyder ever entered the door, but the family didn't feel comfortable telling Snyder that in person.

A battle Snyder continually fought was school image. First, rival recruiters would remind prospects that Kansas State was an agriculture school, which the coach had an immediate answer for.

"What's the matter with that?" he asked. "Agriculture touches the lives of every human on the face of this earth and we have so much to offer in other areas."

Still, with an 18-year-old, it does carry a stigma.

To some, Kansas State was known as a basketball school from the 1950s through 1980s. And, Manhattan is predominately a white community with limited entertainment options for minority students.

"When I first got here there were some places, even around campus where some of our young men were not welcome, which made for the perception that there was a racial issue," Snyder said.

And no matter the sport, coaches at Kansas State were recruiting to a geographically-challenged area with a small population base and a two-hour drive to the nearest major airport, whether Kansas City to the east or Wichita to the south.

For example, a player from Florida on a recruiting trip to Kansas State would fly to Kansas City, where he would make a plane change, which could include a lengthy layover, before departing on a two-hour car ride to Manhattan. Not exactly the image you want to create when trying to impress big-time recruits.

Sure, K-State wanted the 6-6, 290-pound offensive lineman, but to Snyder, the intrinsic values carried an equal importance in recruiting. "We can make life better for this man if he would allow us to do so."

To a large degree, the Wildcats did what many said could never be done with the two- and three-star athlete, many of whom later played multiple seasons in the NFL.

Jon McGraw, a third-round draft choice by the New York Jets, came to K-State as a walk-on out of Riley County High School, located just 20 minutes to the northwest of Manhattan. Terence Newman, a first-round choice of the Dallas Cowboys, was one of the last to receive a scholarship in the 1998 recruiting class out of Salina, an hour's drive to the west of Manhattan and was only recruited by the University of Kansas and Kansas State. Jarrod Cooper, a fifth-round choice of Carolina, received little recruiting interest outside of K-State.

Mark Simoneau, from Smith Center, Kansas, a third-round selection of Atlanta, and Ben Leber, from Vermillion, South Dakota, a third-round choice by San Diego, were not high-profile recruits by any stretch of the imagination.

"They weren't recruited by many schools because they didn't fit the standard player profile, but they definitely fit ours," Snyder said.

If there was a particular turning point to the Snyder era, it may have come by striking gold with the 1997 recruiting class that included a blend of community college signees and prep players.

Community college gems included quarterback Michael Bishop (Blinn Community College), offensive lineman Brien Hanley (Coffeyville Community College), linebacker Jeff Kelly (Garden City Community College), receiver Darnell McDonald (Garden City Community College), defensive lineman Andrae Rowe (Fort Scott Community College), Cephus Scott (Garden City Community College), and return specialist Gerald Neasman (Coffeyville Community College).

From the prep ranks were multiple-year Wildcat starters Monty Beisel, Jerametrius Butler, Andy Eby, John Robertson, Aaron Lockett and Leber. Of those, Bishop, Kelly, McDonald, Beisel, Butler, Leber and Lockett would eventually go in the NFL draft.

Ironically, the highest-profile signee of the class was receiver Julius McMillan out of Altus, Oklahoma, who couldn't handle the structure of the K-State program and never played a down before leaving school. Another example of a player who couldn't adapt to the Wildcat-way was Chris Boggas, a mega-star lineman out of Irving, Texas, in 2000.

With both individuals, Snyder said, "Recruiting is such an inexact science. You never know how a young man is going to handle the rigors of the college environment, homework, study table, meetings, a higher level of practice, dealing with a more regimented lifestyle, and a collegiate social environment.

"It has always been my feeling that it would take two years to determine the capacity of a young man to adapt to our program and the college experience and become a productive student, person and player. Some make it just fine, and others do not."

When discussing recruits who stepped into their first workout and made a statement that they were ready to make an impact and play immediately, Snyder mentions only one name. Darren Sproles.

"Darren Sproles had that impact. That first week you thought, 'He can play. We have one very special young man here,'" Snyder recalled. "Nobody could get their hands on him. He made everyone miss. It was really that simple. It was a no-brainer with Darren. You liked everything about what Darren brought with him to the field. He just had that special presence."

If Snyder has a co-favorite player to go with Sproles, it would be Simoneau. "Mark was so consistent and seldom, if ever, made a mistake on or off the field."

K-State made a steady diet of recruiting for needs from the community colleges of Kansas, Texas and California, in particular. While having success in earlier recruiting classes, the 1997 headliners were, well, just that. Headliners.

Bishop came out of Blinn with a perfect 24-0 record as a starting quarterback, but was recruited by most schools as an athlete.

"We were the only school to tell Michael that he was definitely being recruited as a quarterback," Snyder said. "There were others who had an interest in him, but not as a quarterback. And to be honest, Michael could have played almost any position—receiver, defensive back, running back, linebacker—you name it, he was that good and that competitive."

Snyder liked Bishop's ability, but since he would not arrive on campus until July, there was a question of whether he could pick up the complexities of the Wildcats' offense in time for the 1997 season.

But Snyder did know this: "Michael was the proto-type single-wing tailback, which fit to a 'T' the type of quarterback we wanted to build our offense around. He could throw it, he could run it, he could punt it if needed, plus he was as competitive of a young guy as I have ever coached."

Jeff Kelly at linebacker "didn't jump out at you like Michael did, but Jeff was an athletic guy and he had a wonderful personality. He was just an easy going young man. You'd watch him on video tape, and his personality would stand out."

There wasn't a great recruiting battle to sign McDonald because of a lack of blazing speed. But he did have size at 6-3, and was sure-handed.

"Darnell had a knack of getting himself in position to catch the ball and make big plays," Snyder said. "But he wasn't what other people wanted speed-wise."

Snyder believes that the success Bishop, a native of Willis, Texas, had at K-State would later help in the recruitment of Ell Roberson out of Baytown, Texas.

"Michael was from the same general area. When we got Michael, no one thought too much about it, but when Michael became Michael, that gave Ell reason to think he could be the next one to pull the trigger for us," Snyder said.

While K-State developed a reputation for taking the community college player, Snyder said the concept started, and continued, based on need.

"If you don't have a freshman or a sophomore in your program on track to be 'the guy,' then you better concentrate on filling that void with someone who is ready to play quickly," Snyder said. "We weren't just going out to find community college guys. We had a need to fill."

Though many of the better KSU players came from two-year schools, of the 30 NFL draftees dating back to 1999, 20 were recruited out of the high school ranks and matured through the Wildcat program to star-status.

"We took great pride in our evaluation process. That in itself is the essence of successful recruiting and at the same time, the most difficult element," Snyder said. "A lot of schools went out and committed scholarships early, but we were a little more cautious and wanted to see a high school player's performance on Friday night during his senior season."

Plus, Snyder said, "I never allowed our coaches to get in the business of over-extending ourselves with scholarship offers. I was not going to make an offer, and then near signing day, tell a young player that we had offered more scholarships than we could accommodate and that we would have to retract our scholarship offer to him. A lot of schools find themselves in that position, but I wasn't going to let that happen."

Snyder also had a philosophy of not bringing many recruits on to campus for official 48-hour visits until after the season was over. The majority of the recruits fans saw prior to games at KSU Stadium were on unofficial one-day visits.

"I always felt that the most important players you have are not the ones you're recruiting, but the ones you presently have in your program," Snyder said. "My feeling was that our coaches couldn't do justice in the preparation for a game if, at the same time, they were focused on the recruitment of a young man on campus for an official weekend visit."

"Young men are so much more worldly today and exposed to so much more information. They live a life centered around a cell phone and the internet, and already know all there is to know by the time they make their visit," Snyder said

Kansas State had the money to do as it wished recruiting-wise, but never abused the athletic department with outlandish expenditures in travel or facilities.

"We wanted good facilities, but we never asked for the Taj Mahal," Snyder said. "We've had efficient facilities, but some of these places today take your breath away and that's going to catch the eye of young people.

"I had the belief that we were an athletic department and not just a football enti-ty," Snyder said. "I'm not sure of the message it sends when you have an unbeliev-able athletic facility, but a chemistry building that looks 127 years old. I truly wanted our young people to understand that their education was more important than football, and not send the message to the contrary through our facility."

Had he been selfish, Snyder could have made life on himself easier, but his phi-losophy was, "Do you do it because it's easier, or do you do it because it's the right thing to do?"

While there are certain conferences that have a shady reputation when it comes to recruiting, Snyder said that in his 17 years at KSU he saw a collection of Big 8/Big 12 coaches with strong character.

"I just don't think there was much cheating taking place within the Big 12. I can not think of one instance where I knew someone was cheating," Snyder said. "I would like to think the reason is that it's just the wrong thing to do. In some cases, it may be that the consequences today are a little stiffer. But I would like to think most coaches are honest people."

That, however, wasn't always the case during his earlier recruiting days at North Texas State.

In a day when coaches could be in the home on signing day, Snyder recalled going to a small-town, down-trodden Texas home in a rugged part of town the night before signing day.

"When I went to the door, I found a representative from another institution in the one-room home visiting with the family," Snyder said. "I was asked to wait outside, but as I quickly glanced back through the door as I was preparing to leave, I saw this briefcase filled with what appeared to be bills of an undetermined value."

After the generous coach left the home, Snyder knocked on the door and told the young man, "Look, here's what I saw.

"He said, 'Coach, you're right. And I'll tell you how much they were offering—$16,000,'" the recruit said. "I said, 'Are you going to do that?' And the young man said, 'I didn't do that, I'm coming to North Texas State.'

"I cherished him for that, and when I was visiting with his mother and shared that story in complimenting her son, I could sense that the mother, who I knew had difficulty in providing for the family, was somewhat upset that he had not taken the money."

Chapter Thirteen
1989: The Drive

I was disappointed that we hadn't gotten the first win (20-17 over North Texas State, September 30, 1989) before that. I was amazed at how excited everybody got about it. No disrespect to anybody we played, but it wasn't as big a thing for me as it was for everybody else.

— Coach Bill Snyder

Snyder went into the 1989 season, his first as a head coach, saying, "I don't have a clue about wins or losses, but we've stressed an understanding of how not to give up, and an understanding of how to avoid beating yourself, and an understanding of how and why we expect to win."

There was reason to believe that nothing had changed through the first three games, and 59 minutes, 59 seconds of the fourth.

In the opener, the Wildcats lost to Arizona State on the road, 31-0.

"I have never gone into a ballgame where I didn't think we were capable of winning if we played like I thought we were capable of playing," Snyder said. "If you're hoping someone else doesn't play up to their capabilities, then you're messing with something you have no control over. I always put it on us. We will succeed if we do A, B, C, and do it for 60 minutes, and if we have prepared in a proper manner during the course of the week."

Against the Sun Devils, William Price intercepted a Paul Justin pass on the first play of the game. The Wildcats moved the ball to the ASU 10-yard line, but David Kruger missed a 27-yard field goal.

After that, Snyder said, "The onslaught was on."

What was more painful than what the scoreboard advertised at game's end was how the Wildcats reacted to the loss.

"I was upset with them because I didn't sense any pain," Snyder said. "My message to the team was the greater the investment, the greater the pain in defeat, and I didn't see any great pain. The pain was going to be equivalent to what you're putting into it during the course of the week."

This first road game was also the site of the infamous Snyder butter story.

After arriving in Tempe, the team gathered for their Friday evening meal. They found mini-tubs of butter for baked potatoes on each table instead of the single pat of butter per athlete that had been requested. Snyder was not pleased.

Smiling at the attention the tale has received over the last 17 years, Snyder simply said, "We want the best possible diet for our players. I've never believed in the saying that if you take care of the little things, then the big things will take care of themselves. I do think, however, if you take care of the little things, it will help you take care of the bigger things.

"To me it was a diet issue that we wanted to control and we did," Snyder said. Pausing and grinning, he said, "That has been relaxed a bit over the years and now it's two pats per athlete."

It was also at that meal where, when service was not up to par, K-State's staff of assistant coaches, along with Snyder, scurried back into the kitchen and delivered meals themselves.

"I've always helped serve at away games," Snyder said. "No task was beneath me. I wanted our players to know that. It was about setting the example."

Returning to KSU Stadium the following weeks, the Wildcats stumbled against non-powers Northern Iowa, 10-8, and Northern Illinois, 37-20.

In week four against North Texas State, K-State improved but still made enough mistakes to trail 17-13 with 1:35 left in the game.

That's when The Drive started.

"We hadn't won a game in years, but I remember the look in Carl Straw's eyes in the huddle," said KSU sophomore receiver Michael Smith. Laughing at the memory, Smith continued, "He said, 'We're going to complete every pass we throw.' The first play he ended up getting sacked, and I said, 'You've got to be kidding me.'"

Straw didn't complete all his passes, but he was pretty darn close.

Here's how The Drive went. K-State trailed by four, 17-13, with 95 seconds left:

1st & 10 at the KSU 15: Carl Straw sacked, -7 yards
2nd & 17 at the KSU 8: Pass interference on NT

1st & 10 at the KSU 22: Straw pass to Michael Smith, 27 yards
1st & 10 at the KSU 49: Straw sacked, -11 yards
KSU timeout: 36 seconds remaining
2nd & 10 at the KSU 38: Straw pass to Smith, 20 yards
1st & 10 at the NTS 42: Straw pass to Smith, 20 yards
KSU timeout: 23 seconds remaining
1st & 10 at the NTS 22: Straw pass to Smith, 10 yards
1st & 10 at the NTS 12: Incomplete pass
2nd & 10 at the NTS 12: Incomplete pass
KSU timeout: 4 seconds remaining
3rd & 10 at the NTS 12: Straw pass to Frank Hernandez, 12 yards, touchdown.

Kansas State 20, North Texas State 17

KANSAS STATE 20, NORTH TEXAS STATE 17!!!

"It was like we had won the damn Super Bowl. People were jumping over benches, little kids were biting me on the ankle. It was only one win, but it felt like winning the Super Bowl," said KSU defensive end Maurice Henry.

Athletic director Steve Miller said, "When we scored, I really thought I was going to pass out. I mean, I really lost it. I couldn't catch my breath and almost fell down."

Joking about the crowds back in those days, Smith said, "All 6,000 or 7,000 fans stormed the field and were on top of Frank, including myself."

Kansas State had won its 299th all-time game on October 18, 1986, against the University of Kansas, 29-12.

Kansas State beat North Texas State on September 30, 1989 for its 300th win.

In between, K-State had lost 16 straight games and was 0-29-1 in their last 30 games.

On the winning catch, Snyder recalled, "I remember Frankie Hernandez coming to the sidelines and saying, 'We can run this particular thing,' I said, 'Okay, if that's what you think you can do, go do it.' And they did it.

"There is a time when you listen to players," Snyder said. Pausing and smiling, he added, "Not all the time, but sometimes."

"It was designed as a five- to seven-yard out, but this one was 11 to 12 yards.

Instead of a three-step drop, I dropped back five," said quarterback Straw.

From the right hash mark, Straw threw across the field to No. 83, who made the catch, and "toe-tapped" into the front left corner of the north end zone of KSU Stadium.

Everyone saw the catch but Straw, who only heard the catch.

"I got belted on the chin. It really hurt, but when the crowd stormed the field, I felt no pain," Straw said. "When I knew Frank caught the ball, all I wanted to do was laugh, cry and scream, but nothing came out of my mouth."

Snyder was not surprised, calling Straw "a tough nut," who possessed an "I will do it" attitude.

Straw completed five passes for 90 yards during The Drive, with Smith catching four of those for 78 yards.

"I'll never forget the array of catches Michael Smith made in that drive," Hernandez said.

But in the end, it was Hernandez who made *the play* in The Drive.

As Smith good-naturedly says today, "I made all the catches until the last one, and Frank got all the love."

Just for the record, the starters in the 20-17 victory over North Texas State were:

Offense: WR—Frank Hernandez and Michael Smith; QB—Chris Cobb; RB—Pat Jackson; FB—Curtis Madden; TE—Alan Friedrich; C—Paul Yniguez; OG—Chad Faulkner and Eric Zabelin; OT—Will McCain and Shawn Fleming

Defense: DE—Maurice Henry and Reggie Blackwell; DT—Ekwensi Griffith and John Crawford; LB—Brooks Barta and James Enin-Okut; CB—Tyreese Herds and Dimitrie Scott; FS—Marcus Miller; SS—Eric Harper

Hernandez, a native of Mission, Texas, added, "The victory was certainly a huge milestone for the stage our program was in at that point. It was one of the components of building that foundation. It was one of the baby steps to where we are today.

"Nobody was happy with a 1-10 year, but that win gave us a taste of what victory felt like," Hernandez said. "It was a sneak preview of what we were capable of doing."

Smith added, "I still think it was the biggest win in the history of the school. For the first time, it showed us that if we worked hard, good things would happen."

Snyder agreed, but at the same time was more realistic about the happenings of the day.

"The law of averages says sooner or later somebody is going to fall down and lose to us," Snyder said. "We got better that day, and that's all that we've ever asked our players to do."

Tom Ross, Snyder's best friend from his days at Iowa, remembers putting in an immediate call after the game to offer his congratulations on his friend's first win Manhattan.

"I said what a great win! This is a wonderful day!" Ross said. "Bill's reply was sort of a calm, 'Well, we all knew it would happen some day, but there's another game coming up.' He was already looking to the next week."

Kansas State would lose that next week to Nebraska, 58-7, and the next six Saturdays as well. But in some of those games, there was reason for hope. The Wildcats played Oklahoma State to within four (17-13), Kansas to within five (21-16), and Missouri to within 12 (21-9).

Overall, Snyder said of the season, "My assessment of 1989 didn't have much to do with that one win. What I assessed the year on was steady improvement made during the course of the year individually, and to some degree, collectively and that we had gotten ourselves into the fourth quarter with a chance to win in four of our games. That allowed me to say that we were going to be a pretty decent program."

He added, "I knew we weren't very good, but I knew we were going in the right direction. I'm sure people were saying, 'Here we go again. It's the same-old, same-old,' but I didn't feel that way. I could see the players and the people associated with the program altering their attitudes."

It was also in this first year at Kansas State that Snyder scored his biggest victory—saving the life of one of his players.

Snyder had gotten word that one of his players was planning to commit suicide and had left a call for help. The Wildcat coach received word that the player would be out around Tuttle Creek Reservoir, just north of Manhattan.

Snyder found his player in a car with a hose going from the exhaust pipe to inside the car with the windows rolled up.

"He was just sitting there listening to the radio," Snyder said. "He let me in the car and we talked for a long, long, long time … close to three hours.

"You had a heartfelt concern for the young man. Life gets over-whelming at times and, unfortunately, some young people do not have the experience to handle it. It was such a relief to find him. I only applied common sense, which can make a lot of positive things happen, especially when facing disruptions in life like that. I was just pleased that I could help," Snyder said, deflecting any notion that he, in fact, did save the player's life.

Billy Dean Snyder with his
mother Marionetta.

Grandma and Grandpa Owens with a young
Sean Snyder.

Bill Snyder, George Olendorf and Wayne Rudloff pose for the camera after graduating from William Jewell College May 28, 1962.

Snyder's senior class of football teammates at William Jewell College:

(Back Row L-R): Bill Snyder, Sam Childress, Tom Travis, Jack Jordan, Charlie Lynn
(Front Row): Bob Huft, Grundy Newton, Don Sporck, Jim Gladden, Art Miller

The 1982 University of Iowa coaching staff

(Bottom Row L-R): Phil Dervrich, Bill Brashier, Bernie Wyatt, Barry Alvarez, Dan McCarney

(Back Row): Bill Snyder, Del Miller, Carl Jackson, Hayden Fry, Kirk Ferentz, Donny Patterson, Bruce Kittle

Hayden Fry and Bill Snyder pose with their prized pupil–Iowa quarterback and Heisman Trophy runner-up Chuck Long.

Snyder made his mark at Iowa as both a coach and top-notch recruiter. He is pictured here with a trio of Iowa recruits out of Omaha, Nebraska *(L-R):* Richard Station, Sean Ridley and Richard Bass. Station and Ridley were considered the top recruits in the country their senior year of high school.

Bill Snyder at his first press conference as the new K-State football coach.

The 1990 Kansas State coaching staff

(Bottom Row L-R): John Latina, Nick Quartaro, John Hendrick, Del Miller, Bruce VanDevelde
(Back Row): Dana Dimel, Jim Leavitt, Jerry Palmeri, Bob Stoops, Bill Snyder, Mark Mangino, Mike Stoops, Ben Griffith

Bill Snyder takes a moment to compose himself after announcing he is stepping down as the head football coach at Kansas State.

Bill Snyder leads the Wildcats onto the field for the last time November 19, 2005.

Wildcat players Jordy Nelson and Jeromey Clary carry a victorious Coach Snyder off the field following a 36-28 win over Missouri in Snyder's final game at Kansas State.

The Snyder family is introduced on the field prior to a Kansas City Chiefs game.

(L to R): Kansas City Chiefs President Carl Peterson, Bill Snyder, Sharon Snyder, Sean Snyder, Wanda Snyder, Shannon Snyder, Ross Snyder and Whitney Snyder.

Bill Snyder at his induction into the Missouri
Sports Hall of Fame.

The KSU fans let their coach know how they feel about him.

Chapter Fourteen
Foundation Players

I so appreciate the players who played at Kansas State and established the foundation from which other teams could be built. These are the guys who had to practice every day out in the cold because there wasn't an indoor facility; these are the guys who never benefited from a bowl game.

— Coach Bill Snyder

The likes of Eric Gallon, Carl Straw, Paul Watson, Brent Venables, Michael Smith, Jaime Mendez, Sean Snyder, Brooks Barta, and so many others never realized the thrill of playing in a bowl game. But if it hadn't been for the foundation established by these Wildcats, the run of 11 straight bowl games would never have been realized.

When 1-10 was followed by 5-6 which led to 7-4, and especially when the program slipped back to 5-6 in 1992, Mendez remembers, "Coach just stayed the course, and that was admirable when things weren't going as everyone would have liked. He always kept us together.

"That was a year when we had closed meetings, and he kept us together by allowing us to coach ourselves," Mendez said. "I'm not sure how he did it, but he kept us feeling positive about ourselves."

That was on and off the field. It's an easier task to be a disciplinarian when things are right, but to go from an anything goes program philosophy to the rigid rules of Snyder was a more difficult transition. Especially since this was before the winning came.

"It's the little things he thought of that went a long way," said running back J.J. Smith, who played for the Wildcats from 1991 through 1994. "If your shirt was hanging out, he would let you know it was inappropriate. I think that was a discipline we gradually learned to take onto the field."

Kevin Lockett, who still ranks as KSU's all-time leading receiver with 217 catches for 3,032 yards from 1993-96, agreed.

Sure, Snyder wanted his players to become the best possible talents they could be, but as Lockett said, "He was more concerned about turning you into a man. A lot of lessons he taught through football were ones that taught you how to provide leadership, have integrity, and have character. These were lessons that would help you in life after football is over."

To get players through the growing-pains of college when football was celebrated only 11 Saturdays a year, Snyder was sure to do his part, but as Venables, a product of Salina South High School and transfer from Garden City Community College, said, "Coach Snyder always gave us a sense of ownership with the program. He had a blueprint, and we knew if we followed his plan, it would pay dividends.

"With Coach Snyder, there was an investment that you had to be willing to make if you were in the program," Venables continued. "There was never an option of having one foot in the boat and one foot out. If you were going to be involved in this program, both of your feet were going to be in the boat, and you had to be willing to stay out to sea until the very end."

It was still a time when few thought a 10-victory season was an achievable goal. But Snyder did, and he convinced these players of the early 1990s that while they may not realize it personally, they would always be a part of, and a reason for, the success of future Wildcat teams.

Recalling how Snyder worked the minds of the Wildcats in those days, Mendez says, "The only people who know what it was like are the ones that were here in the beginning. No one remembers what it was like to have facilities that were worse than the ones at the high schools where several of us had played. When I got here and saw the facilities, I just thought, 'You've got to be kidding.' But Coach Snyder had a vision, and he made us believe in that vision."

Neujahr said it was a bit of "Us against the world," that Snyder portrayed, an attitude that allowed the players to fight through those long days of early August practices. Days Neujahr defined as, "You got up with the sun and were still up when the sun went down. (Laughing) They weren't two-a-days, they were one-a-days that lasted all day.

"There are two types of commitment," Neujahr went on to say. "Commitment where you agree, yeah, we're going to do this, but when times get tough, you're not as committed as you once thought you were. And, there's commitment without exception. That's what Coach demanded. I equate Coach to that horse at the Kentucky Derby who had blinders on. He was going only straight ahead. This is the way we're going to do things. If we fail, it's due to my decision."

Carl Straw, a junior, and Paul Watson, a sophomore, were already on campus when Snyder was hired.

"Demanding, but fair," Straw said of his first impression of Snyder. "He didn't know us, but he instilled a belief."

Watson added, "You can't call him an excellent coach because that would be selling him short. He's better than that."

Chapter Fifteen
1990-1992: Years Of Growth

These were years where we still weren't very good, but we were getting better every day. You could start to see it on the scoreboard, but more important than that, our players could feel it every day in practice.

— Coach Bill Snyder

The fall seasons of 1990 and 1991 would be ones of growth and maturity.

Five wins came in 1990, which had been bettered in a single season only one other time—6-5-1 in 1982—during a 20-year period dating back to a 6-5 campaign in 1970. Prior to that, one would have to journey back another 16 years—7-3 in 1954—to find a Wildcat season with more than five smiling Saturdays.

While five wins may not seem like much, those in the Big 8 Conference lauded the accomplishment by decorating Snyder with Coach of the Year honors.

"I'm sure some were wondering what was going on that a guy would be Coach of the Year with a 5-6 record, but that may have put in perspective what the history of this football program was all about," Snyder said. "What it meant to me, and what I wanted it to mean to our players, was now you're hearing from the people we play on a weekly basis that they see the improvement. We know where you've been, and we can see the improvement. What it was saying was, 'We respect you.'"

The 1990 Wildcat wins came over Western Illinois, New Mexico State, New Mexico, and in the conference against Oklahoma State, 23-17, and Iowa State, 28-14. The victory over the Cyclones was KSU's first Homecoming win since defeating Iowa State in 1981.

"That year was really positive for our players," Snyder said. "We had quite a few back from the year before, and the guys who were left were those who had declared an intent to buy-in to the program. They had a pride in it, while the other guys were gone."

Had there not been victories to celebrate, it would have been only natural for doubt to set in.

While the wins during the month of September were against some lesser opponents, K-State's rival coaches understood the method to Snyder's scheduling philosophy.

"Confidence is a quality that allows abilities to surface," said rival coach Bill McCartney of Colorado in defending KSU's light early schedule. "Everybody has talent, but not everybody sees those abilities come to the front. With their scheduling, they had a chance to gain momentum and cohesiveness. Gain a rhythm. When you over-schedule, you never get a chance to allow everybody's talents to blend."

At the time, McCartney had been given a 15-year contract by the Buffs leading him to joke, "That's why I was willing to schedule Stanford, Texas and Miami of Florida."

Even more fame and fortune came with the 1991 season when the Wildcats went 7-4. It was a win total that had not been matched since the 1934 7-2-1 championship season, and had been bettered only three times in school history—8-2 in 1931, 8-2 in 1912 and 10-1 in 1910.

Snyder was not only decorated with Big 8 Coach of the Year honors, but also the *ESPN* National Coach of the Year award.

The Wildcats opened with wins over Indiana State, Idaho State and Northern Illinois, then defeated Kansas in Week No. 5, and closed out the year by handling Iowa State, Missouri and Oklahoma State.

The lone losses were to No. 4 Washington, 56-3, No. 9 Nebraska, 38-31, No. 16 Colorado, 10-0, and No. 21 Oklahoma, 28-7.

While games at Clemson, Florida and Tennessee were removed by Snyder, the University of Washington was one top-ranked team to refuse K-State's wishes to opt out of playing the game. Snyder personally called Washington coach Don James to say it simply didn't make any sense for either side to be involved in such a game.

"I explained our situation to Don and told him that Kansas State would not be coming," Snyder said. "He said he really appreciated our situation, but he wanted to play the game."

Next, the athletic directors talked, with Kansas State being told, in Snyder's words, "Not no, but heck no."

So, Snyder called James again, "I said, 'Okay, Don, you're going to need to dress your guys in two different colored jerseys because we ain't comin'. You can just play each other.' He chuckled, and said, 'We'll see you on September 28.'"

K-State did go, did get slaughtered, but the team got to see the Space Needle. "That's the only thing we got out of the trip," lamented Snyder.

The 1991 season was the first time K-State demonstrated an ability to make a spectacular play to win a game that looked to be a sure loss, and to actually compete against the best in the country.

In the opener against Indiana State, K-State turned what looked to be a 25-24 defeat into a 26-25 victory when William "T" Price swiped a pass and returned it 102 yards for a two-point conversion with 3:24 left in the game. At the time, Price was the first in NCAA history to provide the winning points to a game on a defensive extra-point since the rule had been put in place in 1988.

For the year, Kansas State averaged 160 rushing yards per game, which was the highest total dating back to 1982 (178); passed for 225 yards per game, which had been bettered only once (234 in 1988) since 1969 when Lynn Dickey threw the ball for 250 yards per game; and averaged 23.9 points per game, which was the highest by any Wildcat team since the '69 Wildcats put up 31.9 points per Saturday. Kansas State's defense allowed just 351 yards per game, the best in nine seasons, and Kansas State held opponents to 20.5 points per game, the lowest figure in nine years.

Eric Gallon rushed for 1,161 yards, making him only the third back in KSU history to eclipse the 1,000-yard mark in a single season; Paul Watson threw the ball for 2,312 yards and 10 scores; and Michael Smith caught 55 passes, running his career totals to all-time Wildcat highs of 179 receptions for 2,457 yards and 11 touchdowns.

All nice looking in the press guide, but to Snyder, the season had more meaning than numbers.

"If I put my finger on the one thing that this football team accomplished, it would be how they came together better than any we've had in our time here. The guys had a single purpose, and were willing to make sacrifices for the success to happen."

Snyder added, "I was probably in the minority, but following the five-win year of 1990, I thought seven wins were possible. But if I say I'm satisfied with seven wins, that means I am conceding the other four. I never want to put myself in a position to do that."

While Kansas State did win seven times in 1991, the Wildcats were not bowl-eligible because two of the victories—Indiana State and Idaho State—came against non-Division I teams. At the time, those games could not be counted by teams trying to reach the magic number of six wins needed for postseason play.

Snyder's teams were getting better, and quickly, going from one, to five, to seven wins. Seven wins with a program that had won a *total* of just six games in the five years prior to his arrival.

At the time, Snyder offered, "You try to get to that level of six, seven or eight wins and maintain that for a while to show you have arrived. Then there comes that time down the road where you come up with an excellent recruiting class that gives you a chance to compete with the best in the conference and have a chance at that major bowl. We just needed to keep in the range of six, seven, eight wins for a while."

While the fans were getting caught up with the scoreboard improvement, Snyder was not. His focus then, and for the entirety of his 17 seasons at K-State, was individual practice improvement, which would eventually equate to on-field team victories.

"We didn't all of a sudden become a better football team. We were a better football team by first being individually better, and then collectively better," Snyder said. "That's when we became a 7-4 football team."

Snyder characterized the improvement between the first year in 1989 to the second in 1990 as improving greatly in some segments, minimally in others, and not at all in others.

The same would be true in 1992 when the Wildcats slipped back to 5-6. A 27-12 win over Montana opened the year. A 35-14 smacking of Temple was followed by a 19-zip handling of New Mexico State.

Perhaps taking victory for granted fresh off the success of 1991, the fortunes changed for the Wildcats. While the players may have been caught wondering why, Snyder understood that the better the team became, the more the degree of improvement would lessen from the first couple years when the team was starting from sub-ground zero.

And 1992 was a year where Snyder said some player issues surfaced that hadn't been there the first couple years. There were some built-in distractions, and players weren't quite as focused as before. Some selfishness set in, not collectively, but just a little here and there, which was enough to throw the team off center.

One who did play with focus, and had paid the price to play, was Gallon, a 6-foot-1, 210-pound running back from Lakeland, Florida, who was coming off a 1,000-yard junior season.

A senior-to-be, Gallon tore ligaments in his knee during the spring season. When doctors told him that surgery would be needed, Gallon literally bolted out of the training room door.

"At that time, such surgery took eight months to recover from, and he knew his playing days were over," Snyder said. "He was upset and ready to leave school. I caught him out in the parking lot and we talked in his car for a quite some time."

Gallon decided to stay at K-State and had the surgery on April 14. Shortly after, he started an intensified rehabilitation program.

On September 19, just five months after surgery, Gallon started in the opener against Montana, and gained 87 yards on 22 carries. Gallon finished the year with 705 rushing yards, running his career total to 1,960, second only in school history to Isaac Jackson's 2,182.

K-State opened Big 8 play with a 31-7 loss at Kansas, then suffered an embarrassing 28-16 non-conference setback at Utah State, followed by consecutive road losses to Colorado, 54-7, and Oklahoma, 16-14, for a month of losses coming all outside of KSU Stadium.

"That year was the most disappointing of my career," said Barta, who would end up the second leading tackler in school history behind K-State Hall-of-Famer Gary Spani. "We had so looked forward to that year because of the people we had back, but we really needed a quarterback."

The Wildcats defeated Iowa State, lost to Missouri, and blanked Oklahoma State, 10-0, to lead to Snyder's first bowl game, albeit an unofficial bowl game. Kansas State gave up its home date with the University of Nebraska to play in the Coca Cola Bowl in Tokyo, Japan, on December 5.

Typically not drawn to a situation out of the norm for his program, this trip intrigued Snyder for a couple of reasons.

First, he said with a smile, "With Nebraska being such a prolific program, and the fact we were still growing, there was the thought of out of sight, out of mind.

If we played the game way across the world, fewer people would even know the game was being played."

But seriously, Snyder had an inkling that the Wildcats were nearing bowl-quality, and this trip could serve as a prep course to what a postseason experience would be like.

The Coca-Cola Bowl also led to more Snyder-isms in terms of his attention to detail. K-State and Nebraska traveled on the same chartered jet, and Snyder wanted to make sure the Wildcats were seated on the side of the plane that would have fewer hours of direct sunlight.

"It's just something I tend to think through, whether it's riding in a bus from the stadium to the airport or going across the world. It only stood to reason that the sunny side of the plane would be much warmer, and I didn't want our big guys sweating until we got them on the field," Snyder said. "It wasn't going to be something where if we didn't get our way, we were going to take our marbles and go home, but it was just something that I asked for."

K-State competed, but lost the game to Nebraska, 38-24, to finish the year at 5-6. Two steps in reverse from the previous year's seven victories. Even with this setback in wins, Snyder's influence with the Wildcats was being recognized.

CU's McCartney said of Snyder, "KSU will be hard pressed to keep him. What's the saying, 'The same things that make you laugh, make you cry.' It's a perfect example of being excited, but at the same time threatened."

He continued, "If I left CU, they wouldn't miss a beat. But Kansas State would be the loser if Bill Snyder left. Kansas State needs Bill Snyder. I'm not trying to be overly modest. I'm just trying to tell the truth."

McCartney then read a phrase from Benjamin Disraeli, the former Prime Minister of Great Britain.

The secret to success is constancy of purpose.

"I firmly believe that the key to Kansas State continuing to improve and continuing to have good fortune is the constancy of purpose, and that means Bill Snyder."

Snyder now faced the task of motivating his players and coaches to maintain what had been accomplished in the first three seasons.

At the time, he said, "I don't think it will be tougher to motivate them because their expectation level is so much higher. As long as you don't allow complacency to set in, there will be motivation because they do expect more out of themselves."

He added, "I don't like 5-6 right now, but two years ago 5-6 would have been a godsend."

"You just can't come up for air. If you do, you run the risk of sinking back," Snyder said at the close of the 1992 season. "There are hurdles to jump, or avoid, every single day."

Snyder: King Cotton

When I think of Coach Snyder, I automatically think of the words integrity, focus, organization, dignity and loyalty.

I give Coach Snyder and the Kansas State administration a lot of credit for helping save the future of the Cotton Bowl. The 1996 game (1995 season) was the most difficult match-up we ever had to promote. We didn't have a title sponsor, and our game was not selected as a member of the Bowl Championship Series. For the first time in 55 years, the Cotton Bowl did not feature a team from the Southwest Conference. On top of that the game was played in poor weather.

With Southwestern Bell (now AT&T) signing on as our sponsor prior to the 1997 game, it was important to produce a big game to solidify the Cotton Bowl's future.

When Kansas State entered the picture the team brought along a wave of 40,000 K-State fans who helped produce the quickest sellout in our history. It was a watershed moment.

— Rick Baker
President of the Cotton Bowl

Chapter Sixteen
Purple Haze On The Horizon

The 1993 season was the culmination of putting it all in place. I will never forget the great following that we had in Tucson. The game and environment couldn't have been better.

— Coach Bill Snyder

In 1993 the Kansas State football program accomplished the following:

- KSU opened a season 5-0 for the first time since 1931.

- KSU's 9-2-1 record was the program's best since 1910.

- The Wildcats were a perfect 4-0 in non-league games for the first time since 1934.

- K-State secured its second straight undefeated home season.

- Quarterback Chad May set four Big 8 records including passing for 489 yards against Nebraska.

- Andre Coleman became the first player in Big 8 history to lead the league in all-purpose yards, kickoff returns and punt returns in the same season.

- Kevin Lockett shattered the receiving record for freshmen with 770 yards on 50 catches.

- Free safety Jaime Mendez became only the third player in KSU history to receive consensus first-team All-America honors, joining linebacker Gary Spani (1977) and punter Sean Snyder (1992).

- Mendez, Thomas Randolph, Quentin Neujahr, Coleman and May were first-team All-Big 8 honorees.

- Bill Snyder was the Big 8 Coach of the Year, and one of four finalists for the Bear Bryant National Coach of the Year.

The Wildcats opened the year with routine wins over New Mexico State and Kentucky, followed by a 30-25 thriller at the University of Minnesota. That win snapped an 18-game non-conference road losing streak that dated back to the 1979 season.

Quarterback May and receiver Lockett worked 53-yards of pass-and-catch magic on the second play of the game, but the outcome was not decided until the final play. Trailing by five points, Minnesota marched to the KSU four-yard line, but four times the Wildcats' defense held the Gophers out of the end zone.

After thumping UNLV 36-20, K-State opened Big 8 play by hosting the Kansas Jayhawks. The Wildcats scored on a May-to-Coleman pass play and a booming 50-yard field goal by Tate Wright, and then handed the heroics over to the defense to preserve the 10-9 victory.

Moving on to Lincoln, Nebraska, K-State did everything but win the game over the No. 6-ranked Big Red. With May completing 30 of 51 passes for 489 yards, K-State totaled a whopping 565 yards on offense, which was the most ever allowed against a Tom Osborne-coached NU team. J.J. Smith rushed for 102 yards in the game, making him only the third back in Wildcat history to crack the century mark against Nebraska.

Final score: NU 45, KSU 28.

Next came a 16-16 tie with No. 16 Colorado.

K-State trailed throughout, but faced the option to go for the win or the tie with 21 seconds left in the game. Down 16-13, May led the Wildcats from their own 20-yard line to the CU 18.

"We had a penalty and it was like 4th and 8," Snyder said. "I know you don't play for ties, but in this case, it was the right thing to do."

Wright toed the game-tying 35-yard field goal, and K-State had its first non-loss to a ranked team since defeating No. 17 Missouri in 1970.

"Jaime Mendez is mad at me to this day for going for the tie," Snyder said. "But before the game, you always factor in where you stand in the standings, and how it might impact your chances for a bowl game. I knew a tie would not hurt us, and in fact could help us, in regard to a possible bowl game."

The tie elevated Kansas State into the national polls at No. 25 the following week, a first for the Purple and White since being ranked No. 15 on November 8, 1969.

"The players were enthusiastic about that. It was really significant to them," Snyder said. "They knew it had been decades, if ever, that the school had been in the rankings, and they were proud of it."

That chest-puffing would increase on the following Saturday when No. 13 Oklahoma marched into KSU Stadium. With a record of 0-74-1 in the previous 75 games against ranked teams, Kansas State ended a 22-game losing streak to the Sooners with a 21-7 victory.

After the game, Gib Twyman of the *Kansas City Star* wrote, "Make no mistake, K-State's abilities equal, or better, anyone in its league."

May threw TD strikes to Lockett and Mitch Running, plus scored on a keeper.

Perhaps spraining elbows and wrists with self-congratulatory back slaps, K-State stumbled and lost the next week to Iowa State, 27-23, in the game that featured a streaker dashing across the field. Rebounding to knock off Missouri and Oklahoma State, the Wildcats finished regular-season play at 8-2-1, Big 8 play in third-place at 4-2-1, and held a No. 20 national ranking.

More importantly, the Wildcats accepted an invitation to play in the Copper Bowl against Wyoming on December 29.

At a pre-game pep rally, athletic director Max Urick announced, "As the sun begins to set on Tucson tonight, you're going to see a purple haze on the horizon because they're coming, and they're coming by the thousands."

An estimated 22,000 K-Staters made the trip to the desert, and they weren't to be disappointed.

With the game billed as a "100-Point Shootout," Kansas State did its part in a 52-17 thrashing of the Cowboys. K-State totaled 227 rushing yards, with Smith accounting for 133 of those. May passed the ball for 275 yards and two touchdowns, and, Coleman had 144 yards in receptions and a score, as well as a 68-yard punt return for six-points.

Throw in the fact that Kenny McEntyre scored on a 37-yard interception and Tate Wright booted a 22-yard field goal, and as lineman Jim Hmielewski said, "Our offense scored, our defense scored and our kicking game scored. That makes it a perfect game."

Even the difficult-to-please Snyder said, "It was a complete ballgame. At that time, we couldn't have played a whole lot better."

Mendez offered, "It's a fairy tale. To win nine games, to win the first bowl game in history, to know we're going to finish in the Top 20 for the first time in history—it's hard to explain."

After returning from Tucson, Snyder had an unannounced visitor from western Kansas arrive at his Vanier Complex office. The gentleman asked for a bit of Snyder's time and proceeded to tell the Wildcat coach that the entirety of the Copper Bowl experience was "the most important event of my entire life."

"That set me back," admitted Snyder. "He had already said that he was married, had children and a career. To me, these were a lot more important than our win in Tucson, and I didn't want to accept the responsibility for him feeling that way.

"It was an occurrence that allowed me to truly understand, for the first time, how much the success of our program meant to those who remained loyal K-Staters throughout the unproductive years."

To this day, Snyder says he continues to get mail referring to the Copper Bowl game and what a magical night it was.

Chapter Seventeen
Game Week and Game Day

I keep long office hours because I just think that's what it takes to be successful. I honestly wonder about what other people do with their time. I guess I'm just slower than most coaches.

— Coach Bill Snyder

Bob Elliott had known Snyder at the University of Iowa. He had seen firsthand the mastermind at work, and since Iowa, he had heard about Snyder's overdose of work as a head coach at Kansas State.

But when he joined the KSU staff as defensive coordinator in 2002 he marveled at the three- to four-hour marathon meetings.

"Bill Snyder can concentrate all day and never lose focus. I don't know how he does it." Laughing, Elliott added, "How old is he? I've never known a guy who could go longer without a bathroom break. He must have a tube or something!"

Even Snyder laughs at that, saying, "I constantly have a cup of coffee in my hand, but I seldom drink a full cup. To me, if we took breaks, it would break the concentration and then you'd have to start over."

While several coaches begged not to be quoted when calling the meetings long and boring, well, that's how they described some of them. To Snyder, however, each item on the agenda was a part of a puzzle that wouldn't be complete if not attended to.

A typical in-season work week with the coaching staff required seven full days:

Saturday evening after the game the coaching staff was free to leave, but Snyder—often to the tunes of Kenny G, Ella Fitzgerald, or the Jackie Gleason Orchestra—stayed and watched every second of the just-completed game, completed a hand-written report for each assistant, and viewed at least one game tape of the next opponent.

Sunday morning, Snyder was in early, held an informal press conference at 10 a.m., and met with his coaches at 10:30 for an overview of the Saturday game. The coaches then evaluated their film, wrote corrections for each player and graded tape prior to a 4 p.m. meeting when they provided detailed grading information to Snyder, plus identified the Players of the Week.

Also during this time Scott Eilert and his video staff constructed situational tapes for the next game. Tapes would be made for all drop-back passes, 3rd-and-short from the right hash mark, 2nd-and-long from the left hash mark, and so on until every possible game situation was covered.

Around 6:45 p.m., after a short dinner break, coaches returned to continue studying tape and begin the early stages of formulating a game plan for the upcoming opponent. These sessions usually lasted until midnight, but sometimes much later.

It wasn't unusual for Snyder's phone to ring around midnight during late nights in the office. On the other end would be Jim Colbert giving him a jingle from his home in Palm Desert, California.

"I didn't want him to go buggy-eyed," laughed Colbert. "I knew he needed a break, something to break the monotony."

Snyder chuckles about some of the calls that had Colbert suggesting, "Hey, how about if we do this? What about this play?"

Snyder would respond by saying, "Hmmm, okay."

After up to an hour of conversation, Colbert would then sometimes call right back to say, "Hey, now I'm not telling you how to coach your team."

The friendship was tight enough that Colbert, along with Jack Vanier, were two of a very short list of people Snyder allowed on the KSU sidelines during games.

On Monday through Wednesday, days were much the same. The coaches began with an 8 a.m. meeting to re-discuss the previous game and talk about the next foe, recruiting, and academic issues. Throughout the morning, Snyder met with the offensive coaches, defensive coaches, and special teams. Assistant coaches then scripted, in play-by-play fashion, each snap of that afternoon's practice so that Snyder had it in his hands by noon. Practice sets were organized in eight-play sequences: eight plays coming off KSU's 20-yard line; eight plays in the Red Zone; eight plays from the middle of the field, with three coming on the right hash mark, three on the left hash mark, and two in the middle of the field; eight plays on 3rd-and-long; eight plays for fourth-down, and so on.

Monday also included a players' meeting at 2:45 p.m., a break for dinner, and practice at 7:15 p.m. The rest of the week, it would be players met at 2:45 and practiced from 4 until 6:45 or until Snyder was satisfied.

The coaches meetings were long, twice a day, and with every minute utilized for the betterment of the football program.

"He'd have a dozen pages of notes of things he wanted to do," Brent Venables, a former linebacker and linebacker coach for the Wildcats, said about Snyder. "It might have to do with X's and O's, but just as important to him would be improving our players academically or even getting an extra desert for the guys at the cafeteria. You'd shake your head sometimes, but he had such an attention to detail for absolutely every facet of our football program."

Whatever the topic of discussion, Greg Peterson said, "You always knew every detail had been thought out. He might ask you for your ideas, but he had already thought of everything."

The coaches broke for dinner after practice or had dinner brought in. At least one Wednesday a month a family night was held, where a dinner would be catered for the coaches and their families at the Vanier complex.

After dinner coaches watched film from that day's practice. Defensive coaches watched the defense. Offensive coaches watched the offense. Snyder watched both.

While Snyder was very hands-on with the offense, Stoops remembers Snyder as wanting to be informed of what the coaches intended to do and about match-ups, but left the rest to the defensive staff.

"He would have suggestions, but rarely did he disagree with what we were doing," Stoops said.

Well, except for those early games against mighty Nebraska when the Big Red offensive linemen annually toyed with the undersized defensive linemen of the Wildcats.

"He came up to me in one of those games and said, 'What the heck is happening?' I remember saying, 'We're getting our bleeping butts kicked,'" Stoops said with a laugh. "I quickly found out that he didn't like that for an answer.

"With Coach, there was always a solution," Stoops said. "Find a way. There always has to be an answer. Look for one and exhaust all possibilities."

Throughout practice, Snyder would talk into a tape recorder to note things he didn't want to forget. The poorer the practice, the more active Snyder would become. If play became ragged, he might fire his fistful of papers to the turf or give a slight leg-kick in disgust. After practice, notes from that tape were jotted down and given to each coach before the doors to the offices were closed, usually no earlier than midnight.

Thursday evening, Snyder's assistants would present their leader a detailed game plan, including all situational plays.

"Here's what we expect the opponent to do, and here's what we want to do," Snyder said.

On Friday, there might be a light practice or a walk-through in street clothes. Friday night featured a team meal in the Gold Room of the Derby Food Center. The weekly menu was steak or prime rib. Players would then return to Vanier for more meetings, followed by optional time within the complex to watch a movie, study, or go over more game tape. Players would then have pizza, and return to their homes for an 11 p.m. lights-out.

While many teams stay in a hotel the night before a home game, Snyder said, "In the beginning, that was money we didn't have, or if we did stay in a hotel, it would be money out of another program's pocket. I wanted the players to feel I trusted them and allowed them to have that luxury as long as they proved they could be trusted. There have been only a couple of times where there was anything that led me to believe I was being taken advantage of."

Each meeting throughout the day was conducted on Snyder time. Snyder time? If the meeting started at 1 p.m., it was best to be seated by 12:55. Brent Venables learned the hard way in his first year on staff in the summer of 1996.

He thought he would dash down Kimble Avenue to grab a quick Coke and hustle right back.

"It was dead around the office and I needed my battery charged up for the rest of the day," Venables said. "It was customary that if you were going to leave the building, you checked out with Joan (Frederick, Snyder's secretary). I was only going to be gone five minutes, so I just dashed out without saying anything to anyone."

The timing couldn't have been worse, as Snyder called an immediate coaches meeting to discuss academics. Venables walked in late for the meeting, and later in the day there was a sticky note on his office door: "If you ever leave this building again, you're fired!"

Venables said he was scared to death, and just as mad. The incident was never mentioned again, but Venables added, "I also never left the office again."

While miffed, Venables got the message loud and clear. This was a team that played by one set of rules. It was a program of checks and balances, and everyone had to work hard. There was never a resentment of a coach not doing his share because those duties were divided nine ways. One share for each assistant coach, multiple-shares for the head coach.

Extras on Snyder's plate included a 15-minute Big 12 Conference call with the media on Monday; a weekly press conference each Tuesday from 1:00 to 1:30; a session open for the visiting media to call in on Wednesday evening; and his call-in radio show on Thursday night at the Vanier Complex.

For a 1:10 p.m. Saturday kickoff, the staff met at 8:45 a.m. for 15 minutes, then players bused to Derby for a breakfast pre-game meal (chicken if it was an evening game), and then back to the stadium by 10 a.m.

"There would be some dialogue, but if they wanted music, they had to use headsets," Snyder said. "At meals, there was some talk between coaches and players, but often you could hear a pin drop."

From 10:30 to 10:45 a.m., an optional chapel service was offered which Snyder would always attend, followed by a team meeting where each coach would stand up in front of the entire team and quiz his players.

"This was a way to have players perform under pressure," Snyder said. "You knew they were going to answer most of the questions right, which allowed the team to gain confidence."

This was followed by a five-minute motivational tape, and then another meeting with Snyder and the quarterbacks.

Forty minutes before the game, the team was on the field for stretches, with Snyder briefly visiting each position group.

The team returned to the locker room 20 minutes prior to kick-off, while Snyder and his assistant coaches visited with recruits before retiring to his office.

Ten minutes prior to kickoff, Snyder maneuvered down the inside steps to the locker room, sitting on the second to the bottom step to await a point of the finger from strength and conditioning coach Rod Cole, who would coordinate to the minute the pre-game routine.

Two-and-a-half minutes prior to taking the field, the team often chanted briefly—"Roll Purple Roll" or "This Is Our House"—and then Cole called them up.

Snyder entered the locker room and briefly addressed the team, stressing the 3 Es—enthusiasm, effort and execution.

The lights went out for 30 seconds to mentally prepare, and the team took the field.

After the game, the routine began all over again, with the goal of being better than the day, and the game, before.

It wasn't unusual for Snyder to come to each assistant coach and say, "Make sure you take five minutes today to come up with something that can make you a better coach." Whether it be on the practice field, getting your position players to play harder or more efficiently, or getting through to your players the importance of academics, it was to be thought through with a sense of purpose.

Snyder's belief in the program that he was building was unwavering. Players came and went, coaches did the same, but from 1989 to 2005 the system was as constant as a white yard line.

"It's not that I don't have a burning desire to win championships, but my only goals are to achieve the things that will allow that to happen," Snyder said. "Sitting on top of the peak is not the exhilarating part. It's the climb. I really believe that.

"My only burning focus is to get better every day. You start focusing on championships, then you're looking right over the top of things that really matter. When you do that, you run a serious risk of skipping steps."

"He forced you to be better. If there was a weakness, address it as a player and a coach," said Venables. "There was a consistent message to address deficiencies. He did that every day in meeting every single need of the program."

With Snyder, there was seldom a shade of gray. Only on a rare exception was anything other than black and white.

"You always understood that everything was for a common goal," said Michael Smith. "He only wanted the best from us, because it was the best for the team."

Mark Mangino left the program after the 1998 season to join Bob Stoops at Oklahoma, and is now the head coach at the University Kansas. Always knowing that he was working with brilliance, he realized that his Wildcat boss had a higher level of expertise than he ever dreamed when he started running his own program.

"I'm surprised at the number of times something comes up, even something little, and I catch myself saying, 'So that's why he did it that way.'"

Mangino added, "He's very demanding, but he demands more of himself than anyone else. You don't mind working for a demanding person if he's asking a lot of himself. I know when I would be trudging down that hallway and out the door, his light would still be on. He was an example to all of us. Nobody was going to out-work him."

Wearing a headset on the field, Snyder would get input from offensive coordinator Del Miller, but also receivers coach Greg Peterson and offensive line coach Bob Stanley.

"I was just amazed at how he could process information," Miller said. "The more information he had, the better he felt about calling a play."

Shaking his head, Miller added, "How he could filter it all out, I'll never know. To me, it was a zoo. But he was a perfectionist and always wanted to call the perfect play."

Chuckling, and getting a dig in on his head coach, Miller said, "Of course, now you know why we got some of those delay of game penalties."

As a play-caller, running backs coach Michael Smith said, "Coach Snyder was a genius."

Snyder called nearly every game in his 17 years. But it was prior to the 2005 season that he privately told Miller that he wanted him to call the plays. Miller said his head coach stayed out of the mix in a 35-21 win over Florida International.

The second week against Marshall? "Then he started asking some questions. 'What are you calling that play for?' 'You sure about this?' I finally had to say, 'Coach, you're driving me nuts.'"

While 3-1 at the time, Snyder decided to take the controls for the rest of season.

Well, almost.

After announcing his retirement on the Tuesday prior to the season finale against Missouri on November 19, 2005, Snyder told Miller that with the emotions and distractions of the week, he was going to need help.

As steady as Snyder was Sunday through Friday, on the seventh day look out!

"Dr. Jekyll and Mr. Hyde," said more than one assistant.

"I wouldn't say he was totally different, but there was an extra gear on game day. A stronger fire," said Bob Stoops.

That's regardless of whether Snyder was talking to a player or coach.

Laughing at the memory, Matt Miller recalled his first game at quarterback. He had called the right play, but in the wrong formation.

"He called me every name in the book," laughed Miller. "You tried to use it to your amusement at times. It was tough, but you also knew that everything he was saying was right. The things he told you on the sideline, you knew if you did it the way he said, it would work."

Miller added, "I will say on game day he was wired a little differently. He acted different, he talked different. He could definitely say some things that wouldn't make you feel too good about yourself."

Del Miller agreed, but said, that's just football. Things are said that a person just has to get over. "You have to understand what he's saying, and not how he's saying it."

On Saturday's, Snyder had an extra shot of adrenalin that made him more of a yeller in the heat of battle. As Miller said, there were times when you had to tell your quarterback, 'Be prepared,' when he went to talk with Coach Snyder.

To all of that, Snyder gives a "Who, me?" type of response. Snyder says fans constantly comment to him about how calm he seems on the sideline. "That may be how it seems," he says, "but they don't have a microphone in front of me all the time."

The coach admits, "I run in a high gear, but never to the point of losing focus on the task at hand. I can get upset, but you have to pick and choose your battles."

And he does admit to being harder on the quarterback than any other position on the field.

"I try to have the same tone of voice during the week as I do on game day with the quarterback," Snyder said. "You want to put your players under fire during the course of the week because that makes it a heckuva lot easier to respond on Saturday. I don't want anything on Saturdays to come as a surprise. I want them to experience a pressure during the week of practice that is greater than that they feel in the heat of battle on game day."

Chapter Eighteen
1994-1995: Keeping It Rolling

People often asked me if it was more difficult to build a successful program or to maintain a successful program. My answer to both questions is it's hard. It's not easy.

— Coach Bill Snyder

Kansas State had won 18 games in the previous two years. National rankings were no longer news. A Top 25 listing was the norm.

Once again Kansas State had a top-flight quarterback in Chad May, who didn't skip a beat from where Carl Straw and Paul Watson had left off before him.

May, a 6-2, 220-pounder, had transferred prior to the 1992 season from Cal State-Fullerton.

In comparing his new signal-caller to Straw and Watson, Snyder said, "I think Chad has the quality traits you could draw from both of them; consequently, it's made him a little better quarterback than the other two."

Snyder liked Straw's toughness, and while saying that other quarterbacks demonstrated great toughness, "Carl was an unbelievably tough young man."

May had a mental toughness and the respect of his teammates, and he could throw the nice tight spiral that Snyder appreciated, as he had with Straw. Watson may have had a better feel for the offense, but Snyder thought May just may have taken that concept a step further in terms of audibles, seeing the field and throwing efficiency.

Kansas State opened the 1994 season with four straight wins, which included a 21-13 victory over Kansas in Lawrence. May was on target with 33 of 44 passes for 379 yards. J.J. Smith rushed for 44 yards and caught nine passes for 82 more, while Lockett snared eight balls for 116 yards.

Afterward, May, who set a school mark for completions in a single game, said, "I played okay. I made a couple mistakes, but I'll work on it next week and get it corrected."

K-State would lose its next two to a pair of No. 2 ranked teams in Nebraska, 17-6, and Colorado, 35-21.

The Wildcats would then win out, including a 37-20 win over No. 25 Oklahoma, and a season-ender at UNLV, 42-3, upping their ranking to No. 11 in the country, the highest in school history.

The 9-2 Wildcats would be paired with Boston College in the Aloha Bowl, where the worst was saved for last:

Boston College 12, Kansas State 7.

"It was not our day," Snyder summarized, after watching his team rush for a negative-61 yards, credited to eight sacks by the Eagles. K-State's first eight plays netted a negative-23 yards, and the Wildcats' lone score came on a Joe Gordon blocked punt that Chris Sublette recovered for a touchdown. May did pass for 165 yards, but was just 13 of 31.

"I didn't think this could ever happen, but it did today," May said.

To Snyder, part of the problem was focus during the last week of preparation, or the lack thereof. Leading up to the game there had been some trash-talking between the two schools, which disappointed the coach.

"We let our players have some freedoms that you always cringe about, but we allowed it because it was Hawaii and none of our players had ever been there. I wanted them to see as much as they could and enjoy the experience," Snyder said. "Some things started innocently, but then there were some hassles. As I remember, we didn't practice well when we were there."

Still, K-State had a chance, trailing by five and with the ball at the BC 45. A last-ditch heave into the end zone intended for Mitch Running was swatted away as the buzzer sounded.

The 1995 season was much like 1994. Kansas State defeated all comers, except Nebraska, 49-25, and Colorado, 27-17.

The Wildcats continued a trend of doing whatever was necessary to win games that went down to the wire. Playing at Cincinnati, K-State was on the short end of a 21-17 score with the seconds racing off the clock.

Despite turning the ball over a half dozen times, a 22-yard pass from Matt Miller to Lockett on the final snap of the game proved to be the difference-maker. Cincy had just scored to take the lead with 44 seconds remaining, but after Derek King returned a squib kick to the KSU 41, Miller went to work.

Key plays were passes of 20 yards to Tyson Schwieger, and 9 to Running, putting the ball on the Cincinnati 22 with three seconds left.

"Those plays were really important because we knew where we needed to be to throw the pass we wanted to throw to score," Snyder said.

That pass had Miller rolling left, setting, and throwing cross field to Lockett at the goal line.

"We were learning lessons about finding ways to win, instead of how to lose," Snyder said. "In reality, this program was still in its infant stages, and those lessons were important. Play until the end. Never give up. It's one of our Goals To Success that we build each season around."

The other lesson learned is that you better come to play or you risk the chance of defeat.

K-State would next post shutouts over Akron, Northern Illinois and Missouri, winning the three games by a combined score of 141-0. Later, the Wildcats would hold Kansas, Iowa State and Oklahoma to a combined 24 points, not allowing more than one touchdown in any game.

K-State defeated a No. 6 Jayhawk team, 41-7, for the first win over a Top 10 program in the history of the school.

Cornerback Chris Canty and lineman Tim Colston won at least one first-team All-America honor, while linebacker Percell Gaskins was a second-teamer, and Joe Gordon honorable mention. All were first-team All-Big 12 selections, while Chuck Marlow was also a first-teamer, and Dirk Ochs was a second-team selection.

The 1995 season was capped at the Holiday Bowl. Wildcat fans got a glimpse of the future when Matt Kavanagh was summoned out of the bullpen to relieve Miller, who had gone down early in the first half with a cervical sprain.

"We knew we had to pick Kavanagh up, but really, he's the one who picked us up," said wide receiver Kevin Lockett.

Entering the 7-7 game at the 11:22 mark of the second quarter, the right-hander completed 18 of 24 passes for 242 yards and four touchdowns. In his first eight possessions, Kavanagh directed the Wildcats to six touchdowns in what would be a

54-21 win over No. 25-ranked Colorado State at Jack Murphy Stadium in San Diego.

"I'll bet his heartbeat didn't go up two counts from the time he was on the sideline to the time he got on the field," Snyder marveled. "It was a heart-warming story. Brian didn't have all the innate ability in the world, but he was a very intelligent young guy, who was not prone to making mistakes or running free-lance plays. He just knocked them dead."

"I had a blast out there," said Kavanagh, who engineered two touchdowns on his first four snaps.

It was a night for all to celebrate as seven different 'Cats scored—rushes by Mike Lawrence (2), Hickson and Dederick Kelly, and receptions by Brian Lojka, Lockett, Tyson Schwieger, and Mitch Running.

Chapter Nineteen
Birth of the Lynch Mob

My mother told me a story that one time some vigilantes went to the jail house in St. Joseph, broke in, and took a prisoner out and hung him. She saw that. She talked to me about how horrible it was, and that if she ever saw me becoming prejudice, she would break every bone in my body.

— Bill Snyder

In 1995, Kansas State's defense was ranked No. 1 in the nation in team defense, allowing 250.8 yards per game, a miniscule number by football standards. The Wildcats' 13.2 defensive scoring average ranked No. 2 in the country. The team's relentless style of play led to a "don't mess with me" attitude born by some swash-buckling players, and coaches, too.

Bussing to and from workouts and functions at the Holiday Bowl, the players began to organize themselves—Bus No. 1 was for the offense and Bus No. 2 for the defense.

"I remember instead of Bus No. 2, the guys put 'Lynch Mob' on it," said Bob Stoops, defensive coordinator at the time. "There was a pride that went with that name. Politically correct or not, it just meant highly aggressive defensive play. It was just a two-word phrase that the kids took pride in. Playing defense in an aggressive, tough way."

As for the sensitivity of the slogan, Snyder said, "I was well aware of the connotation of the phrase, but within our family, it had nothing to do with race. We had more black players than white players. To the players, it is just verbiage amongst themselves, and it didn't leave the football family."

Snyder admitted to getting a handful of letters from fans unhappy with the new nickname. To each, he penned a personal note, explaining the K-State definition of "Lynch Mob" which was coined by William Price, one of the Wildcats' black players.

Terance Newman, who joined the Wildcats from 1999-2002, explained, "We have black, white and Asian people on this team. Within our family it means an attitude, nothing more. It means people standing together as one. Players united. It's playing with an attitude of not taking anything from anybody. You don't mess with the 'Lynch Mob.'"

Linebacker Terry Pierce, 2000-2002, added, "To me, it means unity. We stress having 11 people in the screen at all times. Everybody playing together; a spirit of one."

Or as Jarrod Cooper, 1997-2000, simplified, "We play with one heart and 11 heads."

That tradition continued over the years, and the "Lynch Mob" was known conference-wide.

On September 19, 1998, Heisman Trophy candidate and eventual winner Ricky Williams moseyed into KSU Stadium with his Texas Longhorns.

The "Lynch Mob" put this Longhorn to the turf all afternoon. Twenty-five times Williams ran the ball for a grand total of 43 yards. His longest run of the day was a seven-yarder, and 11 of the 25 carries netted no more than one yard.

"They came and came every play," Williams said of the KSU defense. Jeff Kelly and Travis Ochs each had 11 tackles with Cooper adding 10 and Mark Simoneau eight.

"I started helping him up. I let him know I'd be there, but I also wanted to be a nice guy and wanted him healthy," said Kelly. "I wanted him to come back and run the ball every play."

Later in the year, Kansas running back David Winbush got a taste of what Williams had experienced. In a 54-6 loss to the Wildcats, Winbush said of Kelly, "Everywhere I went, he was there. I cut, he cut. I went out for a pass, he was already there. At times, it looked like the entire sideline was chasing me."

No, it was the "Lynch Mob."

Through the years, mini-slogans were given to the different positions. In 2002, the secondary had t-shirts that read, "Swangin and Bangin."

Newman, an All-American said, "We swing first, and then we come up and bang."

Decorating the shirts of the linebackers was, "Knock-out Kings."

"We're hitting all the time," said Pierce. "No matter what, we're always hitting."

And the shirts of the defensive line read "When we mob, we mob deep."

Snyder noted that with each new set of players, "there was a sense of obligation to continue the tradition."

And with each new defensive coordinator came a slightly different approach, but with the exact same result—"Lynch Mob" football.

About defensive coordinator Bob Cope, Snyder said, "He was a matter-of-fact guy, but with humor. He could be razor-sharp with his comments, but at other times he showed down-home humor."

Bob Stoops and Jim Leavitt followed as co-coordinators. Snyder admitted that not many other head coaches favored the co-coordinator system, but it was his way of rewarding two deserving coaches who were proficient at what they did.

"Bobby was a highly motivated and demanding coach. Where Bob (Cope) would get on a youngster and have a sense of humor that was a little biting, Bobby would make corrections and do it in a way where you sensed fear in a player. But the results were positive.

"Jim had such a great sense of detail. He was always on the move, but in a productive way. He was a pacer, who became actively involved in practice. He was a demonstrator," said Snyder.

Phil Bennett came onto the scene next.

"Phil was one of those guys who knew exactly how to get on a player pretty good, but also knew exactly when to put his arm around him and give him a hug," Snyder said. "Phil had an excellent mind for the game. He had a tremendous understanding of what the opponent was doing."

Bret Bielema and Bob Elliott followed Bennett as another set of co-coordinators.

"Bret was one of those guys who had a real knack for recall," Snyder said. "He could read things quickly. He could call a ballgame without a lot of paper in his hand. He had a good vision for the field."

Elliott, "was well-prepared. He was a good multi-task guy, who stayed in tune to his recruiting when he was coaching."

To a certain degree, Kansas State's defense developed in the early years when it simply wasn't good enough to win enough one-on-one battles at the line of scrimmage to defeat the better teams in a run-oriented Big 8 Conference.

That meant putting an extra Wildcat, or two, at the line of scrimmage, and playing man-defense in the secondary.

"It was really a no-brainer if we wanted to stop the run," Snyder said.

As for going man-on-man in the secondary, Snyder said, "That's what we worked on, so we became better at it, and it became a bit of an attitude position. We didn't have the fastest guys in the world, but they played with a competitive spirit.

"In many cases, they won the battle through persistence. I think our players mentally wore down receivers," Snyder said.

When the Big 12 hit mid-stride going into the 2000s, a balanced offense became vogue, with some teams, such as Texas Tech, going to an aerial circus. It was a time when K-State was forced to change schemes going to more zone looks in the secondary.

"It took us away from what we had made a living on," Snyder said. "Then it became more of a guessing game. If we thought they were going to run it, we'd get one more guy up there. If we thought they were going to throw it, we'd add a guy to our coverage. There was just a lot more guess work involved."

Snyder admits today, "It was a difficult change from the old way we had done things. We were doing something diametrically opposite of what we had made a living on."

When things turned a bit sour with the 2004 and 2005 seasons, Snyder put his foot down saying the "Lynch Mob" slogan could not be used.

"That's because we weren't playing well enough to be described with the same vernacular as some of those other teams," Snyder said.

Chapter Twenty
A Role Within The Department

Within the structure of our program, I am very proud of the fact that we never over-spent our budget. With myself, and my coaching staff, I always said, 'Spend the money as if it's your own.'

— Bill Snyder

Kansas State's athletic directors of the past 17 years—Steve Miller (1989-91), Milt Richards (1992-93), Max Urick (1993-2000) and Tim Weiser (2001-present)—are united in their opinion of Snyder.

Phrases like "a man of vision" or "a proper man" or simply "a gentleman" are used.

Asked if he was a demanding man, they would respond with a chorus of laughter, but quickly followed up words of sincerity.

"People viewed Bill as being demanding, but you always knew that before he came to you, he had asked himself, 'Is this something that will make the program better, or something we're doing for the wrong reason?'" said Miller.

"Demanding, but fair," according to Urick. "There was always a logical reason for everything he asked for."

A man of discipline?

You bet, in every single area of the program.

"I'll never forget the first time I had a reason to speak to the team," Miller said. "At the end there was one clap. Not four here, six there, but one unison clap. Every part of that program was filled with discipline."

On more than one occasion, Urick said, "I know coaches turned receipts in from recruiting trips only to have Bill not approve a charge that he felt to be too extravagant."

A man of ego?

Richards, who is now director of athletics at Cal State-Stanislaus, said, "Bill's ego was checked at the door every single day. It was never about Bill. It was about the kids and giving each one of them the opportunity to be better students and better players. It wasn't about Bill being in the limelight."

In the athletics arena, every coach has an ego, whether he be the head football coach or the head tennis coach. So, sure, Snyder did have an ego, but he was never brash in nature. He never wanted for himself, only for the student-athletes.

As Urick said, "He has a strong ego, but without any arrogance whatsoever. He's just a man who carries himself with such high self-esteem, with confidence and total focus in what he wants to accomplish, which can be intimidating to some."

Nothing advertised his lack of ego more than his office decor, which included only pictures of family members and a colorful framing of Pinocchio. Rarely would there be a commemorative football on display, and nothing that advertised the fact that Snyder was a multiple-winner of Coach of the Year awards.

"Those family pictures were more important to me than any trophy," Snyder said. "With everything that's in the papers and on the internet these days, I'm sure any recruit has already figured me out. There doesn't need to be a bunch of trophies around my office."

His home is decorated the exact same way.

"I probably have 150 footballs, trophies and plaques, but none are on display."

Each athletic director also knew that while Snyder had his wish list in terms of facilities, he was a company man first.

Nothing advertised that fact quicker to Urick than when Snyder, in two separate fiscal years, put in calls to say that it appeared he would have monies left over in his individual sport budget, and he would be willing to sign it over to the general operating fund.

"As I remember, both years it was about $100,000," said Urick, who in his early years had accepted control of a department that was $3.5 million in the red, and ran an approximately $1 million dollar deficit. "Right there, I knew I had a team player as my head football coach. In all my years in athletics, I had heard that done only one other time, and that was by Woody Hayes at Ohio State."

The first time, Urick accepted the monies and dispersed it within the other sport programs. The second time, he encouraged his head coach to give it as bonuses to his assistants.

Snyder's giving back to the athletic department was a sign of trust from within, and one reason Urick was willing to let his coach have control over his sector of the department.

"Bill pays attention to every single detail," Urick said. "You take comfort knowing that the most significant sport in your program is being run with a meticulous CEO in charge."

Richards, who was just 32 years old when he became athletic director at a Big 8 Conference school, added, "Bill had a total, total control over every single thing in that department, but he didn't abuse it. It worked because he was such a good person, such an honest person."

And that's the way Miller saw his head coach in his first year on the job. Especially during those early days when there were multiple needs on a daily basis.

"It was tough staying up with his needs. I thought he was a junkie," Miller quipped. But he added, "He was a guy you didn't have to say 'No' to because he didn't ask for frivolous things."

Never said no?

"Never. I can't think of one time," said Miller.

"He didn't make demands, he made suggestions: 'If we do this, this can happen.' It was Bill being Bill and wanting things done right."

Snyder suggested, Miller agreed, and the results were not only recorded in the Kansas State record book, but eventually ended up in the Wildcats' bank account.

Kansas State went from a deficit near $5 million, and season-ticket sales numbering 7,175 in 1988 when the average attendance was 18,205, to a $3.5 million shortage and season sales in the high teens in the mid-1990s, to operating in the black with ticket sales of 30,000-plus and an attendance average of 43,000-plus by the late 1990s.

"Had we not won in football, I don't know what the hell would have happened," Urick said.

Urick felt a common bond with Snyder from the day of his hiring in 1993. Maybe it was because both came from Iowa—Urick from Iowa State and Snyder from Iowa—and maybe it was due to Urick's background as a former football coach.

Urick remembers a lunch date he had with Snyder shortly after his hire.

Good-naturedly, Urick said, "Are we going to be able to work together? People tell me you want to control everything." Bill chuckled and said, "I always respect authority."

As a former coach, Urick knew not to bother his head coach during the season unless the issue was truly pressing. Basically, he took an attitude of "don't sweat the small stuff."

As for having total control over his program, Urick's philosophy was, "If he wants to do it, and is going to do it well, let him go with it. If he wants to be the one to write up some of the financial reports, go for it. I honestly can't remember one time that we weren't on the same page."

Wait!

There was one time.

Urick wanted to bring in a circus-like bell-ringer who would slam the hammer down after touchdowns so a metal weight would go up and smack a bell. It was going to be placed in the northwest corner of the field, well beyond the end zone.

"I didn't even mention it to Bill. I didn't think he would care about it," Urick laughed. "Well, he did."

After one game, Snyder sent word through his son, Sean, his administrative assistant, that Kansas State didn't need a bell-ringer.

"It's something I could have pressed, but why? It wasn't that big of a deal."

Weiser was continually amazed at how each and every detail was monumental in Snyder's mind. He recalled that Snyder was not happy with the representation K-State had received on the game program at the Black Coaches Association game the Wildcats played against Iowa in Kansas City's Arrowhead Stadium in 2003.

"I got word about that and just shook my head. I thought, 'How could something like that be a concern?'" But Bill was concerned about everything, and that's how Kansas State football became what it is."

Richards recalled taking charge of handling the officials for a non-conference game against Temple in 1992.

"Where I came from, the AD handled that, so I agreed that we would have officials from the Big East Conference," Richards said. "I thought Bill was going to rip my head off on that one."

Weiser had heard the Snyder stories while athletic director at Colorado State prior to his hire in 2001.

"No one in my profession envied my hiring as AD with Bill Snyder as the football coach," Weiser said.

But that would soon change.

"I quickly found out how comforting it is to have your most important sport in every perspective from revenue to exposure, being coached by a tireless worker, and someone who had a concern for the total department," Weiser said.

While K-State had the monies to compete in the Big 12, in no way were the Wildcats lavish in their spending.

"I've always thought there was too much money being wasted in college football," Snyder said. "I wanted what was right for football, but I wanted every program to have enough money to operate and to compete."

Whether giving money back to the athletic department or supporting other programs like baseball or women's basketball by attending games, Snyder said, "I came here because of the people and stayed because of the people. From day one, I've had affection for Kansas State. If that's the case, then it's only right to try to help the entirety of the athletic department and the school."

Snyder has an appreciation for all sports, which includes women's athletics. His daughter, Whitney, is a current member of the equestrian team. What he doesn't agree with is the concept of numbers equality which stipulates that if there are 90 male student-athletes, then there must be 90 female student-athletes.

"This concept of, 'Let's start an archery team to meet our quota. Let's go out and get 500 young ladies, who may or may not have ever seen a bow before just doesn't make sense," Snyder said.

Snyder wants those individuals to have the right to compete, but not at the expense of dropping programs such as wrestling and baseball to balance the numbers.

"The needs football had were genuine," Snyder said. "We didn't go out and buy every new piece of equipment that came out. We were frugal with our spending, and hopefully, that was for the good of the entire athletic department."

Weiser noted that one conference school made sure each of its coaches rented Hertz cars because they were perceived to be the best.

"I didn't have to worry about things like that with Bill. Does that make your program better? I don't think so. It's what's in the car that makes the program better," Weiser said.

To his staff, he made it clear that staying in the fanciest hotels and eating $100 meals on recruiting trips was not the answer to winning games on a Saturday afternoon.

Snyder has one regret about his relationship with all of his athletic directors, and that was that they often took the heat for his scheduling philosophy.

"They didn't deserve to take shots for that, when it was in my contract that scheduling was my responsibility," Snyder said.

Chapter Twenty-One
The Big 8 To The Big 12

My reasons for not wanting to enter the Big 12 Conference were not valid. Because I had grown up in the Big 8 days, I always thought it was a great conference. I balked at the Big 12 just because I loved the Big 8 Conference and admired the success it had enjoyed through the years.

— Coach Bill Snyder

Jon Wefald almost always said "yes" when Bill Snyder had a wish, but that wasn't so when it came to forming the Big 12 Conference.

"He said that from a football standpoint, he didn't like the idea," Wefald related. "He was starting to have his way with the teams in the Big 8. We hadn't beaten Nebraska, but he was competing favorably with everyone else."

But Wefald envisioned the possibilities had K-State not followed suit with its rival cousins, and the options were not good. Arkansas had already left the Southwest Conference for the Southeastern, and Wefald could see Texas and Colorado moving west to the Pac-10.

Wefald says when the Big 12 Conference was going from blueprint to reality in 1993 through 1995, a lot of folks said Kansas State couldn't compete. Urick was the director of athletics at Iowa State at the time, and denies that there was any conversation between the league's athletic directors that Kansas State would not be included in the new 12-team alignment.

"We were a very family-like conference and no one was ever going to kick a school out of the league unless it was for gross misbehavior," Urick said.

But he knew schools like Iowa State and Kansas State would have to aggressively improve their facilities to compete with the wealthier half of the new league.

If that wasn't possible, he said, "It would have come down to a Kansas State decision, not a Big 8/12 decision. The question would have been asked, 'Is the value of staying in the conference worth it to the total university? Was a school like Kansas State willing to pay the price or would the school look to a conference like the Missouri Valley?'

"To me, that was unthinkable, but at the same time realistic," Urick said. "It's hard to play the 'what if' game, but it does make you wonder."

Wonder, because in the late 1980s, Kansas State's home attendance had dipped into the 18,000 range, and apathy for the most pivotal sport in the program was apparent. The reality is, had Kansas State not had an immediate dose of success, the "what if" game would have been very real.

Snyder had just become comfortable with the Big 8's rival coaches as well as administrators and faculty reps that he had met through league meetings. When he thought of Texas, he envisioned all of the high-financed programs that he knew his little school in the flint hills had no chance of keeping up with, at least monetarily.

"It was easy to see that the price of poker was going up," Snyder said. And it was a no-limit game, especially with the Longhorns and the Aggies.

On the field, Snyder had no reason to believe his Wildcats couldn't keep competing. In just six years, his K-State program had already surpassed all but Nebraska and Colorado in what would be the Big 12's North Division, and the only real question marks were Texas and Texas A&M in the South Division.

The conference would move from seven league games to eight, but that was okay.

August, 31, 1996. 2:30 p.m.

That's when the first toe—belonging to Kansas State's Jamie Rheem—touched a football in the inaugural season of the Big 12 Conference. Kansas State versus Texas Tech.

Of playing Kansas State in the month of August, Red Raider coach Spike Dykes reasoned, "I didn't have a problem with that. I looked at it like gong to the dentist. You have to do it, so you might as well go get that tooth pulled and get it over with."

Kansas State no longer had just an occasional good season; it was becoming a solid program that was establishing deep roots. Snyder had a sneaking suspicion that this 1996 team was going to be pretty good.

"I felt playing Texas Tech so early was one thing they could never take away from us. We will always be a part of the first game played, and people will always remember who won the first game ever in the Big 12 Conference," Snyder said.

After a Tech field goal, Kansas State scored the next 21 points on touchdowns by

Brian Kavanagh, a Kavanagh to Jimmy Dean pass, and a bad snap recovered in the end zone by Mario Smith to make it a 21-3 game with 12:51 remaining.

Kansas State held on for a 21-14 victory, though hardly playing to Big 12 standards. The Wildcats had a negative-12 rushing yards and only 160 yards of total offense compared to 392 on a whopping 119 snaps for the Red Raiders.

"I never could beat Bill, but there are a lot of coaches saying that," said Dykes, who also lost to the Wildcats 13-2 in 1997 in Lubbock. "The only way you beat one of Bill's teams is to have better players because you're not going to be more fundamentally sound and you're not going to out-coach him."

Snyder and Dykes had been friends since the early 1980s. Dykes claims that if Snyder had consulted with him prior to accepting the head coaching position at K-State, "I would have told him to check that menu real good and make sure all the side orders were in place."

Dykes had beaten K-State in 1986 during Stan Parrish's first season, winning 41-7.

"I'll tell you what, that wasn't a very good football team," said Dykes, who now lives at Horse Shoe Bay, west of Austin, Texas. "I mean, we weren't very good, but we were sure better than they were."

Dykes coached at Tech through 1999, but always kept track of the success of the Wildcats and marveled at the manner in which Snyder did his thing.

"He is who he is," Dykes said. "His teams didn't major in being flamboyant. He didn't try to be funny. Humor's not an adjective you use when talking about Bill, but his teams were so fundamentally sound. All those hours that people say he spends preparing were evident on the football field. You could see the value of those hours spent.

"The more you put into something, the more you get out of it. That's just logic," Dykes said. "Well, I promise you, no one put more into something than he did."

Dykes added, "He didn't just go out and buy the success he had, he went out and earned it.

"I'll tell you what, to be in that upper-echelon year after year, and to have done it in Manhattan, Kansas, now that's doing something. That's not a bunch of baloney, that's fact!"

After the win over Tech, K-State disposed of non-conference opponents Indiana State, Cincinnati and Rice by a collective score of 128-10.

K-State would lose to Nebraska, 39-3, but win the next four, which included a 23-20 win over Texas A&M and a 38-12 win over Kansas, making it a clean sweep for the Wildcat Senior Class of 1996 over the Jayhawks. They had won earlier games over their in-state rivals 41-7 in 1995, 21-13 in 1994, and 10-9 in 1993.

Snyder, however, was concerned heading into College Station to play Texas A&M.

"The Big 12 was new and we had never gone to Texas to play some of these teams. We had played games at Nebraska, but still, going into an atmosphere like Texas A&M could have been imposing."

K-State scored the first three TDs to lead 20-3 at the half, and then held on for the 23-20 victory as Chris Canty stripped Albert Connell after a reception down to the KSU 17.

K-State fell to Colorado 12-0, but capped the season with a 35-20 taming of the Cyclones, which earned the Wildcats a spot in the Cotton Bowl against BYU. It would be the program's first New Year's Day bowl game.

"That was neat, except for the 10:30 a.m. start," said Snyder.

At the half, K-State led by the unusual count of 8-5. On the final play before intermission, Kavanagh let fly with a 41-yard "Hail Mary" pass that BYU deflected into the arms of Andre Anderson, who scored the touchdown. K-State kicked the PAT, but BYU was penalized as the teams headed to the locker room.

Snyder opted to take the single point off the board and go for the two-point conversion, which was converted on a Mike Lawrence run.

K-State upped its count to 15-5 on a pass to Lockett in the third quarter, but No. 5 BYU scored twice in the fourth quarter for the 19-15 victory.

K-State wrapped up its first year in the Big 12 with a 6-2 conference record. Detractors, and they included some southerners, who said Kansas State's cheerful Saturdays were over upon their move to the Big 12, had no clue about this guy named Snyder. Tell the man "No, that can't be done," and he'll say, "Why not? Just watch!"

But University of Kansas athletics director Bob Frederick said the movement that

Kansas State was making in football was apparent well before the Big 12 came into existence.

Recalling a Big 8-sponsored Orange Bowl trip, Frederick said, "You would see Bill and Sharon walking on the beach in the morning, but then Bill would disappear. The rest of us would be out on a boat fishing or playing golf, and Bill would be up in his room studying tape or watching another bowl game on television.

"That told you right there that he was something different, and Kansas State football was about to become really different," Frederick said.

"He's not easily frustrated, but it does irritate him when people say, 'It can't be done.'" Weiser surmised. "He looks at everything as a challenge, and says, 'Here's how I think we can do it.'"

And do it Snyder did.

In Snyder's 17 years at the helm, Kansas State's Big 12 record of 53-27 trailed only Texas (62-18), Nebraska (56-24) and Oklahoma (55-25). The Wildcats played in three Big 12 title games—1998, 2001 and 2003. Only Texas, Oklahoma and Colorado had more with four appearances.

In Big 12 regular-season games, Snyder had at least a .500 record against all but two teams: Oklahoma (2-4) and Texas A&M (2-4). His record against the rest of the league: Missouri (10-0); Kansas (9-1); Iowa State (8-2); Baylor (4-0); Oklahoma State (3-1); Nebraska (5-5); Colorado (5-5); Texas Tech (3-3); and, Texas (2-2).

"I don't think anybody in America has done a better job taking a program that was down and building it up to a program of national prominence," said University of Texas athletics director DeLoss Dodds, a former athletic director at Kansas State. "I can't think of anybody who has even equaled what he has done, let alone bettered it."

"I thought Kansas State could win, but he got them playing in the national arena, fighting for a national championship," Dodds said. "It's absolutely unbelievable."

Chapter Twenty-Two
1997: Community Colleges To The Rescue

You had to be impressed with Michael Bishop's physical presence. I mean, to throw a football 70 yards in the air, holy Toledo! That's special.

— Coach Bill Snyder

With seasons of nine, nine, ten and nine wins from 1993 through 1996 and a steady climb up the bowl ranks—Copper to Aloha to Holiday to Cotton—Kansas State was squarely on the college football map. The Wildcats were a perfect 15-0 in non-conference games during those four seasons, winning 11 of those games by at least 24 points.

Still, the Wildcats had no answer for Nebraska and Colorado, going a combined 0-7-1 against the two powers in those four years, which left KSU finishing second once and third three times in the Big 8/Big 12 standings from 1993 through 1996.

Kansas State had traditionally focused its recruiting on the high school ranks, but riding its appearance in the Cotton Bowl, K-State decided to focus attention on junior college players. The move paid off with the signing of quarterback Michael Bishop, linebacker Jeff Kelly, receiver Darnell McDonald, offensive lineman Brien Hanley and defensive back Gerald Neasman.

Bishop had edged out Jonathan Beasley as the starting quarterback, but his early play demonstrated an inconsistency that had the coaching staff wondering what to do.

The 1997 season opened with non-conference wins over Northern Illinois, Ohio and Bowling Green by a combined score of 127-27.

Bishop totaled 270 yards of total offense in the opener against NIU, but completed just 3 of 14 passes for 93 yards against Ohio. In his third game, Bishop directed the Wildcats to a school record 638-yard output against Bowling Green to complete the roller-coaster ride through the non-conference season.

"It was tight between Michael and Jonathan," Snyder said. "It was evident that Michael was going to be a special player, but he was also somewhat of a risk at the position until he learned more about what we were trying to do."

Snyder admitted, "There were moments early on when I thought, 'What the devil did I do?' And at other times, I said, 'Wow, this guy is going to be something.'"

A 6-1, 212-pound quarterback from Willis, Texas, Bishop's on-field heroics were nothing short of Texas-sized. The word was he could throw a football 93 yards in the air and reportedly broke the finger of a Blinn Community College teammate who was trying to catch one of his laser throws. Other Blinn receivers had lacerations from the laces of the football.

Offensive coordinator Ron Hudson said, "He has the strongest arm I have ever seen." And Hudson knew what he was talking about, having coached Kent Graham (Arizona Cardinals) and Bobby Hoying (Philadelphia Eagles) at Ohio State, and Steve Beurlein (Carolina Panthers) at Notre Dame.

Bishop was listed as one of the top three junior college quarterbacks in the nation and one of the Top 25 overall two-year college recruits. He passed for 1,248 yards and rushed for 451 as a freshman, and nearly equaled the stats the next year with 1,121 passing and 379 rushing yards.

Perhaps the most attractive aspect of Michael Bishop's junior college performance: Blinn Community College was a pristine 24-0 with Bishop as the starting quarterback.

One of Bishop's less enduring qualities was that he agreed with, if not embellished, every single compliment sent his way, describing himself as a cross between John Elway of the Denver Broncos and the multi-talented Tommie Frazier, formerly of Nebraska.

The Wildcats opened Big 12 play against No. 3 Nebraska, losing in Lincoln, 56-26, with Bishop's erratic play continuing. The NU Black Shirts smothered Bishop's every move as he netted just 14 yards on 17 rushes, and was only 8 of 24 passing.

K-State responded by thumping Missouri, 41-11, though the Wildcat offense passed the ball just nine times. Bishop led a ground attack that produced 339 yards.

The next victim would be No. 14 Texas A&M, 36-17. The K-State defense held the Aggies to 90 yards of total offense.

Snyder was feeling good about this 1997 team, and thus became even more demanding.

After a 26-7 whipping of Oklahoma, he said, "We played very average."

A trip to Texas Tech was next. The Wildcats played below average, yet were able to post a 13-2 win. Beasley replaced a struggling Bishop who was just 6 of 21 with three interceptions at the time of his benching.

"That was not an easy decision to make because you always knew that Michael was one of those guys who could take the team on his back and make it go," Snyder said of the benching. "I didn't know how the team would respond to the benching, and perhaps more importantly, I didn't know how Michael would respond to being on the bench. It was a roll of the dice."

Snyder would hold a hot hand with the dice as Beasley turned a 6-2 lead into a 13-2 margin of victory with a 33-yard quarterback-keeper with 3:05 remaining to wrap up the win.

Perhaps with the Tech game serving as an attention-getter for the Wildcat players, K-State stormed past Kansas (48-16), Colorado (37-20) and Iowa State (28-3), to finish the year at 10-1.

Kansas State scored a second-place finish in the Big 12 North to a Nebraska team that would finish 13-0.

The No. 9-ranked Wildcats were rewarded with an invitation to the Fiesta Bowl where they would play No. 14 Syracuse. The 'Cats would bring to the bowl game an offense that scored 34.8 points per game, a defense that allowed a measly 14.5 points per game, and special teams units that held up to their name—special. Martin Gramatica won the Lou Groza Award as the nation's No. 1 kicker with 19 makes in 20 attempts, kicker Jamie Rheem consistently sent kickoffs dancing into the end zone, punt returner David Allen averaged 13.9 yards per return, and Gerald Neasman averaged 33.9 yards on kickoff returns.

"We're hard to stop. The defense doesn't know what we're going to do because I can throw or a running back can run it or I can run it myself," said Bishop.

The defense lived up to its "Lynch Mob" nickname allowing just 257 yards per game to rank fourth in the nation, and 14.5 points per game—sixth best in the country.

The Fiesta Bowl would be the 103rd game in the Snyder era, and outside of a series of Nebraska games, the foe would be the toughest the Wildcats had faced.

The Orange were led by Donovan McNabb at quarterback and Quinton Spotwood at receiver. The secondary featured hard-hitting Donovin Darius and Tebucky Jones.

For the Wildcats, the game meant a return to the scene—Sun Devil Stadium in Tempe—where the Snyder era had started nine years earlier.

"A lot of people didn't think we deserved to be in the Fiesta Bowl," said running back Mike Lawrence. "To all those who didn't think we deserved it, how about this? We are good!"

Lawrence was wrong. On this New Year's Eve night, K-State was not good. K-State was great in a dominating 35-18 victory over Syracuse.

Bishop totaled 390 yards of offense—317 passing and 73 rushing. McDonald caught seven passes for a school-record 206 yards and TD balls of 19, 77 and 41 yards.

"Don't credit me," McDonald said. "It was Michael. He put the ball where it needed to be every time."

Leading up to the game there was talk of the McNabb versus Bishop match-up, with the Syracuse QB always getting the better billing.

To that, Snyder said, "Donovan may have been the top quarterback in the nation that year, but on that particular night, he wasn't."

Of the win, Snyder said afterward, "I'm happy about winning 11. I'm unhappy about losing one."

Later, when the magnitude of the victory set in, Snyder said, "That was really a significant ballgame from a national perspective. It made a statement. We really were a good football team."

Chapter Twenty-Three
When Life's Not Fair

Any time you lose somebody within your family, it's hard. You just have to be there for people who you care about. That's all I ever attempted to do.

— Coach Bill Snyder

Sudden death is a sports term. But when it touches human lives, sudden death becomes something totally different.

Within the Kansas State football family during the 17 years of the Snyder era, death became a reality four times.

Assistant coach Bob Cope died of cancer in the summer of 1997. Nancy Bennett, the wife of assistant coach Phil Bennett, was killed after being struck by lightening in 1999. Wildcat defensive tackle Anthony Bates passed away in 2000 due to an enlarged heart. And Troy Miller, the son of assistant coach Del Miller, succumbed to a rare cancer in 2004.

Today, limestone monuments stand in front of the Vanier Football Complex in celebration of those four lives.

Here are their stories:

Bob Cope

Throwing a damper on the success of the 1996 Wildcat team was the cancer that made its way throughout the body of defensive coordinator Bob Cope during the fall.

Having been given a clean bill of health during a routine physical in July, it wasn't that alarming when a nagging neck pain put Cope in a brace for a few days in August. He thought it might have to do more with his being 59 years old than anything else.

The next month, he was diagnosed with cancer. The deadly disease was in his lungs, brain and bloodstream.

He said at the time, "I was going to work, feeling healthy, jogging every day, feeling normal and strong. All of a sudden, bang!"

Still, Cope was on the sidelines coaching until October 2.

After practice that day, Snyder drove Cope home.

"I sat down with a Nebraska media guide and all of a sudden I was in a coma. I guess I was out three or four days," Cope said later that fall.

Cope would receive a total of 14 radiation treatments, and throughout the process Snyder kept his coordinator involved, bringing him game tapes to study at his home.

"I'm probably not helping much, but I think I am," Cope quipped.

To Snyder, it was a no-brainer. He had hired Cope as his first defensive coordinator in 1989. Cope stayed for two seasons, and then had gone to USC for two years and to Baylor for three, before returning to K-State for the 1996 season.

In a 1996 Thanksgiving interview, Cope, his voice cracking with emotion, said, "If only people knew all that Coach Snyder has done for me and my family." Pausing, and with tears, he repeated, "If only people knew."

What Snyder did, but kept quiet, was personally finance a trip to Mexico City for Cope to be part of an experimental cancer treatment program.

"It was one of those deals that was in Phase III, right before getting the okay to be accepted as a legitimate treatment for cancer," Snyder said. "Bob and I have always been solution guys. We were not going to accept that cancer was going to win."

For a while, the drug seemed to work, but in the summer of 1997, cancer scored another victory.

Throughout Cope's battle with cancer, Snyder kept him a part of Kansas State football, and Cope continued to touch lives.

Prior to his death, Cope said, "It means so much. You don't think much about it when you're well, but I'm so appreciative of my friends."

To this day Snyder pays tribute to his former coach and friend by keeping his name above one of the side-by-side lockers Snyder has in the Wildcat locker room.

Nancy Bennett

The stinging sensation that ended the 1998 season had just been replaced by the anticipation of a new fall when tragedy struck the Wildcat family again.

Nancy Bennett, the wife of first-year Kansas State defensive coordinator Phil Bennett, went out for a brisk walk on the morning of August 11 through the streets just northwest of KSU Stadium.

It was overcast. There was a hint of a drizzle, but nothing that seemed alarming as Nancy departed her home on Hillview Drive shortly before 6 a.m.

"The last thing she did was come over and kiss me and say, 'I love ya. I'll see you tonight,'" Bennett said.

Thirty minutes later, the drizzle had become rain and there were rumbles of thunder. Bennett decided to hop in the car and retrieve his wife before going to the office.

"I turned the corner on Meadowbrook and I saw the police car with its lights on. It was raining fairly hard and I thought someone had surely invited her into their house. She loved to critique houses.

"I didn't even think about the police, but drove up and kiddingly asked, 'Have you seen a good-looking blonde jogging?'

"I could see it in the officer's eyes. Something was wrong."

Further to the north, in his home atop a hill that allowed a view of the Flint Hills, Snyder remembers seeing, then hearing, the aftermath of a lightening bolt.

"I remember saying, 'That one must have touched down,'" Snyder said. "It wasn't too long after that the phone call came."

Nancy Bennett had been struck by a single jagged lightning bolt that literally knocked her out of her running shoes as it traveled from her upper body to her feet.

For 17 days, Bennett battled the effects of the lightning strike—hypoxia (lack of oxygen), general trauma and electrical shock.

On August 28, she died.

"I woke up about 2:50 in the morning and knew I needed to be at the hospital,"

Bennett said. "I was getting dressed when the phone rang. It was a nurse saying Nancy's blood pressure was dropping and that I might want to come up.

"I raced up there, and walked into her room. Within two minutes she died in my arms."

Nancy was 41.

She left behind Sam, a sixth-grader, and Maddie, a third-grader.

"Coach Snyder tells his players to surround yourself with people who want to make your life better," Bennett said. "If I had to describe Nancy, that's what she did for me. I never was a bad person, but she put something in my life I didn't have before I met her."

For 17 days Bennett spent every waking hour beside his wife's hospital bed. Snyder also spent a lot of time at the hospital with Bennett as the K-State staff was readying for the season at KSU Stadium—across the street from Manhattan's Mercy Health Center.

Bennett said there were decisions that had to be made that he could not have made by himself.

He called Snyder his "clear thinker" in a time when, "I wasn't too rational about many things. But I was able to express myself to him better than to the doctors. Then he would express to the doctors what I was thinking."

Bennett paused as he said, "He's not only my boss, but also a dear friend of my family."

Bennett then reflected on Nancy going to an early-season pep rally and hearing Snyder speak for the first time.

"She told me, 'Phil, we're with somebody special,'" Bennett said. "Nancy knew head coaches. I've worked for some she wouldn't say that about."

He added, "She loved football and was so excited about the opportunity to win and be around good people. In this business, you need a strong boss, and she knew we had one."

Anthony Bates

It was the last week of July, 2000, when Anthony Bates, a Wildcat defensive tackle, called his mom, Sharon, at her home in Phoenix, Arizona. During small talk, he complained of being out of shape, suggesting that maybe too much soda during the summer was taking its toll.

The Mountain Pointe High School and Phoenix College product's voice was alarming enough for his mother to call his K-State position coach, Mo Latimore, asking if he would check in on her son.

Three days later, July 31, Latimore was back on the phone with Sharon, telling her that her son had been involved in an automobile accident and was dying.

Bates was returning to his apartment from what was called a light workout. An autopsy revealed that the muscular 20-year-old had passed out due to an undiagnosed Hypertrophic Cardiomyopathy (HCM), a thickening of the heart for no apparent reason.

Bates' heart weight was 680 grams, or more than three times the size of a normal heart. Bates fell victim to the same disease that claimed the lives of basketball players Hank Gathers and Reggie Lewis.

"I guess how I look at it is the Lord felt Anthony had to have a big heart to handle all the goodness he demonstrated," said Snyder.

He added, "Regardless of your faith, you have to ask why? But some people put more life into 20 years than others do in 80 years. I told his mother, there was enough affection and passion in their relationship to last a lifetime."

But Snyder added, "That one hit us a little differently. We had 20-year-olds all around who knew it could have been them. It was a time when all of us rallied around the Bates family."

A service was held for Bates on August 5 at the All Faith's Chapel.

At the ceremony, teammate Jonathan McGraw played a violin solo.

"Having faith in God, and knowing Anthony, I know things are under control," McGraw said. "It shows you how fragile and temporary life is, but knowing Anthony, he's in heaven. For me, that makes it easier to handle."

Bates was an active kid who had played football since he was 9, as well as any other sport involving a ball.

Each year he would go through a standard sports physical. When he had surgery on his finger in his senior year of high school, an EKG was performed, but no hint of HCM was found. Sharon Bates would learn that HCM is a genetic heart disease that forms in the heart muscle, typically during adolescence. The surest way to detect the disease is through an echocardiogram of the heart.

Soon after her son's death, Sharon Bates founded the Anthony Bates Foundation in an effort to promote heart health and education through fund raisers and events.

"I needed to heal," Mrs. Bates said. "This was a very unfair thing for a parent to go through, and I want to prevent it from happening to others."

She promoted free cardiac screening events in Kansas, Arizona and Nevada, targeting young student-athletes aged 14 and older.

She says of her mission, "With education there is power; with power comes life."

"She has attacked this mission with as much persistence as I have ever put into the game of football," said Snyder.

Troy Miller

"Coach Del Miller, this one's for you and your son! We love you all. Keep the fight."

The words were those of Ell Roberson, who was talking into the lens of an *ABC* camera.

Kansas State had just scored its biggest win in the history of the school, winning the 2003 Big 12 Conference championship with a shocking 35-7 victory over the No. 1-ranked Oklahoma Sooners.

Troy, was Troy Miller, the son of Del and Jan Miller.

The Wildcats' offensive coordinator, Del Miller, didn't attend that December 6 game. He was bedside with his son Troy in an Iowa City hospital.

"There were some tears shed when Ell said that," said Jan Miller, Del Miller's wife.

Two years later, in a voice still choked with emotion, Del recalled, "Troy said, 'Dad you shouldn't be here, you should be at the game.' And I said, 'No son, I need to be with you. I love you, son.'"

Two weeks later, back at his Manhattan home, Troy said, "For Ell to think about our family after a big game like that was really meaningful. Those were powerful words for me. Sometimes words are stronger than medicine."

It was in September of 2001 when Troy, a model of health, suddenly urinated blood. A CAT scan revealed that a six-inch tumor in his kidney had exploded.

Snyder personally rented the K-State plane, which jetted the Miller family to the Mayo Clinic in Rochester, Minnesota, where the tumor and his kidney were removed. The cancer, however, had already entered the lymph nodes.

Through chemotherapy treatments, Troy's cancer went into remission, but only for 12 months.

Troy died on June 23, 2004, from an extremely rare transitional cell cancer, diagnosed in only about 500 individuals a year, and most commonly in persons in their 70s and 80s.

Through the fall of 2003, Snyder took time out of game preparations to help track down the best doctors, and made it known to Miller that his son came first.

"That's just doing the right thing," Snyder said. "We were going to look around for something that might work. We wanted to find a solution to a problem."

"I shed a lot of tears in his office. It was a difficult time for me," Miller said.

Of the Wildcat football family losses, Snyder said, "Death tends to make us put things in perspective. Athletes and coaches often view defeat with far less significance than we otherwise might once we've encountered a death. The loss of these four members of our family has had an accumulative effect on so many of us in the program.

"To experience the pain first hand, and at the same time attempt to ease the suffering of the family members of the deceased, is indeed a heartbreaking experience that lingers on," Snyder said. "All four passed long before their time and with so much yet to give. There was no better coach or family man than Bob Cope. No better person than Anthony Bates. No better wife or mother than Nancy Bennett, and no better son than Troy Miller."

KSU Plays with the Big Boys

Some who follow the Big 12 Conference hold to the notion that only the high budget, big stadium football programs can thrive in the Conference's rigorously competitive environment. It seems these concerns are regularly voiced to imply that the only factor determining success is the amount of money a program has to spend.

Fortunately for the Big 12, there will also be the example of Bill Snyder. Coach Snyder's legacy to college football demonstrated that hard work, a single-minded focus and attention to detail can be equally important in determining success. He devised a blueprint that put Kansas State on the national map.

Coach Snyder not only created a great learning environment for players, but also for young coaches. Current Big 12 head coaches Bob Stoops and Mark Mangino worked under Snyder at Kansas State.

Through his vision and leadership, Bill Snyder showed that the right plan, well executed, can lead to sustained success in one of the nation's most competitive conferences.

— Kevin Weiberg
Commissioner of the Big 12 Conference

Chapter Twenty-Four
1998: No Higher Highs; No Lower Lows

I'm not sure any one was projecting winning them all, but we knew we were going to be a good football team.

— Coach Bill Snyder

There were plenty of reasons to be optimistic about the 1998 Wildcat season.

Kansas State returned 18 starters. Among them were Butkus Award candidates Jeff Kelly and Mark Simoneau at linebacker; Eric Hickson at running back, who was on target to become KSU's all-time leading rusher; Martin Gramatica who was returning as the Lou Groza Award-winning kicker; and Michael Bishop, a Heisman Trophy candidate at quarterback.

This was testament to the Wildcats' potential for success, but it was more than that to Snyder. He had seen the gradual maturity of the program, and with this team, the intangibles were in place. In Snyder's words, "A lot of things you can't see and you can't touch but are necessary for success were there."

K-State was no longer the Mildcats. The days of being a team that others tried to schedule as a Homecoming opponent were long gone. Kansas State was one of just six schools to win at least nine games for five consecutive years. The others? Nebraska, Ohio State, Penn State, Florida and Florida State. Yes, K-State had become a big boy.

Kansas State started the season No. 6 in the national preseason polls. The 'Cats had now been ranked for 51 consecutive weeks.

"They said it couldn't be done" had been replaced with "What will they do next?"

Season tickets were now difficult to get. Single game tickets for the likes of Nebraska and Oklahoma were next to impossible to buy, with scalpers charging $150 for these showdowns.

All of this just 10 years removed from selling only 9,336 season tickets and averaging just 20,000 per home game.

And you know what? Snyder was not surprised.

"It boiled down to people. Good people with a similar vision as mine," Snyder simplified.

With a tireless work ethic and a weekly work week in excess of 100 hours, Snyder found ways to take that extra difference-making step.

Snyder warned, "This is a new year. The chemistry could be better, or worse, but it won't be the same." And he said, "There is a difference between being potentially good and really being good. That difference is doing it."

Kansas State did do it winning three non-conference games against Indiana State (66-0), Northern Illinois (73-7) and Louisiana-Monroe (62-7) by a combined score of 201-14.

Weaker teams? Yes. Games that proved little? Perhaps.

But it was also in September that the Purples blasted Texas, 48-7. That Longhorn team had a young man in the backfield named Ricky Williams.

Ricky Williams, who entered the game averaging 237 rushing yards per game; Ricky Williams, who would later win the Heisman Trophy.

"I think he came into that game averaging six million yards per game, which made our players really excited to play that ballgame," Snyder recalled. "But there was also a motivation to play Texas for the first time."

On this day, K-State had two backs—Eric Hickson with 124 yards and Marlon Charles with 44 yards—surpass Williams' total of 43 yards on 25 carries.

"I'm not sure if we could have played a much better game defensively," Snyder said. "It wasn't like we put 11 guys on Ricky. There was definitely a motivation to stop Ricky, but also a team discipline that shut down Texas."

The Wildcats had opened a 35-0 lead by the time Texas put its first points on the board on the first play of the fourth quarter.

Bishop completed 14 of 20 passes for 182 yards, plus rushed for 41 more, and Darnell McDonald caught 11passes for 159 yards. In addition, the defense scored with a Jeff Kelly pass interception, and the special teams scored on a 93-yard punt return by David Allen.

It was an afternoon when talent teamed with motivation, maturity and discipline.

Now No. 5 in the polls, K-State went on the road and surprised No. 14 Colorado, 16-9.

After that, a No. 4 Wildcat team disposed of Oklahoma State, Iowa State, Kansas and Baylor, scoring at least 49 points in each game, and not allowing more than seven points in three of the four.

The 49-6 win over Baylor in Waco, coupled with a 28-24 Ohio State loss to Michigan State, lifted K-State to No. 1 status in the *USA Today* coaches poll and to No. 2 in the Associated Press' media poll.

"Our young men were proud of that, our fan base was proud of that, and I was proud as well," Snyder said of being billed No. 1 in America. "My caution to them, though, was let's wait until it's over to celebrate.

"I wanted them to have a sense of accomplishment. I wanted the players to have that, but what I shared with them was that we had another game coming up, and another one after that. We're No. 1, but let's get the celebration behind you and go on to the next one."

The next game just happened to be against No. 11 Nebraska on the turf of KSU Stadium's Wagner Field. Nebraska was a team that Snyder had yet to defeat. In fact, the Big Red was an intercollegiate franchise that K-State had not defeated since a 12-0 win in Lincoln in 1968, and had not beaten Manhattan since a 29-14 win in 1959.

Yes, three decades, 10,962 days until November 14, 1998: Kansas State 40, Nebraska 30

"It's gotta be the greatest feeling ever," said KSU offensive tackle Ryan Young.

With a record 44,298 crammed into the 42,000-seat KSU Stadium, the Wildcats found themselves on the short end of a 17-7 count late in the second quarter.

But with Bishop scoring once by land and once through the air to McDonald, plus two Gramatica field goals, K-State had a 27-24 lead at the mid-fourth quarter mark.

Nebraska reclaimed the advantage on a Sheldon Jackson catch of an Eric Crouch pass with 8:22 remaining, but the PAT failed, giving the 'Huskers a 30-27 edge.

With 5:25 remaining, Bishop rifled an 11-yard pass to McDonald, and with Gramatica's kick, K-State led 34-30.

Nebraska went back on offense, but Joe Bob Clements jarred the ball loose from Crouch and Kelly scooped up the fumble and rumbled 23 yards for the score with just three seconds left.

Kansas State had cleared its last hurdle in Big 8/Big 12 football: defeating the University of Nebraska.

"We addressed it as something we had not done before," said a pleased but subdued Wildcat coach. "That was how I perceived the victory."

Bishop had never been better. He accounted for 446 total yards—140 rushing and 306 passing—and accounted for four touchdowns, two rushing and two throwing. With this game, he became the first Big 12 player to rush for 100 yards and pass for at least 300 in a single game.

"What he did tonight, well, I've never coached a guy like that and I don't think may people in the stands have ever seen a guy like that," said offensive coordinator Ron Hudson.

"With Michael, you knew there were going to be bad plays, but you also knew that there would likely be more good than bad. There was always a comfort with Michael because of his competitive spirit. His teammates responded to his nature of never say die, never give up," Snyder said.

The win gave K-State a first-ever 10-0 start to a season, and extended its win streak to 18 games.

While others celebrated, Snyder did as he had done after the first win of the season over Indiana State.

He met with the team, he met with the media, and then he spent the night reviewing the game and looking ahead to Missouri.

"Some coaches say to celebrate tonight, and worry about the next game on Sunday," Snyder said. "While I let my coaches go after games, I just feel it is a chance to get a heard start. It is finding a crease, and taking advantage of it. This profession is never-ending. There's not a night when you can go to bed and not think of something you could be doing."

Snyder doesn't say that this is the right way nor the only way to coach, but it works for him.

Kansas State entered the regular-season finale at Missouri having won games by margins of 66, 66, 41, 55, 7, 32, 45, 48, 43 and 10 points.

"I really don't think that team felt any pressure until maybe the last week of the season," Snyder said. "Then, I think some of us had that home-free feeling, and some of us were feeling the pressure of the game, and what if we lost."

Against Missouri in the regular-season finale, K-State found itself down 13-10 at the half. They also faced a second half without Eric Hickson, who had sprained an ankle, and without his backup Marlon Charles, who was carried from the field after fracturing his hip.

Snyder's halftime message to the team was "championship teams win this type of game."

And Kansas State had a championship quarterback in Bishop. "I enjoy games like this," he said. "The pressure is on, the games get tougher, and there are chances to step up and make the great run or great pass. You just have to take advantage of it."

Bishop did just that, scoring on a 1-yard step-in just four plays into the second half, which was followed by a Frank Murphy dash for six on KSU's next possession that was set up by a 47-yard punt return by David Allen, making it a 24-13 Wildcat lead.

Mizzou closed the difference to two, 24-22, but Murphy would score K-State's final touchdown in a most unique way, fumbling at the MU 1 but recovering his own mistake in the end zone for a TD.

After the game, the difficult-to-please Snyder would only say of the Wildcats' 11-0 record, "It's better than losing one, or two, or three. I think it's a special achievement."

While never mentioning it as a team goal in any of his years at Kansas State, Snyder and his team, using a one day at a time philosophy, were now one game away from a Big 12 Championship and a possible opportunity at a national crown.

"I wouldn't know how to coach for a national title. The only way I would know how to coach is to do it a step at a time for the betterment of the program," Snyder said. "Then maybe you have the season that goes right, you win a championship, and you have that opportunity to play for a title.

"But I can't say, here's how you coach for a national championship, other than to say, you better take care of today."

But K-State didn't take care of this day. K-State didn't know it at the time, but the dream season would soon turn ghoulish.

Kansas State had won its first Big 12 Conference North Championship, and would now travel to the Trans World Dome in St. Louis to play the best from the South in Texas A&M.

On this night, the South won, or some might say, the North lost.

The final: Texas A&M 36, Kansas State 33, in double-overtime.

"It's a sick feeling," said Bishop.

"It shouldn't have happened, but it did," said d-back Jarrod Cooper.

Yes, it did.

After leading the Aggies by 15 points, 27-12, in the second half, and with a national championship on the line, the Wildcats could not complete the task.

Saying he didn't want to be disrespectful, Snyder compared the loss to losing a family member.

Snyder took heat over such a comparison, but he later explained, "All I was trying to say was that it felt bad, but to equate a ballgame to being as significant as a human life wasn't the meaning I intended."

But it was a sickening feeling.

Golfer Jim Colbert, the most loyal of KSU fans, compared it to the feeling he had when he lost the Masters by two strokes in 1974.

"That's a tournament I'll take to my grave. With all I've won in golf, that's the moment I remember most," Colbert said. "I don't think there's a win in Coach Snyder's career that will ever be more vivid than this loss."

After the game, Snyder said, "The Lord tests us in a lot of ways. This team has a lot of love and affection, which is important. We have to show that care and love, and hang together even tighter."

"It's painful now, it will be more painful later this evening, and even more painful tomorrow," Snyder said. "This team had invested a lot into this season, and they were pained."

Receivers coach Michael Smith said of Snyder, "He was distraught. We all knew that this was our opportunity. In a 10-year span, we were going from one victory to the opportunity to play for a national championship and we didn't get it done."

Pausing to reflect on the memory, Smith said, "Like Coach said, it really was like somebody had died."

Pausing again to go back in time, Smith said, "We had put so much into that season. It was a team that had no weaknesses. It was a coaching staff that had no weaknesses."

If A&M had an MVP on this night under the dome, it might have been the public address announcer, who announced that UCLA had lost to Miami, 49-45, which assured K-State a spot in the Fiesta Bowl to play for the national championship if it could hold its lead over A&M.

That the Bruin/Hurricane game was set for a late-afternoon start had already crossed Snyder's mind. He forgets who, but he had instructed a K-State official to ask the Trans World Dome staff not to announce the score of that game, and not to display it on the scoreboard during the playing of this Big 12 title game. In his mind, "It could have an impact on the performance of players."

Shortly after K-State went up 17-3 in the second quarter, though, the score was announced.

A&M scored the next 10 points and the battle was on.

With a headset on and focused on the game, Snyder said he didn't hear the score.

When asked if that might have been the turning point of the evening, Snyder said, "I would like to think that didn't have an effect, but you never know. We made some mistakes and let them back in the ballgame."

Like their coach, the players were certainly not using it as an excuse. "It didn't matter," said linebacker Travis Ochs of hearing the score. "It didn't change anybody's play."

Jeremy Martin said, "If anything, it gave us a boost."

The scoreboard, however, said otherwise, as A&M battled back to tie the game at 27 when Sirr Parker caught a nine-yard pass, plus added the two-point conversion, with 1:05 left in regulation.

With one last chance, Bishop let fly with a 54-yard Hail Mary pass that was batted by McDonald and caught by teammate Everett Burnett at the A&M 2-yard line as time ran out, sending the game into overtime, a first in K-State history.

The teams traded field goals in the first OT, and Gramatica gave KSU a 33-30 lead with a 25-yard three-pointer in the second OT.

Down three and facing a 3rd and 17 from the KSU 32, A&M's Randy McCown threw a slant to Parker.

"We were just trying to get in field goal range," Parker said.

They did better than that.

Parker shook off Jerametrius Butler and then beat Lamar Chapman to the right corner of the end zone.

"I thought it was in slow-motion," said receiver McDonald, who watched the play unfold from the sideline. "I thought they would tackle him, but he kept running for what seemed like days. Even when he was in the end zone it didn't seem like he scored."

Instant replay was not in vogue in 1998, but replays later showed that Parker was out-of-bounds at the 1-yard line. Still, it would have been 1st and goal and likely wouldn't have changed the outcome of the game.

Did Snyder forward the tape to the Big 12 office?

"If I did, it's between me and the Big 12," Snyder said. "I never made that public."

After the game, Snyder did as he always does. He took his first-row aisle seat on the right side of the bus headed for the airport and started watching the game on his portable video player.

And once seated on the late-night charter back to Manhattan, he hit the resume button on the tape machine, perhaps in hopes that the outcome would be different.

"You just keep fretting over games like that," Snyder said. "You fret if it's 55-0. But with a chance to win it in the fourth quarter, a chance in overtime, and a chance in the second overtime ... it was difficult."

"We were all in the doldrums for quite some time after that one," said tight ends coach Matt Miller. "It wasn't just the loss, but the way it happened."

Martin said, "Today, we tripped and fell, but we have to get up and take more steps."

Kansas State did get up, but would trip and fall again in a 37-34 loss to unranked Purdue in the Alamo Bowl in San Antonio.

Alamo Bowl chairman Ernesta Ancira Jr., said, "To be host to the No. 4 team in the nation is an unbelievable opportunity for us."

For K-State, it was a slug to the chin.

Not only had the Wildcats lost the right to play for the national championship in the Fiesta Bowl, but the pecking order for bowl games with Big 12 ties crumbled before the Wildcats' very eyes.

Tennessee and Florida State were locks to play in the Fiesta Bowl for the national title, while the Rose Bowl went with its anchor conferences in selecting UCLA from the Pac-10 and Wisconsin from the Big Ten.

That left the Sugar Bowl and the Orange Bowl with Syracuse and Texas A&M getting automatic entries because they were conference champions.

The Big East was tied to the Orange Bowl, so Syracuse locked up one spot, and with Miami based in southern Florida, the Orange Bowl took the Hurricanes as the opponent because of the local fan base.

That left A&M in the Sugar Bowl. A rematch with K-State was not logical, so Ohio State became the Aggies' opponent.

Feeling sure that No. 1 ranked K-State would win the Big 12 title, the Cotton Bowl worked to get Texas, with Ricky Williams, while the Holiday Bowl liked the idea of bringing Nebraska and its Big Red fans to San Diego.

That left Kansas State, only two weeks prior the No. 1 team in the country, to play in the Big 12's fourth seeded bowl game in San Antonio.

"Things tumbled down hill pretty fast," Snyder said. "We called the Sugar Bowl and soon realized that wasn't going to work. We called the Cotton Bowl and realized that wasn't going to work. We called the Holiday Bowl and realized that wasn't going to work.

"There was a rule in place where you couldn't negotiate with teams for bowl games until after the season was over," Snyder said. "It didn't take long to realize that rule meant nothing.

"I used to believe that everything was good about the bowls. Growing up, January 1 was my favorite day, watching those four games back-to-back-to-back-to-back," Snyder said. "I thought the bowl system was loyal to the world, and I remained loyal to the bowls until 1998.

"All of a sudden that bowl system I had counted on was not being loyal to us," Snyder said. "I just said, 'Hey, I no longer have the same stance.'"

Nothing hurt worse than getting the cold shoulder from the Cotton Bowl.

It was in 1995 that the Dallas-based bowl was teetering on the brink of distinction when Kansas State was invited to play BYU and brought an estimated 44,000 fans to the game.

"That was a magical year for us," said Rick Baker, executive director of the Cotton Bowl. "At that time, Kansas State helped save this bowl. We were in trouble. We weren't going out of the bowl business, but we were back on our heels."

Looking at the decision with objective eyes, the Cotton Bowl choosing to go with Texas made sense.

The Longhorns hadn't been to the Cotton Bowl since 1991; Ricky Williams was a mega-attraction; the Cotton Bowl is played in a stadium known as "The House That Doak (Walker) Built"; and it was the 50th anniversary of Walker winning the Heisman. Walker, who had died earlier that year, would have been 72 on January 1,1999, the day of the Cotton Bowl.

As for the Holiday Bowl wanting Nebraska, that was due in large part to the name recognition that went with Cornhusker football and the following of Big Red fans that would journey to San Diego.

To all of that, Snyder said, "I understood why they did it, I just never agreed with it.

"The bottom line was, if we were out there, and if we were as good as everyone perceived us to be, there should have been a bowl game available to us. After all, we were 11-1 with our only loss coming in overtime."

"Was I naive to all that takes place in the bowl business?" Snyder asked. "Apparently, yes. I learned quickly that this is a business, and loyalty took a back seat to that. They have to make money."

Snyder said it crossed his mind to opt not to play in the Alamo Bowl, but added, "That was short-lived."

He explained, "I was angry, and wrongly vindictive for a short period of time. I knew that wasn't right."

The players were, using Snyder's phrase, "a mixed bag" as to whether they wanted to play in the game, and that would become even more apparent on December 29 in the Alamodome.

First, the mindset was not right. In K-State's mind, it deserved better than the bowl to which they were going. Maybe it was only natural then that once the team arrived in San Antonio, practices were mediocre and curfews were missed.

"We had some issues. Nothing serious, but just issues showing our lack of respect for the game and our teammates," Snyder said. "We were not as selfless as we had been throughout the season."

Purdue gave K-State some issues early that the Wildcats would never overcome. Behind Drew Brees, the Boilermakers opened a 17-7 half-time lead and extended that to 27-13 at the end of three periods.

Snyder called KSU's play "lethargic," and called the first 30 minutes "a disastrous half."

The 'Cats rallied to take the lead, 34-30, on a pair of Bishop TD passes of 88 yards to McDonald and 2 yards to tight end Justin Swift, with the second coming with just 1:24 left in the game.

Brees then orchestrated a six-play, 80-yard drive capped by a 24-yard strike to Isaac Jones with 30 seconds left for the 37-34 final.

Not even Brees could comprehend how Purdue ended up winning the game, stating, "I remember thinking, 'How did we win this game?'"

In the end, Snyder said, "Tonight was the culmination of three weeks of disappointments." The year ended with an 11-2 record and a boat load of records set:

- 73 points in a single game

- The 73 touchdowns bettered the former record of 53

- Hickson became KSU's all-time leading rusher

- Bishop accounted for a record 37 touchdowns and 3,130 total yards

- McDonald and Aaron Lockett caught 119 passes for 2,020 yards, nearly 500 yards more than any other KSU receiving duo

- KSU was No. 2 in the nation in yards allowed per game and second best in points allowed

- Gramatica hit a record 65-yard field goal and ended up with 52 field goals, shattering Steve Willis' record by 15

- David Allen tied an NCAA record with four punt returns for touchdowns

- Punter James Garcia was used just 30 times in the 13-game season

Chapter Twenty-Five
Loyalty

I made it pretty clear across the nation that I wasn't interested in other jobs.

— Coach Bill Snyder

During his 17 years at Kansas State, Bill Snyder orchestrated such a successful turnaround that he became a hot commodity in coaching circles. The most attention came in the late-1990s, after the Wildcats bolted up the Big 8/Big12 ladder, rising from obscurity into the Top 10.

Snyder received a half-dozen college head coaching offers, as well as three offers from the National Football League ranks. Among the offers most advertised were Minnesota, UCLA and LSU.

"I had conversations," Snyder says, reluctant even today to talk about the opportunities. "I was honored because of how I felt about those programs and schools, but not to the extent that I thought about leaving."

At one time, returning to Iowa as a successor to Hayden Fry might have been a thought, but when the opening occurred in 1999, Snyder said, "I realized I was already where I wanted to be."

Snyder always said he came to Kansas State because of its people. And after he constructed the Wildcat Nation for those people, they truly became his extended family. As corny as it sounds, he felt a loyalty to his kingdom.

He had handcrafted one turnaround, and that was enough. As for taking over a mega-power, like a Notre Dame, Snyder said, "A place like Notre Dame doesn't intrigue me. You ought to win a championship at a place like that. From my standpoint, I'm not interested in a position where it's already laid out for you."

Snyder's loyalty started with the Wefald administration and extended to his staff. Snyder hired 34 different assistants over his 17 years and never dismissed one.

No, the only coach Bill Snyder ever fired was himself.

In that regard, Snyder wasn't much different from Fry.

Laughing, Del Miller said, "At Iowa, if you stayed any length of time at all, you'd be fired three or four times. Hayden fired everyone, at least for a few hours."

While Fry would never mean it, the threat was always there.

At K-State, Snyder was loyal to his staff, perhaps to a fault. Oh, he held the door open for some who opted to leave, but with most, he did everything in his power to keep them as Wildcats.

Many believe Snyder has the qualities to be the head of a Fortune 500 company. But those closest to him say that if he had a CEO weakness, it was his tendency to be too loyal. His heart is too caring to let go of those not pulling their weight.

Never before was Snyder's loyalty tested as it was after the 1998 regular season.

Bob Stoops had left the program to become defensive coordinator at the University of Florida after the Wildcat recruits had been signed for the 1996 season.

At the time, Stoops was the lone assistant remaining from the original Snyder coaching staff of 1989.

"That was a good move. I didn't want to lose him, but I understood," Snyder said. "We were working our way up, and [Florida] was already there."

Though the 1995 season saw Stoops put his thumb print on the No. 1 defense in the nation, he felt it was time for change.

"I had been at Kansas State for a long time by coaching standards. This was an opportunity to broaden my horizons under Coach (Steve) Spurrier at Florida," said Stoops. "I was going to be defensive coordinator for a team that just played for a national championship, in a wonderful part of the country. Shoot, it was another way to learn things."

Giving a slight chuckle, Stoops said, "I don't think people cared when I left then, but they cared when I went to Oklahoma three years later. Then it seemed like they developed a sense of owning me and I was a traitor."

Or perhaps purple-clad fans were more offended that after taking the Oklahoma position, Stoops, and understandably so, went to coaches he knew and trusted to form his first Sooner staff.

It only made sense that he would offer a position to his brother Mike, who had been on the K-State staff for the previous seven years.

"How could I not offer Mike a job?" Stoops asked.

Brent Venables had been a fulltime KSU assistant for three seasons, and he was the second choice to co-head the OU defense with Mike Stoops.

"He was a perfect complement to Mike," explained Stoops.

"It wasn't an act of treason, as some people took it. It wasn't like I wanted to leave in the worst way, but it was just a professional move," said Venables, who was 28 at the time and indicated that it was the hardest decision he's ever had to make. "I appreciated Coach Snyder very much. He encouraged me to stay. He didn't say I was nuts or crazy which made it that much more difficult of a decision. Everyone had worked so hard to have success at Kansas State, so it was very difficult to leave."

The third to be invited south of the Kansas border was Mark Mangino, the Wildcats' assistant head coach and running game coordinator, an eight-year veteran of the Snyder staff.

Mangino didn't make his decision until a couple days prior to the Alamo Bowl in San Antonio.

"That was a difficult day for me. I had invested a lot of work and effort, and my family had made sacrifices during my eight years at Kansas State," said Mangino. "I never wanted to disappoint Coach Snyder. I did everything he asked, at times more than he asked, so it was difficult."

But while at K-State, Mangino had developed a very close personal link with Bob Stoops and after all, it was an opportunity to coach at tradition-rich Oklahoma.

"In the end, I just felt that I had contributed everything I could at Kansas State and I was ready for a new challenge," Mangino said. "The fact that that challenge was with a very good coaching friend confirmed to me it was the right thing to do."

As head coach of the University of Kansas, Mangino understands the importance of keeping a staff together.

"As a head coach, you always want to keep continuity," he said. "It's never easy when coaches leave because it disrupts the continuity. In this instance, three were leaving KSU at one time."

Distraught Kansas State fans were wondering if the sun would ever come up again after being stunned in the Big 12 championship game by Texas A&M and losing the fiasco in the Alamo Bowl.

Now, Stoops, Venables and Mangino were depleting the Wildcat coaching staff by one-third.

Mangino heard the whispers about Snyder' resentment, but he hopes that was not, and is not, the case.

"In the end, we shook hands, exchanged a hug, which I know was very sincere on my part, and I believe was sincere on his part," Mangino said. "I have never seen a hint of Coach Snyder holding a grudge."

Of the trio of hires, Stoops said, "It was a tough decision, but I was in charge of putting together the best possible staff I could find for the University of Oklahoma," Stoops said. "I knew these guys and I trusted these guys. It wouldn't have been right to not at least offer them this opportunity."

Snyder also said the bitterness talk was primarily chat-room hearsay that made good print for papers.

"You want all your coaches to want to better themselves and become head coaches," Snyder said. "You want that ambition, and you always try to prepare them the best you can. There's that natural progression from position coach, to coordinator, to assistant head coach. You're constantly trying to prepare them for that highest rung."

One way Snyder made his assistants attractive to other schools was by giving titles. He may have been the first coach in the country to name co-defensive coordinators—Bob Stoops and Jim Leavitt—in 1995. In 1997, he went with Greg Peterson as passing game coordinator and Mangino as running game coordinator, while Ron Hudson was the overall offensive coordinator.

The thought was that if schools didn't have the opportunity to hire a sitting head coach, a coordinator's title would advertise that this coach had accepted additional responsibilities.

That was one reason. The other was, "I wanted to reward coaches for their loyalty and years spent within the program," Snyder said. "Sometimes you're not able to give them the kind of money they deserve, but this was another type of reward."

Snyder's loyalty certainly didn't stop with his nine top assistants. He was true to his word with graduate assistants. If they came, did the grunt work and earned their stripes, Snyder would do his best to reward them with fulltime positions.

Examples of coaches who followed this path are Michael Smith, Greg Peterson, Mangino, Joe Bob Clements, Bob Stanley, and even the likes of Del Miller and Dana Dimel, who both left the K-State staff to become head coaches—Miller at Southwest Missouri State and Dimel at Wyoming and Houston—only to return to the Wildcats as GA's until a fulltime spot opened.

Snyder respects and honors loyalty. He admires no one more than three individuals who stood by his side for all 17 years.

That's equipment manager Jim "Shorty" Kleinau, secretary Joan Friederich, and building supervisor Lyle Hasenbank.

"You talk about people who love their job, those are truly dedicated individuals," Snyder said.

Friederich is in her 35th year in the Kansas State athletic department, with the last 33 of those being with the football program. She started as a secretary for the assistant coaches, and has since been the go-between for all callers to head coaches Dickey, Parrish and Snyder.

"She just loves being around the players," Snyder said. "She's a mother to the players. Her care is so genuine and as loyal as they come."

Starting in 1998, Snyder developed the Joan Friederich Award, which goes to the individual who demonstrates an unselfishness, leadership and commitment to the team concept of K-State football. In 1999 at the Holiday Bowl, Friederich was presented the Admiral U.S. Grant Sharp Trophy for the person who best exemplifies the spirit of unselfish dedication and teamwork, which resulted in little recognition or acclaim, but contributed significantly to an outstanding season for the team.

Kleinau has been in charge of everything from socks to chinstraps since 1979.

"Shorty lives and dies with this football program," Snyder said. "People don't look at it this way, but Shorty, and individuals in his position, play a vital role to the success of a football team. If things don't go well out on the field, it pains him. I love him to death because of that."

Kleinau doesn't just hand out towels. It is a profession, and he prides himself on the fact K-State has become a bit of a "Cradle of Equipment Managers." Six of his former assistants are in programs around the country: Jeff Parsons, South Florida;

Jeff Cook, Houston; Will Rodecap, Colorado State; Chuck Hall, Louisville; Scott Jean, Tulane; and Scott Gifford, Detroit Lions.

The Jim "Shorty" Kleinau Award goes annually to the Wildcat who best represents loyalty, hard work, commitment and dedication to a common cause.

Hasenbank has kept things tidy around the football plant since 1977. In 1990, he was promoted to custodial supervisor of the Vanier Football Complex, and now serves as the coordinator of facilities management of the complex.

"It's just like with Shorty and Joan," Snyder said. "If Lyle is in charge of doing something, you know it will be done as well as it can be done. Lyle keeps this building impeccable."

Chuckling, Snyder added, "Lyle is the only one who ever beats me to work. There are mornings he even makes my coffee for me."

Each pre-season, Snyder makes it a point to introduce his entire support staff to the team and define what their job is and to announce the respect that each of them deserves.

To Snyder, they're part of Team KSU.

Chapter Twenty-Six
1999-2000: The Beasley Years

We had just lost a Davey O'Brien Award winner at quarterback, but Jonathan Beasley stepped in and did a marvelous job. He wasn't the dynamic personality that Michael Bishop was, but he was always setting an example in regards to all the values that are important. He was a positive reinforcement to other players.

— Coach Bill Snyder

Jonathan Beasley proved there would be K-State football life after Michael Bishop.

The sun would rise over the Flint Hills, and Kansas State would keep on winning. In fact, as with Bishop before him, Beasley was a 22-game winner in his two seasons as a starter, and to this day is the only Wildcat quarterback to win two bowl games.

The Glendale, Arizona, native wasn't the fastest or the strongest or the shiftiest, but he could do the one thing that counted most—win. The Wildcats went 11-1 in 1999 and 11-3 in 2000, which included defeating Washington in the 1999 Holiday Bowl, 24-20, and Tennessee in the 2001 (2000 season) Cotton Bowl, 35-21.

"Michael Bishop always believed as long as the ball touched his hands, the play was going to be a good one," Snyder said. "Jonathan had a great command of the offense, knowing what the defense was allowing, and then taking advantage of it."

The 1999 team didn't have the high-profile talents of past years, but there was a team-wide belief in each other and the system.

"You didn't see anybody outside the circle, so to speak," Snyder said. "It was a bunch of guys who wanted to continue to be successful. I really think how the '98 season ended served as motivation."

K-State opened the year with nine straight wins, the biggest a 35-17 victory over Texas in Austin.

"That one came relatively early in the year and told this team that we can really do this," Snyder said. "It was the turning point to that season."

The Wildcats scored 35 points on the Longhorns, but the offense scored only one of those TDs, on a David Allen run.

Allen also returned a punt for a TD, the seventh of his career, which tied the NCAA record. Mark Simoneau intercepted a pass for a score and Jamie Rheem kicked five successful field goals.

Overall, it was a strange early-season as the Wildcats rallied from a 28-7 half-time deficit to defeat Iowa State in Ames, and beat Oklahoma State in Stillwater 44-21 after trailing 21-0 just 16:36 into the game.

K-State stayed perfect through nine games before losing to No. 7 Nebraska, 41-15, in Lincoln.

"That game carried a significant disappointment because we really believed that we were capable of winning," Snyder said. "It was a locker room that I visibly remember. Our players were crushed by the loss. I didn't like the loss, but I appreciated the attitude our players had."

K-State would "Rout 66" Mizzou, 66-0, the next week and accept an invitation to play Washington in the Holiday Bowl, which it would win, 24-20.

Down by three points, Beasley led K-State on a 20-play, 92-yard drive that ate 9:54 off the clock and was capped by a Beasley option-run for the winning score.

Going 11-1 in 1999 and sharing the Big 12 North Division title with Nebraska, K-State had the opportunity to attend the Cotton Bowl, just a year after believing it had been snubbed by the folks in Dallas.

"I let our players vote which bowl game they would like to attend, and the players voted on the Holiday Bowl," Snyder said. "It was a tough decision, but one you could make without feeling an obligation to the bowl system because the bowl system hadn't treated us very well the previous year."

Snyder says he's not saying that the the Cotton Bowl's treatment of the Wildcats in the previous year went unmentioned, but he emphasized, "The bottom line is that it was the choice of the players."

In 2000, K-State opened the year against Snyder's old school, the University of Iowa, in the Eddie Robinson Classic staged in Kansas City's Arrowhead Stadium.

The Wildcats won, 27-7, but Snyder remembers more about playing the game on a late-August afternoon when the field temperature was 120 degrees and a KSU fan died from heat stroke in the stadium.

While Iowa will always be dear to his heart, Snyder said that he had been removed from the Hawkeye program for enough years that there weren't great emotions involved in the game other than to get the season off to a winning start.

"I had Eddie Robinson come in and speak to the team before that game," Snyder said of the Grambling University coaching legend. "He was just delightful for me, but I got the feeling that our players didn't quite know who he was."

Snyder, however, could have listened forever.

"Eddie Robinson was a titan in our profession," Snyder said. "He was a coach who for so many years cared about young people and always did things the right way."

Kansas State was 8-2 heading into a November 11 meeting with Nebraska on a snowy night at KSU Stadium when a Beasley to Quincy Morgan 12-yard pass with 2:52 remaining gave K-State a 29-28 victory.

"Jonathan showed such poise, sitting back there with snow flurries all around him and as cold as it was," Snyder said. "Jonathan Beasley was a winner."

While the Wildcats had the lead with just under three minutes to play, Snyder still had a significant concern.

"When the snow started to fall, we ended up being in the wrong shoes, and knowing that Nebraska was going to pass the ball, I was scared to death that one of our defensive backs would slip," Snyder said. "I've never been in a game where the clock seemed to move so slowly."

When the clock finally ticked down to 0:00, the Wildcats celebrated with snow-angels on the Wagner Field turf.

After edging Missouri, 28-24, K-State had yet another Big 12 North title, and returned to the scene of the season-opener, Arrowhead Stadium, where it would face No. 1 Oklahoma in the Big 12 title game.

The Sooners had won earlier in Manhattan, 41-31, and would win again on this night, 27-24.

With a quartet of former Wildcat coaches on the Sooner staff—the Stoops brothers, Brent Venables and Mark Mangino—Snyder admitted that it forced his hand to change.

"We had to be a little more protective with the things we were doing," Snyder said. "We had to change our signaling system, we had to change our audible system, and because of that, we were not as adept at what we were doing."

Snyder frequently says that nothing surprises him, but on this night, the Sooners did.

With OU clinging to a 21-17 lead late in the game, the Sooners faced a short-yardage fourth-down snap.

"Oklahoma had not run an option play all season, but as soon as they came up to the line, I started hollering, 'Option! Option! Option!'" Snyder recalled. "I don't know why I knew it was coming. I guess because that's the play we would have run in that situation, but Oklahoma hadn't shown it all year."

With Josh Heupel at quarterback, OU converted the fourth-down option run, kept the ball, and eventually kicked a field goal to make it a 10-point game with 1:25 remaining.

With the loss K-State once again earned an invitation to play in the Cotton Bowl, and this time accepted. The Wildcats would defeat No. 15 Tennessee, 35-21, in a game played on a frigid, snowy turf at the historic stadium located on the Texas State Fairgrounds.

With the experience of playing in the snow against Nebraska six weeks earlier, K-State used the unusual winter-like conditions in Dallas to its favor.

"I don't think the weather bothered us one bit, but I do think it affected them," Snyder said of the Volunteers. "Our players knew the mental toughness that it took to play a game in those conditions, and I don't believe Tennessee did."

Josh Scobey rushed for 147 yards, Beasley completed his career with 98 rushing and 210 passing yards, and Quincy Morgan caught seven balls for 145 yards in the win.

The win, said Snyder, "might be as big as we've ever had just because of the perception of the team we defeated."

With the two seasons under Beasley's guidance, Kansas State had now won 11 games in four consecutive years (44-7-0), which had been accomplished by only Nebraska and Florida in college football history. KSU also had one Big 12 North title to itself, and two more shared in 1999 and 2000.

Kansas State had posted a four-year Big 12 record of 28-4 with the losses coming to No. 3 Nebraska in 1997, No. 7 Nebraska in 1999, No. 8 Oklahoma and unranked Texas A&M in 2000.

Chapter Twenty-Seven
2001: America Attacked, A Loss Of Focus

I'm very much apple pie. There wasn't so much a fear as there was an anger over 9/11. I wasn't angered so much by why it was allowed to happen, but angered that someone could actually do this.

— Coach Bill Snyder

Bill Snyder was sitting in his office on the morning of Tuesday, September 11, 2001.

Suddenly, Snyder heard an urgent rap on his door and was told by his secretary, Joan Friedrich, to flip on the television.

In Snyder's office, the set is normally tuned into one of the news channels—*Fox* or *CNN*. With the flip of a switch, he saw the billowing smoke from the World Trade Center.

Our country, his country, had been attacked. "It's one of those things I will never forget.

"It's like always remembering where you were when President John F. Kennedy was killed. I was standing in line at a cafeteria in downtown Portales, New Mexico, where I was attending Eastern New Mexico," said Snyder. "I've never watched so much television in all my life as I did on September 11."

Snyder didn't personally know anyone killed or injured in the destruction of the twin towers, but so many thoughts raced through his mind, which included what he had always preached to his players.

"I'm constantly telling young people not to take anything for granted, and it just made me think of how I, like so many others, had taken for granted the security of this country and our safety," Snyder said. "There was never a thought that something like this could happen on our soil."

Snyder said the enormity of the incident gave him a new perspective on worldly affairs and how they should be important in every person's life.

On the field, K-State had opened the football year 2-0, prior to having the game with Louisiana Tech rescheduled for November 17 following 9/11.

The Wildcats would open the Big 12 season at Oklahoma, where they would lose 38-37, and then lose on the next three Saturdays—Colorado, Texas Tech and Texas A&M—to fall to 2-4, the poorest start to a season since 1989.

Ell Roberson's performance in the Oklahoma game would be a microcosm of the season, if not his career. The sophomore rushed for 115 yards, passed for 257, and accounted for four touchdowns.

With the game on national television, the Wildcats called an option play on their first series. Roberson went left and made a blind pitch. One problem: the rest of the KSU team had gone right. OU's Roy Williams picked up the one-hop fumble and raced 18 yards into the end zone for a 7-0 Sooner lead.

"Ell was a young pup and all the television people applauded his play and forgave his mistakes to the point of being detrimental to him," Snyder said. "He was hearing too much of what a talent he was, and it was too much for him to carry at that particular point in time."

Snyder said that Roberson had a little bit of Michael Bishop in him in that he just wanted to play the game. That's what he had done at Lee High School in Baytown, Texas, where he succeeded by simply being better than the other guy.

"He was never belligerent about it, he just didn't think the game was that hard to comprehend and that got him into trouble at times early in his career," Snyder said.

But the sporadic play of the Wildcats was not all a Roberson-factor. The team seemd to lack selflessness.

"That can get you into trouble, and it did us. It had nothing to do with talent," said Snyder, "but just people being into it for the wrong reason."

Snyder said he could see glimmers of trouble from the start with "little things that become big things." Players' work habits were iffy, they missed classes, and there were more reasons for athletes to be disciplined with the 8- 8- 8 drills. Too much, said Snyder, had been taken for granted.

K-State would defeat Kansas and Iowa State, but then lose to Nebraska to fall to 4-5 with two games to play against Louisiana Tech and Missouri. Both were must wins if the Wildcats expected to keep alive a streak of eight straight bowl games.

"That drew the team together a little better and there was a better acceptance of responsibility," Snyder said. "They knew that one loss and they were out. They didn't want to be the team to break the string."

The Wildcats whipped Louisiana Tech, 40-7, and then Mizzou, 24-3, earning a trip to the Insight.com Bowl to play Syracuse.

The night at the Bank One Ballpark was a football disaster, at least on offense. It was a quarterback carousel. First Roberson, then Marc Dunn, then Roberson, then Dunn. Roberson again. Dunn once more. Each tried to generate an offense, but failed in what would be a 26-3 loss.

Roberson was 2 of 15; Dunn 12 of 35. Each threw an interception. The team rushed for a paltry 33 yards.

"It was like playing the slots," Snyder said of rotating QB's six times. "You play one for a while, and if nothing happens, you move to the next."

No fault could be given to the defense, as it held Syracuse to just eight first downs and 222 yards of total offense and blocked two extra point attempts.

A DIFFERENCE MAKER

There are two kinds of coaches, those whose primary concern is their win-loss record and a select few who are teachers and by example, are leaders of young men. Bill Snyder has been highly successful at both.

The Bill Snyder record of achievement is unmatched in turning around a football program that was mired in years of defeat and threatening K-State's loss of conference participation. He reversed that record to make K-State one of the top teams in the country, took the team to 10 straight bowl games and made K-State players well known in the NFL. This turnaround is unmatched in collegiate athletics.

Additionally, his achievements were a catalyst for alumni interest and renewal of financial support throughout the university.

He has led us out of the Death Valley days of defeat to great and lasting victories.

I have had the privilege of knowing Bill as a coach and personal friend. Simply put, he has been a class act, a great coach and a wonderful mentor of young men.

Like all K-Staters, I wish him and Sharon the very best and thank him for great memories.

Thanks Coach.

Every Man A Wildcat!

— Senator Pat Roberts

Chapter Twenty-Eight
2002: Cats Of Old Return

We demonstrated some renewed enthusiasm with a turnover of players. A lot had been taken for granted in 2001, and the 2002 players seemed committed to realizing that they had to do something about achieving success. They realized it wouldn't just happen.

— Coach Bill Snyder

Kansas State played with a bounce in its step in 2002. They won 10 regular season games, with their only two losses coming by a total of seven points to Colorado, 35-31, and Nebraska, 17-14.

The Wildcats advanced to the Holiday Bowl, where they scored the last 15 points of the game on a TD by Ell Roberson and a 10-yard Roberson to Derrick Evans pass with 1:15 left to defeat Arizona 34-27.

In its last six games, K-State rattled the scoreboard for 44, 64, 58, 49, 38, and 34 points. The play-calling returned to that of 1997 and 1998 when Michael Bishop was quarterbacking and Snyder was perfecting the quarterback-run game.

While Roberson, at 6-1, 190 pounds, didn't quite pack the bulk of the 6-1, 210-pound Bishop, he still possessed a similar athleticism to his game, and he had an arm that was strong enough to get the ball to the desired destination.

It wasn't impossible to imagine the quarterback-run game went back to Snyder's days of single-wing football at Lafayette High School and William Jewell College. That's when the spinner-back (quarterback) would be joined in the backfield by a blocking back (fullback) and a wing back that would be a stride to the outside of the tight end.

Snyder began feeding single-wing plays into the playbook when Matt Miller was at quarterback in 1995, with the format blossoming under Bishop in 1997 and 1998. Even more nuances were invented for the talents of Roberson beginning in 2001.

In coaching vernacular, it became a numbers game, with the Wildcats having that X-factor of an extra running back who happened to be the quarterback. In the majority of offenses, the quarterback would just throw or hand the ball off. But with Bishop and Roberson, the defensive plan of going hat-for-hat was thrown out of kilter because of the threat of the quarterback.

The solution for most defensive coordinators was to commit another player to the line of scrimmage to account for the quarterback, but that forced the defense into one-on-one coverage in the secondary.

Defenses evolved and tried slanting techniques along the defensive front, which in theory would make it the task of two offensive blockers to account for one defender. In response, the Wildcat offense developed a true option look with its QB-run game, which, while common today, was a bit of an anomaly 10 years ago.

First with Bishop, and then with Roberson in 2002, at least half of the plays came out of a shotgun formation, which enabled the quarterback to avoid the rush a second longer. As for the shotgun set benefiting the passing game, Snyder never bought into that line of thinking.

"With a shotgun your quarterback had to wait for the ball and his focus could be on nothing but that long snap. While there is more initial separation from the defense, by the time he received the ball, so many things had already happened with the coverages that he had not been able to see. Where the shotgun was beneficial was in our running game. No matter the play, he was always a threat as opposed to when he was under center and could really only run sneaks or the option. When he was lined up deep, he had access to every play we had in the book."

Making Roberson's task easier in 2002 were the heroics of Darren Sproles, who quickly became the Big 12's greatest show on turf.

In 2002, Sproles burst onto the Wildcat landscape with a sophomore season total of 1,465 yards, while Roberson gobbled up 1,032 yards from his quarterback position. Sproles' total was a single-season record; Roberson's ranked fifth in KSU history.

The 5-foot-7, 170-pound Sproles ended the year with nine straight 100-yard rushing games, while Roberson accounted for 86 yards per game rushing, plus another 132 passing.

Chapter Twenty-Nine
The Wefald Factor

I think a lot of other college presidents were frustrated with Jon Wefald because he put them in a position to have to do the same things for athletics at their schools.

— Coach Bill Snyder

Barry Switzer never coached a game against Bill Snyder, nor did he really know Snyder other than through his friendship with Hayden Fry.

But the Oklahoma Sooner coaching legend goes into an instant storytelling mode when asked about his thoughts of what Snyder accomplished at Kansas State.

Switzer was at a Big 8 Conference reception prior to the 1986 Orange Bowl game in Miami.

Picking up the story, and with enjoyment in his southern voice, Switzer began, "We were at this cocktail party and here comes this little guy approaching me with his hand out, saying, 'I'm Jon Wefald. I'm the President of Kansas State University.'

"Well, we had both had a few pops, but I remember him saying to me, 'Coach, I'm excited. I can't wait to win like you do. I can't wait to bring my team down here to the Orange Bowl.'

"I was stunned, literally stunned," Switzer said. "This was a team that we would hang half-a-hundred on by the half, so our other guys, who only got to practice, could actually play in a game."

Switzer said he hollered at his athletic director, Donnie Duncan, to join the conversation.

"I remember saying, 'Donnie, this is Dr. Wefald, and he says he's going to have a program like ours and play in the Orange Bowl.'

"Well, I've had quite a few by then, and I'm laughing even harder, which I think embarrassed Donnie, but then [Wefald] repeated it. 'I can't wait to bring a team to the Orange Bowl.'

"I was rude. I couldn't help laughing," Switzer said. "I'm not sure how it came out, but I tried to say, 'President, I admire you, and I hope it really happens.'"

Fast-forward 12 years to the 1998 Big 12 title game in St. Louis where Kansas State is playing Texas A&M, and Switzer again picks up the story.

"I'm sitting there watching the game on TV, and I turn to a friend and say, 'I owe that President an apology. He knew what the hell he was talking about. I'm going to call and apologize."

As Switzer recalls, he called Wefald the next Monday and located him at a dental appointment.

"I just said, 'I'm Barry Switzer, and do you remember our conversation of 10 years ago? Well, I'm calling just to apologize,'" Switzer said. "I know Bill is a helluva coach, but I also know he didn't do this by himself. It starts at the top, and you should be commended. If I ever get back into coaching, you're the type of president that I want to work for."

Breaking into a hearty laugh, Switzer repeated, "But I'll never forget looking down at this little guy and having him tell me how he was going to win."

But in 1986, when Wefald was hired at Kansas State University, even he will tell you, "Most of our people were just hoping for a 5-6 season, then maybe a 7-4, and an 8-3 in the best of times."

Instead, in Wefald's third year in office, a man named Snyder was hired as the Wildcats' football coach. Wefald says, "We not only met expectations, but we exceeded them, all of them. This is what America is all about. Everybody has the opportunity to pull himself, or herself, up by the bootstraps and do things no one would have ever expected."

When Wefald was hired by the Kansas Board of Regents, he was told to clean house of the existing vice-presidential staff. He then received a list of expectations.

On the second page of that checklist was, in his words, "Oh, by the way, when you find time, give us a little better football team."

There's no question the Regents were chuckling at the thought. Sure, they were tired of their football team being considered a patsy, but if the team failed to improve, the Regents wouldn't give it much thought.

This 47-year-old president, however, had a vision, and he thought constantly about how success on Saturday afternoons in the fall might impact the overall university community.

"There was a chance we were going to get our heads blown off, but I was going to try," Wefald said of his commitment to football.

After firing "at least 20" university-types and replacing them with Wefald's Warriors, he went to work on that checklist.

Enrollment had dipped from nearly 19,000 in the early 1980s to 15,000 in 1986. Three years later, there were 20,000 young Wildcats buzzing around the KSU campus.

Fundraising was $5 to 6 million in 1986. During the 2005-2006 school year, KSU raised $85 million. Funding for research projects zoomed from $17 million to over $110 million.

Wefald wanted to restore hope, and how better to get the Wildcat-nation, present and past, feeling good about Kansas State University than to win a handful of football games?

"You can't do much moving forward when people are depressed about their surroundings," Wefald said. "You have to have a vision and articulate that vision."

Nothing made Wefald's fantasy come to life more than the hiring of Bill Snyder on November 30, 1988.

But Wefald will openly announce, "There would have been no Bill Snyder at Kansas State if Jon Wefald doesn't come to Manhattan, Kansas."

It's true that in 1985 Wichita State defeated Kansas State in football, 16-10, and promptly dropped the sport prior to the next season.

"Under the former administration, it is very possible that there would have been an attitude of 'Why fight it?' Let's just follow the model Wichita State had set," Wefald said.

Pausing, he continued, "It really is serendipity that I came here."

Wefald remembers a chat with Kansas City booster Rick Harman, a basketball great for the Wildcats in the late 1940s.

"He tapped me on the shoulder and said, 'Son, your enthusiasm is great, but I'm afraid you're going to run into a cold stone wall if you think we're going to have a competitive football team.

"'I think you can do that other stuff with the school, but don't waste too much time on this football thing. Others have tried, and it hasn't worked,'" Harman said.

With Snyder and Wefald or Wefald and Snyder, it did work. Success began with the administration tossing the keys to the Wildcat vault and saying, there's not much in there, but go for it.

Snyder wanted higher salaries for his staff; Snyder wanted to spruce up the locker room; Snyder wanted better offices for his coaches; Snyder wanted new turf for the field; Snyder wanted a new press box; Snyder wanted, and wanted, and wanted some more.

"His middle name was 'Demand,'" laughed Wefald.

Had K-State not started to win, would Wefald's gamble have put him out of his Anderson Hall job?

Pausing and smiling, he said, "Could be."

"I think guys like Wefald and athletic director Steve Miller would have been lined up against a wall and executed," Wefald joked.

But there was a core of Kansas State people who shared a united vision.

As Snyder said, "We had people who believed enough to make what many may have considered bad investments. These were smart people. They didn't just arrive on a load of lumber. They were people who believed in Kansas State."

Wefald called it Kansas State's field of dreams. "If we built it, they would come."

Or, if you win, they will come. To Snyder, "My belief and my projection to our fans was that they would first need to support these young men and the success would then come. And that's the way it went. Our fans were great."

Kansas State did build better facilities, Snyder's teams did win, and the Wildcat fans did come, with average home attendance growing from 20,975 in 1988, to 32,980 in 1996, and after stadium expansion, to 41,136 in 1999.

In his 20 years in office, has Wefald ever taken a bigger risk than his commitment to football?

"No," he admits.

And while he bubbles and gushes over his Truman and Rhodes Scholars, he somewhat sheepishly admits that his single-greatest high as leader of the university came on December 6, 2003, when the Wildcats trounced the No. 1-rated Oklahoma Sooners, 35-7, for the Big 12 Conference championship.

"It was a game nobody said we could win," Wefald said. "There have been some great moments at this university, but that one would be pretty hard to beat."

Miracle Behind The Miracle

Bill Snyder's transformation of the K-State football program is in and of itself miraculous. Its impact on the entire university—its national visibility, its self-perception, its ability to unite as a K-State family and achieve goals beyond the wildest of imaginations—is also nothing short of miraculous.

Snyder's tenure at K-State is a testament to the belief that one person can make a significant difference and that big dreams can be fulfilled. Snyder's accomplishments explain the respect, affection and gratitude K-Staters around the world have for the coach.

The miracle behind the miracle is that Bill achieved all of this while adhering to a set of core values that mirror the historic values of Kansas State University—having a caring attitude toward others, working hard, and maintaining a sense of fairness and decency and a love for Alma Mater and especially her people. There were no shortcuts. The foundation was laid brick by brick; progress was measured inch by inch by the tape measure of daily improvement; and a plan was implemented detail by detail. There were no unlimited resources—no bags of money from heaven, no silver bullets—just a relentless, unwavering commitment to guiding values in pursuit of excellence on and off the field.

The playing field of major college football is not level; disparities exist in resources, talent pools, media venues, institutional agendas and a host of other things. It's a lot like life. Bill Snyder is living proof that you can succeed without taking shortcuts, and how you get there is as important as getting there. By the manner in which he transformed K-State's football program, Bill gave a gift to all of us and reaffirmed the values of the university as a place where people can bring their dreams and, if they work hard and are willing to make personal sacrifices, be successful.

Bill is a miraculous person and we all owe him a huge debt of gratitude. It personally has been a privilege to work with Bill and I will always treasure his friendship and be grateful for all he has taught me.

— Bob Krause
Vice President for Institutional Advancement, Kansas State University

Chapter Thirty
The Leaders

I don't know if there's a single definition for leadership. It's a broad-based term.
It's guiding others to become successful in whatever venture that's important to them.

— Coach Bill Snyder

Bill Snyder's teenage years in St. Joseph, Missouri, were far from pristine, but the Wildcat coach never hesitates to share his background with current day Wildcats.

"I want them to know I'm not just spouting off on all these righteous things," Snyder said. "Like many of my players, I have been through some battles and done things that should have been done differently."

But Snyder can also speak of changing the direction of one's personal life through academics and athletics.

At Kansas State, football leaders normally come from a group of individuals who have already been decorated with honors that other players would like to achieve.

While Snyder is the authoritarian of the Wildcats, he has also established a buffer system which includes team captains and player representatives. In addition to the seniors, player representatives are players who have demonstrated the ability to provide leadership and serve as a bridge between the team and the coaching staff.

"The player representative concept is a way of consolidating some of the decision-making process," Snyder said. "We make it clear that the player representatives should not simply be youngsters who absorb information, but youngsters who the players will go to for guidance, for direction, and for leadership."

He added, "If you have a coach constantly repeating the same thoughts day in and day out, the players begin to tune you out. But if a player stands up and says the same thing, it may regain some of its significance."

Normally, the player reps come from each segment of the K-State team: quarterback, offensive line, receivers, linebackers, etc. All are individuals who have demonstrated team-oriented values and principles and are capable of setting an example.

If player reps, who are voted on by the team, violate team rules, they are stripped of their status.

While Snyder's office door was open to all players at any time, the Wildcat coach did meet with the captains and player reps on a regular basis to discuss team issues, to identify solutions to problems, and to identify motivational needs.

Laughing at the memory, center Quentin Neujahr (1990-93) remembers one of his first visits to Snyder to ask for a little lighter practice schedule as the players were beaten down by the rigors of the season.

"I went into his office and he had those low slinky chairs that you fell to the bottom in with your butt no more than a couple inches off the floor," Neujahr said. "You were automatically looking up to this God, telling him that his players were tired."

As Neujahr recalls, he was thanked for coming in and told that the idea would be considered.

On the practice field later that day, Snyder instructed his team to take off the pads, so while the team did practice, the session was a little easier.

"Coach would always listen," Neujahr said.

While some players may be born with some God-given leadership traits, Snyder believed leadership could also be developed over a period of time, whether it be by voice or via work ethic.

"A vocal leader is not someone with a non-stop motor-mouth, always spitting things out," Snyder said. "He can be one of those guys who doesn't say much, but when he does speak, a teammate really listens."

Josh Buhl and Elijah Alexander were ones who led by voice, while Wildcats like Neujahr, Brooks Barta and Carl Straw were examples of those who led by the E.F. Hutton rule—when they spoke, teammates listened.

"Quentin and Carl were guys who wouldn't say boo until they needed to say boo," Snyder said. "For that reason, and because they cared and they set the example, they had the attention of their teammates."

Barta said, "I think my leadership came from teammates appreciating my work habits. I think they saw me as a guy who over-achieved and was totally committed to what we were doing."

Two others with very different leadership styles were Mark Simoneau and Jarrod Cooper, who played on the same Wildcat teams from 1997 through 1999.

Snyder called linebacker Simoneau "as old fashioned as I was." Snyder said, "He was the one in the front row, sitting on the front of his chair, soaking up every bit of information that he could. He had great respect and trust in the program, and what it stood for. Mark knew what to do, and how to do it. He clung to values he was raised with. He did, and I did. We were virtually the same type of person."

As quiet as Simoneau was, Cooper, with a variety of hair styles and colors, was brash.

Cooper went unrecruited out of Pearland (Texas) High School. Raised by his mother and brought up in a trailer court, Cooper played with a chip on his shoulder seen in few other Wildcats.

"He always spoke highly of his mother, but Jarrod liked attention, and could be swayed in a direction you didn't want him to go," Snyder said. "But he was normally a leader in his own way through his enthusiasm for the game."

It was important to Snyder that, along with the coaches, the Wildcat players felt they had ownership of the program. This included accepting responsibility for both successes and failures.

J.J. Smith remembers when the Wildcats were 5-0 to start the 1993 season and were playing at No. 6 Nebraska. Early in the game quarterback Chad May fumbled, which set up the Cornhuskers for an easy score.

As Smith recalls, "Coach looked at Chad and said, 'You got us in this position, now you get us out of it.' He could have said, 'It's okay, don't worry about it,' but he put it squarely on Chad's shoulders because he knew Chad could handle the criticism and respond to it."

K-State lost that day, 45-28, but May passed for 489 yards. Smith says, "I think that was the day Nebraska started recruiting more defensive backs because they knew they would play the Wildcats each season."

Michael Bishop didn't have a lot to say off the field, but in the huddle, he became a tremendous leader because of both his ability and his confidence.

"Michael didn't always do everything that you wanted him to do, but Michael was so competitive. What made him a great leader was the passion that he had not only for the game of football, but also for winning," Snyder said. "He could bark at someone in the huddle, but players would respond to him. He wasn't the type to step up in front of the class off the field, but he would get in a player's face if he wasn't working. He was a consummate teammate in that respect."

While some might accuse Bishop of being a little too high on himself, Snyder said that was not the case. Sure, there was a dose of ego, but Snyder said, "Not once did Michael go to the field thinking of himself first. He had that burning desire to win, and was more than willing to put the team on his back and deliver a win.

"If that took him keeping the ball on every play, he could do it," Snyder said. "But only if it would help the team win the game."

If a Wildcat player did advertise a bit of himself over the team, Snyder was known to immediately address the situation.

Jaime Mendez was reminded of that entering his senior season in 1993 after being decorated with preseason All-America honors.

"My head got a little too big during spring practices, and I started a fight with an offensive player for really no reason," Mendez said. "Coach literally grabbed me and told me if I didn't straighten up, he would send me home. Looking at him, I knew he meant it."

The message was, "I was supposed to be one of the leaders and I wasn't setting a good example. Ten minutes later he looks at me and says, 'Are you really going to be a leader, or are you ready to go home?' In our program, there was never one player better than the program."

After being beaten out for the starting quarterback position by Bishop, Jonathan Beasley demonstrated his own style of leadership. First of all, had it not been for Beasley's helping Bishop learn the offense during the summer, the transfer from Blinn Community College would never have been ready to play.

Against Ohio in the second game of the season, Bishop suffered an injury late in the first half. Snyder's plan that season had been to redshirt Beasley and use Adam Helm as Bishop's backup. Without knowing the seriousness of Bishop's injury, Snyder had to make a decision.

"I've never forgotten Jonathan coming up to me and saying he was ready to go in," Snyder said. "For the good of the team, he was willing to lose a year of eligibility to perhaps help our football team for maybe only one series of plays in one game."

Snyder elected to go with Helm, and Bishop did return, but Beasley's willingness to put the team before himself spoke of what a great leader he was.

Then there was the ever-silent Darren Sproles, who led through example in everything he did for the Wildcats.

"He worked, but seldom said a word. He just loved to play the game," Snyder said.

As good as Sproles was, in his own mind he was never good enough.

Snyder remembers a game early in the 2004 season when Sproles fumbled a couple of times. Sproles was by himself on the Wagner Field turf the next afternoon, working on ball-handling skills and catching punts shot out of a jugs machine.

"Most players would make it a point to stick their head in the office and let me know they had been working out," Snyder said. "Well, I have a window. I would have known, but Darren would never say a word. He wasn't looking for a pat on the back. He was just trying to improve."

Frustrating to Snyder is the fact there are fewer and fewer Simoneaus, Beasleys and Sproles in today's instant gratification society that has complicated leadership in any team of any sport.

Too many players have read their press clippings during the recruiting process and have come to believe how good others perceive them to be. Without question, there's more selfishness today than existed at the beginning of the Snyder years at K-State.

"I think the increased player focus on individual achievement makes quality, inclusive and caring leadership tougher," Snyder said. "It's reduced the number of potential leaders in Pool 1, and reduced the number of followers in Pool 2.

"Not every player has to present himself as a leader. But if he doesn't, then he needs to be a productive follower. Those two areas are equal," Snyder said. "It's when you have a third pool of players trying to disrupt the team concept that you have trouble."

That, Snyder said, was partially the reason that the Wildcats dipped to 6-6 in 2001.

"There was a greater number in that third circle than there had ever been," Snyder said. "We are constantly talking about crossing the line into the circles, but we had more and more players outside the circle."

Snyder stops short, however, of saying that was also one of the main reasons for the Wildcats slipping to 4-7 in 2004 and 5-6 in 2005.

"In those years, it was more a fact that we had inexperienced people. We had a lot of young players on our two-deep," Snyder said. "I'm not using that as an excuse, because if you're old enough to play, you're old enough to play, but I think we did have a slippage in terms of leadership just because some of our players hadn't yet developed into capable leaders.

"In 2001, we had the capacity for good leadership, but we didn't get it. We had too many players capable of quality leadership pulling in the wrong direction," Snyder said. "In these last two years, I think it was more a problem of age, and not having had the time to develop the needed leadership skills, but many were getting very close, and we will see them evolve into excellent leaders before they complete their careers."

Along with leading within the program, Snyder wants leadership demonstrated within the community.

Players make annual treks to a variety of area retirement communities, present values programs at middle schools and take time to read at elementary schools, and help within the community in times of disaster, such as the 1993 flood when they took on sandbagging assignments.

In addition, Snyder instituted a VIP program for area 9th through 12th graders considered to be "at risk" students. Before reaching VIP status, the young people had to demonstrate an improved effort in the classroom and in their overall behavior.

If meeting all criteria on a Snyder-designed contract, "The students would come out and spend time with our players, go to meals with our guys, things like that. We had our players accept mentoring roles. It was a positive experience for the young people, but also for our players."

Chapter Thirty-One
2003: One Wild Ride

There comes a certain degree of satisfaction of playing that ballgame (a 35-7 Big 12 title win over Oklahoma) as well as you can play it. I valued that win because of what it meant to the many Kansas Staters out there who cared so much over the years. But in another way, it didn't feel like I expected it to feel because of the games we let slip away earlier in the year. There was an emptiness as well as a feeling of great accomplishment. Again, we had a chance to be in a national championship ballgame, but we didn't take care of business early in the year.

— Coach Bill Snyder

It was the night of December 6, 2003. A 65-35 split of 79,451 Wildcat and Sooner fans had assembled at Arrowhead Stadium in Kansas City, Missouri, where Kansas State was to play undefeated and No. 1-ranked Oklahoma for the Big 12 championship.

The most die-hard of K-State football fans held out hope for a purple victory.

But 35-7?

No one could have or would have predicted such a decisive victory, at least not by the Wildcats.

After all, Kansas State was a team with three losses—Marshall, Texas and Oklahoma State—and carried only a No. 13 national ranking.

But the coach of the Wildcats had a feeling on this December eve.

The Wildcats had won their last six games over Colorado by 29, Kansas by 36, Baylor by 28, Iowa State by 45, Nebraska by 29, and Missouri by 10 points.

"Our attitude was great, and we had two great weeks of practice," Snyder said. "I was almost to the point of cautioning the players about being over-confident. No one was uptight. The practices were good and crisp. I was happy."

Just 2:49 into the game, the Sooners had taken the opening kick-off and scored on a Kejuan Jones 42-yard run.

Just like that, Oklahoma 7, Kansas State 0.

"I don't think that score impacted our players, but I think it may have had an impact on theirs," Snyder said. "I think it made our kids toughen up. I think for theirs, it may have created an attitude of, 'This is going to be easy.'"

Easy it was, but for Kansas State, as the Wildcats won the rest of the game 35-zip.

OU's Trey DiCarlo missed a 44-yard field goal try on the first play of the second quarter, only his second misfire of the year. Later, the Sooners drove into the red zone, but there for the pick was Wildcat defensive back James McGill to deny another scoring opportunity.

K-State went from playing on their heels to on their toes, with Roberson working the pass-and-catch game to perfection with a number of receivers.

And of course Darren Sproles was never better. Of all of 43's greatness in previous games, he was at his best on this chilly December night in his home town. The second quarter provided K-State with a number of big plays:

13:57—A 55-yard dash, including a 360-move by Sproles, set up the 19-yard strike to tight end Brian Casey.

11:34—James Terry runs a curl-and-go, then goes over Will Peoples, and shakes away Donte Nicolson for a 63-yard score.

Of the one-play drive, Terry, who set a KSU single-season record for receiving yards, said, "OU has a physical defense. It's just like a dog. It has instincts to bite when they see a route like that, and they did."

3:18—Sproles takes a short pass, and with those little-bitty steps quickly marks off 60 yards, just five plays after McGill's interception.

"I just dumped it off to the little-man and let him go to work," Roberson said.

"I turned around and thought someone would be there, but I was wide open," Sproles said. "All I saw were receivers blocking down field."

So after a 16-play, 41-yard first quarter, the Wildcats snapped it another 16 times in the second stanza and gained 221 yards.

"Those weren't magical plays. They were plays we had seen from them all season, but they executed, and we didn't," said Sooner coach Bob Stoops.

The Sooners now trailed 21-7. It marked the first time OU had been on the short end of the score by more than three points all year. In fact, prior to the Wildcats taking the lead at the 11:34 mark, the Sooners had trailed for just 5:58 of clock time the entire season.

OU was fighting to regain momentum to open the second half, but a 14-play drive stalled at the KSU 11, and DiCarlo missed a 28-yard three-point attempt.

"It was a big factor because you think you have a chance to close the gap, and you come up empty," said Stoops. "Then they come right back with big plays."

The Wildcats countered OU's seven-minute scoreless drive with an 80-yard march of its own. Set up by a series of dashes by Roberson and Sproles to the OU 10-yard line, Roberson armed yet another TD toss, a 10-yarder to Antoine Polite.

At the time, Roberson had been on target on six of his last seven passes for 167 yards and four TDs.

The rest of the game was left to the defense as it held the Sooners' offense in check, plus scored the final points on a 27-yard interception return by linebacker Ted Sims with 12:34 remaining.

It was KSU's second pick of the game, significant because OU's Heisman Trophy winner Jason White had thrown only six interceptions all season.

For the Wildcats, it was a near perfect 39-degree December night.

Roberson passed for 227 yards and four touchdowns (a title game record), plus rushed for 62 yards. Sproles rushed for 235 yards, the most ever yielded in a single game by a Sooner football team, and had 345 all-purpose yards, a KSU single-game record.

The defense held the White-led Sooners scoreless for the final 57:49 of the game. The "D" notched a pair of interceptions, plus sacked White three times.

As linebacker Josh Buhl said after the game, "That was the true 'Lynch Mob.' They are a great football team, but we were definitely the better football team today. The 'Lynch Mob' ruled."

KSU tight end coach Matt Miller called Snyder's play-calling "masterful."

"We knew their guys would be coming at the ball hard, so we had a collection of mis-direction plays and screens we thought would work, and they all did."

Laughing, he added, "Plus, we made sure that little No. 43 guy had the ball in his hands as often as possible."

The joke spread like wildfire across the Flint Hills. If it's 6:25 in Manhattan, what time is it in Norman? Answer: 35 to 7.

Yes, Kansas State won the Big 12 Championship, 35-7!

"Kansas State just came out and out-played us and out-coached us," said Stoops. "Our hats are off to them. They really took it to us in every phase of the game."

K-Staters accepted the compliment with glee.

"This is one of the happiest moments in my life. I can't find words for it," said KSU President Jon Wefald. "To come into Kansas City and beat a team that people have been saying is the best in 30 years, and win a Big 12 Championship—it just doesn't get any better than this."

Quarterback Ell Roberson said, "I can't describe it. Nothing can touch this."

And defensive lineman Jermaine Berry proclaimed, "We ARE the No. 1 team in America. We ARE the best!"

Even the coach, always careful with flowery comparisons, said, "I think it probably becomes the most important win as we have never won a conference championship before. This one is maybe the most significant."

True, Kansas State had won a title in 1934, but even the stars of that team— Maurice Elder, George Maddox, Ralph Churchill—were tipping their leather helmets to Snyder's men.

Immediately after the game Snyder was captured by the folks at *ESPN* and asked about the heroics of Sproles. Snyder took the opportunity to put the onus on these self-proclaimed experts of college football.

"I remember saying, 'Who are you going to vote for the Heisman? Don't you think Darren's deserving?' I didn't know if they had a vote, but I had been angered by the lack of respect for Darren as a legitimate Heisman candidate."

Snyder received a hug from his son Sean, and as his wife Sharon made a rare appearance on the field, he remarked that he had never seen a bigger smile on her face.

"It was a resounding victory, and I understand why our fans felt it was the biggest ever. But in my opinion, we had others just as important. The Cotton Bowl win against Tennessee, to me, carried great significance. A first win against Texas, winning at Texas A&M, beating USC for a second time," Snyder listed. "I was happy, but part of me was saying, 'Why did we have to have those three losses?' It was another opportunity that we would have had to play in a national championship game, but we lost it early in the season. There wasn't the feeling that I expected would go with a Big 12 championship."

As for the Oklahoma game itself, at least for Snyder, it wasn't so much winning a Big 12 title as it was "beating a team perceived to be the best in the country."

Snyder enjoyed the win, but as those in the locker room said, he wasn't jumping up and down.

"It was a ton of weight off his shoulders, but he got on that plane, flew back to Manhattan, and started recruiting and preparing for our next game," laughed Matt Miller. "But sure, it was a huge moment for him."

Running backs coach Michael Smith added, "Coach doesn't wear his emotions on his sleeve and act crazy, but he was happy. But he expected to win. To him, it was supposed to happen."

The victory earned Kansas State a trip to the Fiesta Bowl where it would play Ohio State. At the time, there was every reason to believe that an all-time single-season record 12th win was attainable.

After all, this K-State team had Sproles as its all-time single-season and career rusher. Roberson was the all-time career leader in total offense and No. 2 in career rushing, and James Terry was tops in receiving yards for a single season.

They were a three-pronged attack that covered 5,373 strides of turf with Sproles rushing for 1,948, Roberson passing for 2,351, and Terry catching for 1,174.

That total was over 500 yards more than the splendid threesome of Eric Hickson (902 rushing), Michael Bishop (2,844 passing) and Darnell McDonald (1,092 receiving) in 1998.

The team had withstood off-the-field flirts with the law, overcome a series of pre-season injuries, come back from losses to Marshall, Texas and Oklahoma State, and now stood as 2003 Big 12 Champions.

All was good until the wee morning hours of January 1, 2004.

Chapter Thirty-Two
Discipline In The K-State Camp

I believe in second chances in most instances. When it comes to discipline, every situation is not the same. I tell our team, when it comes to making decisions regarding discipline, I do what is in the best interest for our football team, as opposed to any individual in our program.

— Coach Bill Snyder

The Ell Roberson incident still tugs at Snyder more than any other football moment in his 17-year stay at Kansas State University.

Roberson, 22, a team captain and Kansas State's three-year starting quarterback, was accused of a sexual assault by a female acquaintance at the team hotel, the Scottsdale Plaza resort, at 2:00 or 3:00 a.m., on January 1, 2004.

Roberson did not deny that there was sexual activity, but said it was consensual.

The timing couldn't have been worse.

"Words can not define how much that pained me," Snyder said. "It wasn't just anger. I was devastated. Embarrassed that a young man brought up through this program for five years, who had heard the message forever, was now saying, 'It doesn't matter to me.' With so much on the line for this team, he was putting himself first."

K-State was scheduled to play in the Fiesta Bowl against Ohio State on the evening of January 2. The game was arguably the biggest stage ever for Wildcat football, as Kansas State, ranked No. 8 in the nation, was entering the game as Big 12 champions, and playing the No. 7-ranked Buckeyes.

Because K-State was playing in the Fiesta Bowl, the news, including Ell Roberson's name and the Kansas State football name, went national faster than one can say *ESPN*, which irked Snyder.

While not defending his quarterback, Snyder did say, "There was an issue, but what Ell was being accused of and what actually happened were two different stories and the accusation by the media was incorrect, inappropriate and premature."

Punishment was in order, if for no other reason than the fact that Roberson had violated the team's 11 p.m. curfew by three hours.

So the decision had to be made whether to start him, hold him out for the first quarter or half, or not play him at all. Snyder said it came down to the consistency factor in regards to actions taken before, and how the consequences would be in the best interest of the team and not the individual.

"Holding him out for a quarter or two would only be for show and that's not what we are all about," said Snyder.

The decision was not only to play, but to start Roberson. As later announced, Roberson's punishment would be the loss of his scholarship ($8,481 for the spring semester), not receiving the Fiesta Bowl ring, and performing public service work addressing youth groups within the community of Manhattan, which was consistent with the consequences for other wrongdoings in previous years.

But as it turned out, the entire K-State team was affected by Roberson's play. His final numbers of 20 of 51 passing for 294 yards, plus 32 rushing yards, were deceiving. In the first half, Roberson was just 5 of 20 passing, and the Wildcats did not cross midfield until the final 5:47 of the game.

"I'd be lying if I said it didn't distract us," said KSU cornerback Cedrick Williams of the Roberson controversy.

"In hindsight, he was not fair to his teammates," Snyder said. "He wasn't ready to play. He had been through a lot and was not emotionally ready to play. He had gone through so much, and it had become so public."

The next week, Snyder penned a letter of apology to K-Staters in every part of the world for the embarrassment that the incident had caused the school.

While emphasizing that "no criminal incident occurred," Snyder wrote, "I want all K-Staters to know that this incident has hit at the core of my value system. I do not condone any form of sexual abuse, or, for that matter, sexual activity for young, unmarried males or females."

Nothing in the 17 years Bill Snyder coached at Kansas State had challenged this disciplinarian like this incident.

Snyder has few rules, but the ones he has he means.

If he wants you to do x-y-z, you do x-y-z. If you can't do x-y-z, that's okay. You're not a bad person, but you're not going to be a member of the K-State football team, either.

Remember his words as a young adult growing up in St. Joseph? How to some extent he understood and appreciated his mother taking away his bike and car when he violated the house rules. How he understood and appreciated the after-school discipline at Lafayette High when he was caught cutting classes.

Well, Snyder carried that same philosophy to Kansas State. If there was a so-called crime, there would be a time to pay.

Snyder encourages his student-athletes not to take discipline personally, that responsibility and discipline are a part of each team's goals.

Those goals are spelled out in the Wildcat Playbook—do what you're supposed to do, when you're supposed to do it, the way you're supposed to do it, and do it that way every time. If you are a responsible person, none of the penalties will apply to you.

The disciplinary penalties are also described in detail in the Wildcat Playbook:

• Unexcused and late to a meeting, study table or trainer's appointment: 250 yards of updowns after practice.

• Unexcused and absent from study table or a trainer's appointment: 500 yards of updowns after practice.

• Absent from academic class: First offense—600 yards of updowns at 6 a.m. on Sunday, followed by a 7 to 9 a.m. assisted study table; Second offense—1,200 yards of updowns; for each additional missed class monthly NCAA allowed housing paychecks will be withheld; three tardies constitute one absence—8-8-8 (eight laps around the field, eight trips up and down the stadium steps, eight 100-yard updowns).

• No hats in the upper level of Vanier Complex/training table.

• Be on Wildcat Time—be in attendance at least three minutes before meetings or practices are scheduled to begin.

Snyder set the rules for no drinking by team members on Thursday and Friday, with the team voting on the other five days of the week.

The rules applied not only to student-athletes, but to coaches as well.

Should a coach be guilty of driving while intoxicated, he would forfeit one month's pay. Much of the punishment was just sitting across the desk from Snyder in his office. Insiders called it going to the "West Wing for a confessional."

Snyder imposed discipline, but never with the intent to break the spirit of the student-athlete. Much like his mother and grandfather, Snyder had a knack for encouraging the athlete to do a self-evaluation, resulting in the athlete wanting to rectify what he had done wrong.

With young people, Snyder says, "If you read what psychologists say about today's human behavior, you find that young people have somewhat lost the ability to discipline themselves, to circumvent road blocks that keep them from reaching a certain achievement level. If something gets too hard, whether academics or in other areas of society, there becomes an acceptance of not wanting to do it any longer."

Snyder said this can start by being pampered by parents or by being given a green light through difficult times in the high school classroom. It's an attitude that says it is okay to behave whatever way one wishes, whether throwing a tantrum or quitting when things get tough.

"We live in a society today that doesn't always provide consequences when a young person is growing up. There are parents wanting to be the best friend of their child instead of a parent," Snyder said. "The message is preached, but sometimes there's not enough following through with a consequence for inappropriate behavior."

Snyder admits to being more conservative than most, but the few times he tunes in to a television show he is amazed at what he sees. "You have 9-year-olds watching things on television on a nightly basis that you can be put in jail for doing."

Yes, Snyder is well aware of constitutional rights, but he also guesses, "I would believe Thomas Jefferson is doing an about-face in his grave when people keep coming back to the Constitution to justify some of the freedoms that are taking place."

To Snyder, we are moving toward an "it's about me" society. What our youth read in the newspapers or see on television about professional and collegiate athletics today is frequently about sexual abuse, alcohol abuse, drug use, steroid use, and violence both on and off the field.

"The true role models of the game are not headline news," Snyder said. "The media gravitates toward the sensational. Grabbing a pen and signing an autograph after a touchdown is a story. There is no longer a selflessness that promotes teamwork."

Those around Snyder, however, say while standing his ground in the majority of the areas, he has softened in others.

"He's adjusted with the times, but only to a degree," said former player and assistant coach Michael Smith. "I know if some of the incidents that have happened had taken place when I was playing—BOOM!—you would have been gone. It had to be that way. But coach has always been one to give a kid an extra chance.

"You're dealing with more and more kids who don't have fathers. I was raised in a 'Yes, sir' 'No, sir' family, but some of these kids today just look at you, shake their heads, and say, 'What the hell do you know?'"

Under the Snyder model, with each student-athlete—whether the son of a doctor, a lawyer, a factory worker, or a convict—the goal was always the same. Snyder wanted the Kansas State football experience to have a positive impact on a player's life.

Sometimes that happened quickly, sometimes it took longer. Sometimes players needed more than the four years they were part of Kansas State. But at some point, most Wildcats got the message.

"Words can not adequately express how meaningful some of the letters and phone calls I receive are to me," Snyder said. "'Coach, I didn't recognize it then, but it's hit home now. I'm 30 years old, and now I understand the Goals For Success, the values you tried to instill in us. Thank you.'"

"Moments like that are why someone should want to coach," Snyder said. "If you're getting into coaching for any other reason, then maybe coaching is not the best career choice."

As for the no cap, no earring policy, Snyder said, "They knew how I felt about that from the first day in camp. Just because a young man wears an earring does not make him a bad person. It's just a sign of our times and part of the youth culture. I understand that.

"They understood that when they are John Q. Student, and whatever they do outside of football, I had no issues with wearing an earring," Snyder said. "But they had to understand that when they walked through the doors to our complex, this was a special time in their life. I want it to be a reminder that K-State football is unlike anything else that they do, and it needs to be special."

"With caps, it was the same philosophy, plus it was a simple matter of respect. When these young men graduate and pursue career fields, they will be interviewing neatly dressed and probably in a coat and tie," Snyder said. "I wanted to set the example. That is also one of the reasons for issuing blazers to our lettermen to be worn at team functions."

"We have young people who have not been accustomed to proper manners, and this is part of the education that we are trying to give them," Snyder said.

Through Snyder's urging, Kansas State instituted a two-credit class for all freshmen student-athletes called Freshman Transition. It includes sessions and speakers on alcohol, sexual abuse, drugs, gambling, and etiquette.

Snyder tells the story of when he was at a letterman's banquet at William Jewell College. In front of him was a plate and a collection of three forks.

"I was clueless about what I was supposed to do with three forks. I had been raised using one fork," Snyder said. "I just figured if I dropped one, I had two to go."

But in all honesty, Snyder said, "I was embarrassed."

Of concern to Snyder today is the fact that young people are no longer embarrassed when they are socially inept.

"There is a certain percentage of young people who think anything is okay," Snyder said. "'Whatever I want to do is okay.' Not that many years ago if you did certain things in public it was embarrassing. Today, it's okay, as long as it makes you feel good. That's our fault. As parents, and coaches and mentors, we have failed them by not getting the message across."

Knowing of Snyder's leadership abilities, when Kansas Governor Kathleen Sebelius started Kansas Mentors—a program that encourages adults to serve as mentors to young people and provide encouragement, motivation and support—her first choice to lead the curriculum was Bill Snyder.

"He is a role model who has had an incredibly positive influence on his own team, and thousands of Kansans who look up to him," said Sebelius, who also named a nine-mile stretch of highway, from I-70 north into Manhattan, Coach Bill Snyder Highway.

Snyder liked the mentoring concept, and accepted the non-paying position in January of 2006, following his November resignation as coach of the Wildcats.

"I applaud what she's attempting to do. It's something coaches do all their lives, mentor, and it seems like a neat thing for the state of Kansas."

He added, "Depending on how you define mentoring, I learned a lot from people who were in my life, my mother, my grandparents, coaches that I had in high school and college, as well as friends I have had throughout my coaching career."

Chapter Thirty-Three
Snyder And The Media

I don't want this to sound disrespectful, but during press conferences many of my comments were directed to the players.

— Coach Bill Snyder

During his year's at Kansas State, Snyder's were hardly press conferences full of quips and sound-bites.

He never predicted victory. In fact, most Wildcat opponents were made out to be USC-like, injuries were a taboo subject, and at times, he was the single voice of the program.

In his final season, assistant coaches were off limits, and in 1998, Heisman Trophy candidate Michael Bishop was muzzled.

The media restriction for Bishop was due in part because Bishop was a quote machine. During the summer of 1998, he had been charged for being involved in a fist fight on campus, though those charges were later dropped.

"I did not like the way the incident was handled. To me, the media judged him guilty before all of the facts were in place," Snyder said. "I was miffed at the way the media handled that incident, and I didn't want Michael to be distracted with on-going dialogue about the incident during the year."

Prior to playing Nebraska on November 14, 1998, *Sports Illustrated* visited the KSU campus to do a feature story on Bishop, which Snyder allowed without giving the cast of weekly beat writers from towns across Kansas the same opportunity.

Later, Snyder said, "I had second thoughts about that decision. It was a mistake."

The decision to make the assistant coaches off limits to the media for the entire 2005 season came at a time when the program needed "one voice."

"When things aren't going well, it's a burden for an assistant to have to speak to the media, so I was going to take that pressure off of the coaches," Snyder said.

"By and large," Snyder said, "I had great respect for the people of the media. I'm not sure if it showed, but I knew it was their job. I respected that, but I also had a job and a desire to protect our university, our program and the people in it."

Snyder didn't make a steady diet of reading newspapers, but he said that all the stories have been kept in 20 to 30 scrapbooks. Giving a slight wink, "Now, maybe I'll have time to go back and read them."

Clippings were saved for bulletin board use, but normally they were saved for informational rather than motivational purposes.

Overall, Snyder said that players were never told not to go on internet sites or read papers, but at the same time, "They were not encouraged to."

"Reading all those pats on the back can move you in the wrong direction," Snyder said.

Though players were requested by the media for either the weekly Tuesday press conference or the postgame sessions, Snyder would not require players to attend, but did encourage them to make an appearance.

"What I told them was to be consistent," Snyder said. "I didn't want them show-ing up after wins and not after losses; showing up after a successful game, but not after a bad game."

For Darren Sproles, facing the pens and microphones was always an uncomfort-able experience. A speech impediment had the greatest running back in K-State history far more anxious about facing an overweight, gray-headed writer than the most talented linebacker, who he could leave grasping for air with a 360-spin move.

"You were never going to get into a 10-minute dialogue with Darren, but he made progress in that area," Snyder said. "At one time he came to me and said it embarrassed him, and he asked if he had to do interviews."

"I didn't say he had to, but I encouraged him to continue to present himself to the media, and through some assistance, he improved through the years," Snyder said.

Few things miffed Snyder more than media questions on breaks, strains and sprains.

"What I didn't understand, and still don't understand, is why the media would take issue with my stance on injuries. It makes all the sense in the world to me that if a youngster is injured, and I share that with the press that Player B has a gimpy arm, the opponent is going to read that, which in turn could help them develop a game plan. I'm not saying that a team is intentionally going to try to take that player out of the game by taking aim on the injured part of his body, but knowing a player is injured in a certain way may affect his performance level. Providing that information could give an advantage to your opponent."

The Wildcat players were well schooled on dealing with the media, a topic covered in a section of the playbook issued each August.

First, all interviews were scheduled through sports information, and in nearly every case, they took place from 1:30 until 2:00 on Tuesday afternoon following Snyder's 30-minute weekly press conference. The only other availability would come after games. Players were encouraged to be courteous, friendly and punctual, though interviews were not to cut into class time.

Players were to be neatly dressed, clean shaven, with no earrings or caps. Players were told never to trash-talk opposing players, and that "Yes, sir," and "No, sir" always made a good impression. Players were also encouraged to drop writers a thank you note after feature stories.

If a reporter started to go too deeply into game play or personal matters, players were to steer questions in another direction, but not by giving "no comment" as a reply. Players were not to give "off the record" answers.

"We are a close-knit family," Snyder said. "Not every family matter—yours or ours—is for public record."

He Did What None Before Had Done

Kansas State's football program had been nearly left for dead several times in the decades before Bill Snyder's arrival.

It was not uncommon that Bill's quiet manner and studious demeanor sometimes confused those with whom he had dealings. "No ma'am, that wasn't my kid's granddad ... that man is the most unrelenting head coach in college football." Of course, everyone in Kansas, Nebraska, Iowa and Missouri recognized the grey hair and professor's face framed by the trademark glasses. They had seen firsthand how he had changed history at Kansas State.

What nature of man could come to Manhattan, Kansas, and build something from nothing? Well, the history books would tell you a good man ... a man who cared about his players and his coaches, but also a man who wasn't afraid to exercise authority and a man who was willing to stand up and be accountable for all the decisions in his football program.

What Bill accomplished at Kansas State in building a championship contender for conference and national honors may never again be seen in college football.

— John Junker
Executive Director of the Fiesta Bowl

Chapter Thirty-Four
2004-2005: Falls Of Frustration

We were good enough for those narrow losses not to take place, but we didn't get it done. We had command of several of those games. Afterwards, you asked yourself how we could have coached better for the losses not to have taken place? What did we do, or not do, that cost us the opportunity to win those six or seven close ballgames? The bottom line, I didn't coach well enough.

— Coach Bill Snyder

Bill Snyder had always said that no matter how many all-stars returned from one year to the next, the chemistry of each team would be new. Just one player could change the complexion of a team.

At the start of the 2004 season, K-State's football disposition was an enigma. Players returned on the high of being the defending Big 12 champions, but the team was still dealing with the low of the lingering hangover from the Roberson incident.

"It was evident early that we were far from being the kind of football team we needed to be," Snyder said.

Part of it was a "take it for granted" attitude where players figure it's happened before, so it will happen again. In six of the previous seven seasons, K-State had been an 11-game winner, a feat accomplished by only one other school in college football history. Even in the down year of 2001 (6-6), K-State still managed to find the late-season gumption to advance to a bowl game.

The 2004 leadership was not what it needed to be, either. Again, a "take it for granted" attitude prevailed.

Even in 2003 when K-State lost three early games, the Wildcats rallied in the second half of the season.

"When we lost to Fresno State (45-21) early, and then those other three (Texas A&M, Kansas and Oklahoma to fall to 2-4), I still think there was a belief that, 'We'll come out of it,'" said Snyder of the 2004 campaign. "There were still enough youngsters left over from the '01 season who believed you could perform poorly for a good portion of the season, but then come out of it regardless of how well you did or didn't prepare."

This time, that would not be the case.

K-State did blast Nebraska, 45-21, but then lost three of its last four to finish the year at 4-7, the program's most dismal finish since the first year of the Snyder era.

"It wasn't a personnel issue. It had more to do with attitude," Snyder said. "In that first or second year, the attitude was good and they gave their best effort. That wasn't the case in '04."

While having nothing to do with effort, even the numbers of Darren Sproles slipped from his school record 1,986 yards in 2003, to 1,318 in his senior year.

For the first time in his career, Sproles also developed a case of the fumbles. Looking back, Snyder admits, "We probably were asking Darren to do too much. I didn't believe that at the time because I had great faith in Darren's capabilities. But in hindsight, we probably did."

He added, "I don't think he was any better as a junior than he was as a senior, but he just wasn't surrounded by the same talent level in his last year. We had him involved in so many things, I think it ended up causing him some stress."

Twice in early games, against Texas A&M and Kansas, Sproles bobbled away punts that set up easy scores for the Aggies and Jayhawks in what would be KSU losses by 12 and 3 points, respectively.

While always careful about singling out players as favorites, Sproles was one that Snyder did elevate to a pedestal.

Snyder called his 5-foot-7, 180-pound "Tank" a "one of a kind." In Kansas State history, he certainly was.

His career rushing total of 4,979 is 2,161 more than Ell Roberson; his 44 rushing touchdowns are five more than Roberson; his 292-yard game against Louisiana-Lafayette in 2004 is the KSU record; he's the only Wildcat back to ever lead the team in rushing three consecutive seasons; his 24 games of at least 100 yards is 14 more than any other K-State back.

Simply put, the rushing portion of the K-State record book belongs to the Wildcats' No. 43.

Impressive individual numbers? Without question. But Snyder says, "With Darren, it was always about the team. He carried humility in such a unique way. Darren was one who never took his star status for granted. He never looked at himself as being special. He was very selfless."

That is unless K-State was struggling, but even then Sproles always had the team in mind.

"There were times he'd be tugging at my shirt. He wouldn't actually tug, but he was always right beside me saying, 'I'll do it; get on my back and I'll carry you.' That wasn't to promote himself, but to help the team win."

At the press conference following the final game of the 2004 season, Snyder promised that a rededication to the Wildcat Goals of Success would be demanded of every player.

Rumor was that the off-season workouts were tougher than ever before, though Snyder denies the claim other than to say the conditioning period started a little earlier in the day. Sessions initially started at 6 a.m., but if one player missed one of the one-hour workouts, the next workout would start at 5:55 a.m. Another tardy Wildcat would mean a 5:50 start for the entire unit. If the start-time was backed up to 5:30 in the morning, which happened once, then an extra morning session would be added to the next week.

"All it took was six guys out of 90 being late or missing a session and there would be an extra day added," Snyder said. "But other than that, things were pretty consistent with what they had been in the past. The workouts were intense, but they had always been intense. I wanted to see a commitment."

Once the 2005 season started, Snyder heard players saying the right things, but he wondered if every Wildcat truly believed what he was saying.

Season-ending injuries during the month of August to a pair of Wildcat starting linemen—Ryan Schmidt and Michael Frieson—left the line in a lurch, and Snyder felt the team attitude starting to dip.

"When you lose so many potential starters, that can temper some attitudes," Snyder said.

K-State started the season with one significant change, but it didn't last long. Snyder gave the play-calling duties to offensive coordinator Del Miller, giving himself more latitude to focus on sideline duties.

But, "I couldn't deal with it very well. It was like a guy who's used to working 18 hours a day, cutting back to eight. I felt like I was making less of a contribution. It just wasn't a fit. It just wasn't me."

After a 4-1 start, K-State hit the skids, losing to Texas Tech by 29 points and dropping heart-breaking games to Texas A&M, 30-28, and Colorado, 23-20.

Iowa State thumped the Wildcats 45-17, and K-State lost to Nebraska in another close game, 27-25, to end any hopes of postseason play.

Losses by two, three and two in a four week span.

Why? Perhaps it was the lack of discipline to make certain decisions on the field on a consistent basis. There were some choices made on the field that cost K-State the opportunity to win some ballgames.

A play or two going their way and Kansas State would have ended its season with a 7-4 or 8-3 record and an invitation to a bowl game. The team also would have looked forward to 17 or 18 returning starters for the 2006 season.

With the program not finding its way over the hump, Snyder kept constant in his message of it never being the wrong time to do the right thing.

With the team saddled with a 4-6 record following the 27-25 loss at Nebraska, athletics director Tim Weiser remembered Snyder's closing words in his post game message to the team at NU's Memorial Stadium.

"He told the guys to make sure to pick up their towels around their locker, put the trash in the cans, and thank the bus driver for the job he's doing," Weiser said. Pausing, "Now, those are the things K-Staters should be proud about. I'm sure Bill also talked about what did and didn't happen on the field, but what stood out to me were those other things dealing with how you carry yourself. He was equipping these guys to succeed in life."

That was Snyder's message to the team at a time he was in the process of changing his own life's course.

Snyder admits, "That game may have pushed me over the hump to retirement."

Prior to that loss, retirement had been a private though regular consideration.

"It had become an issue," Snyder said.

Entering the 2005 season, Snyder's 17 years (including 2005) at K-State were six more than Dan McCarney's 11-year stay at Iowa State. Heck, add the head coaching tenures at Kansas, Baylor, Texas A&M, Nebraska and Oklahoma State together, and one came up with only 13 collective seasons.

The K-State skipper admitted that years like the 6-6 year in 2001 and the 4-7 mark in 2004 made it truly seem like he had been coaching 40 years.

In August Snyder was charged for another season. Now it was November, and retirement had become a bothersome notion that nudged its way into too many voids in Snyder's day.

"Just wondering whether or not it was the right time? What would be the reasoning behind retiring?" Snyder said. "I always believed that I could get virtually anything corrected. Now I was asking myself about the pros and cons of the position. If not now, when would be the best time to retire?"

On the subject, Snyder never uses the word quit. He has trouble enough saying retire. Normally, he lets the listener fill in the "R" word.

He thought about his family—wife Sharon and kids Sean, Shannon, Meredith, Ross and Whitney—and he thought about the players, his staff of assistants, the fan base, and the ease of transition for the next coach. Snyder knew of his legacy, but he also recognized that there had been 4-7 and 5-6 seasons the last two years.

"It's difficult to replace someone who has had some pretty positive things happen, whether it's in corporate America or athletics," Snyder said. "As the saying goes, the second guy gets the best deal. With that in mind, I thought this would be the best time, following two losing seasons. It wouldn't make it quite as difficult on the incoming coach."

Fair to Bill Snyder? No. A move a little earlier than Bill Snyder would have preferred? Yes, probably.

But, "It's never been about Bill Snyder," Snyder said.

Chapter Thirty-Five
The Decision: 'It's Time'

If you're thinking about retiring and are probably going to do it before too long, maybe not this year, but maybe the next, then it seemed to be appropriate to do what's best for the program and I just thought this was the best time for the program.

— Coach Bill Snyder

Tim Weiser remembers a brief one-on-one conversation with Snyder on the subject of retirement after the 2004 season, and then in July of 2005 there was a private chat that had more to do with what role Snyder might assume within the Wildcat program when he did decide to step aside.

Not another whisper on the subject had taken place until November 13, 2005, the day after the 27-25 loss at Nebraska, which left only a home game against Missouri on the schedule.

Weiser was consoling himself with a trip back to his farm near Great Bend to hunt pheasants.

It was a Sunday about mid-day.

"My cell rings, and it is Coach saying, 'I need to visit with you.' I said, 'I'm on my way.' I knew in my mind what was coming. The phone conversation was no more than 30 seconds."

Snyder said the call was "difficult, but seemingly the right thing to do at the time."

Snyder, Weiser and KSU vice-president Bob Krause met at the on-campus home of President Wefald on Monday morning.

"Bill just said, 'I think we all know why I'm here. It's time,'" Weiser said.

Neither Weiser nor Wefald said they tried to talk the coach out of his decision.

As Wefald said, "He had toiled in the vineyard for 17 years and done what he had done. If it was time for him to have another life, all you could do was say, 'okay.'"

Initially, Snyder wanted to wait on the announcement until the final game against Missouri had been played at KSU Stadium that Saturday.

"It just made sense to me not to have any disruption to the week of preparation," Snyder reasoned.

Weiser knew there would be no way to keep the news private. More importantly, he thought it only fitting that the players knew that they were playing one last time for Coach Snyder, and that the fans of Kansas State would have an opportunity to see him coach one more time.

Thus it was agreed that the weekly Tuesday afternoon press conference would be used for Snyder to announce his retirement.

On the surface, Monday was a normal day in the Vanier Football Complex.

Coaches graded tape, meetings were staged, coaches put together a game plan for the Tigers, players met with their position coaches, and the team practiced.

"I knew what was coming and begged Coach not to make the decision until a week after the Missouri game," said Jim Colbert, one of Snyder's best friends. "I was in Manhattan and went out to practice. I was really hoping he wouldn't say anything.

"He was tighter than a drum during the practice," Colbert said. "He didn't even say hello. He wasn't himself at all."

At the end of the workout, Snyder asked all of the players and coaches to go into the locker room.

"For whatever reason, it hit me right there," said strength and conditioning coach Rod Cole. "I had noticed that Sean had seemed uneasy, and I knew coach was frustrated with the season. It just hit me what was coming."

Surrounded by his Wildcats, coaches, and support staff in the confines of the Wildcat locker room, Snyder quietly said, "After Saturday's game, I'm going to retire."

Those in attendance said that Snyder's lips quivered. His voice broke. His eyes filled with tears.

For one of the few times in his 17 years at the helm, he battled to keep his composure. There was a feeble attempt to crack a joke when Snyder said, "I'm guessing some of you are happy about that."

But no one laughed.

Jaws dropped. Ears heard, but didn't believe.

The visit lasted only three or four minutes, with Snyder reminding them that the rest of the week was not to be about him, but about defeating the University of Missouri.

He reminded his team about all the things he felt were important—the Goals For Success—and hoped that they would retain those without his looking over their shoulder.

After Snyder's departure, defensive coordinator Bob Elliott stepped to the front and challenged the Wildcats to send Snyder out right.

Only family members and the closest of friends, fewer than 10 individuals total, knew of the retirement heading into that Monday evening practice.

"It really wasn't determined that it needed to be made public until later in the day," Snyder said as to why his staff was not told prior to the after-practice meeting. "I would have preferred to tell the coaches and others who were close to me and the program, but there just wasn't a time."

"I had no hint this was coming," Del Miller said. "It came from so far out of left field. No one had an idea. I had told recruits, and I really believed it, that Coach would go until he was in his 70s.

"I still don't believe it," Miller said six weeks after Snyder's retirement.

Tight ends coach Matt Miller said, "We were stunned. We just stood there with blank stares. You had coaches crying. It was a complete punch in the gut to all of us."

Running backs coach Michael Smith said, "I didn't believe what I was hearing. I'm still baffled by it."

Freshman quarterback Allen Evridge said, "When he started to talk, I thought somebody had died."

Past Wildcats were just as stunned when hearing the news the next day.

Former Wildcat center and NFL veteran Quentin Neujahr (1990-93) admitted to crying. Darren Sproles (2001-04) said, "I couldn't believe it. Coach Snyder is always supposed to be the coach at Kansas State."

The rest of the week had Snyder focused on anything and everything but the Missouri game, which finally came on Saturday afternoon.

"That was the longest of all afternoons. I thought I could focus, but my mind wandered all over the place. My mind was going 180 miles an hour prior to the game, and little of it had to do with the game," Snyder said.

He said he thought about past games, former players ... just memories. And, he admitted to silently asking himself: "Am I doing the right thing for the right reason?"

In true Snyder fashion, when the buzzer sounded on KSU's 36-28 win over MU, the coach couldn't help but think "what if?"

"All we needed was one more win to be bowl eligible," he said. "We had all those close games, and all we needed was one more."

Wefald said after the victory, "Knute Rockne would have loved to have had a swan song like this."

And Colbert added, "He's Kansas State's Rockne, for sure."

Chapter Thirty-Six
Questions, Questions, Questions

Did a light bulb go off signaling it was time to retire? No. It was an accumulation of things, but not one particular thing. Was it a year or two earlier than I thought it would be? Maybe, but I believed it was what was best for the program.

— Coach Bill Snyder

Why? When? How come? Borrowing a phrase from Dr. Phil, "What were you thinking?"

"The decision to retire was just a matter of identifying a lot of things in my life, starting with my family, and what was best for the program," Snyder said. "Really, it was nothing more than that."

Winning and losing, was that it? Would a win at Nebraska, followed by one over Missouri, have changed everything?

"A couple more wins? Would winning enough ball games to go to a bowl have delayed the decision? I don't know," Snyder said.

"Was it only the losing? No, that was not the sole reason. We've won a lot more than we've lost, and the future was bright based on the young team we had and the number of first and second-team players returning. If it was just the losing, I was in the profession all these years for the wrong reason. The losing was really not the major factor."

When did you decide to retire? Was there a defining moment?

"I'm not sure. Maybe it was the Nebraska game that pushed me over the hump. I had a feeling the Friday before the Nebraska game, but it was nothing definite."

Did Tim Weiser, President Wefald or anyone else try to talk you out of the decision?

"No, not really," Snyder said. "On the day of the Missouri game, I was sitting in my office 20 minutes prior to kick-off going over tape and the game plan, and Big 12 Commissioner Kevin Weiberg stopped by my office and said, 'Are you sure you can really get away from this?' I wasn't sure how to answer him."

Burn out is a phrase often used with football coaches. Was it burn out?

"I'm not sure what that is, but some day I'd like to sit down with Dick Vermeil (former Kansas City Chiefs coach who once retired from the Philadelphia Eagles because of burn out) and see how he defined that phrase," Snyder said. "But as I understand it, no, it wasn't burn out. It was just time."

Did you ever come close to changing your mind? Did you ever have your hand on the phone ready to call President Wefald and say, "For the first time in my life, I acted hastily. Would you mind if I come back?"

"Come close to changing my mind?" Snyder repeated and took a long pause before answering, "Yes, I may have."

Meaning there has been some regret?

"Am I sorry? No," Snyder quietly said. "But that doesn't mean I might not have that feeling at some point in time."

Is it tougher than ever to get kids today to accept your methods of coaching, to accept your standards through your Goals For Success?

"To a certain degree, yes. But that's painting youngsters with a broad brush, and that's not totally fair," Snyder said. "I will say this, in today's society we have far more followers than supreme leaders. If your base is made up of followers, then you have got to have the right role models in place, and at times, we didn't have enough of them. The pool of role models has become smaller and smaller in recent years.

"Every day the media is deluged with stories on professional athletes who young people look up to. These are our role models, yet they are the ones plagued by narcotic use, alcohol and sexual abuse and a multitude of other social ills."

Did the culture change with today's young people in this era of instant self gratification have an impact on your decision?

"Not entirely. But directing young people is immensely more difficult because we're in a different society than 17 years ago. Young people react, or don't react, far differently than they did 17 years ago.

"We honestly have young players coming to us who have lived in areas where they do not know the difference between right or wrong. Because of that, it is far more difficult to appreciate the values that we have in our program.

"Coaches today are in a difficult profession, but still one where you have the opportunity to impact so many lives in a positive manner," Snyder said. "But in today's society, coaches face a tough question: Is your goal to produce productive young people, or is it wins and losses? For some, that's not an easy choice.

"Most would say why not do both? But we have people in our profession asking themselves, 'Do I promote this set of values or do I win games?' Unfortunately, it's come to that."

At age 66 you often competed against some head coaches half your age. Did you ever feel like you lost touch with today's 18 to 22-year-old athlete?

"No, not at all. I stay very much in tune to the changes in youth and society. That doesn't mean I agree, but I did always understand the wherewithal of our players. And they understood where I was coming from, what my direction was."

Might you coach again someday?

"I haven't thought seriously about that. I just can't envision myself coaching anywhere but Kansas State."

Chapter Thirty-Seven
Family Defines Dad

I've not been the kind of father or husband that I should have been. I'm going to spend some time correcting that.

— Coach Bill Snyder

The words from Bill Snyder, husband and father, hit linebacker-hard, and to his family—wife Sharon and children Sean, Shannon, Meredith, Ross and Whitney—were too harsh.

In the midst of his retirement press conference, Snyder said that his dogged devotion to his Wildcat football family had caused him to neglect his own family.

"We were still in shock over his decision, so I'm not even sure it registered with me," said Shannon, at 34 the second oldest of the five Snyder children. "We were all okay with who he was as a coach and a father. It was touching, but also very hard to know that he felt that way."

Whitney, the youngest at 20, added, "It was touching, but he was definitely being too hard on himself. He's been a great father."

Snyder's personal concern about his life as a father/husband was not totally new. In 1997, he had said, "If I had a regret, it would be that I have five wonderful children and they've all been neglected by me."

His family disagreed then, and still does today.

"Dad has always been there for us," said Meredith. "I can't imagine a more supportive father."

Like everyone else, the Snyder children were caught off guard by their dad's decision.

On Monday, one by one, the coach/father notified his children of his decision.

Sean was first, since his office was only a 10-step walk from his dad's. At around

9 a.m., dad poked his head in his son's office and said, "Need to see you when you get a chance."

The son had a feeling.

"I don't know why, but I knew what it was going to be about," Sean said. "He had not said a thing about it during the season, but for whatever reason, I knew. I honestly just sat at my desk for about 10 minutes to gather myself."

Entering his father's office, Sean found his intuition to be true. "He just said, 'It's time. I'm going to retire.' There seemed to be an ease about him. He seemed comfortable with his decision."

The two talked for about 20 minutes. Sean remembers asking, "Are you sure?" And, "Why are you doing it?" But the answers were typically pretty generic. "I'm ready." And, "It's just time."

At mid-season, Sean said he noticed a slight change in his father. A more "relaxed demeanor," he said. "But I also thought it might be my imagination at work. I just couldn't imagine him retiring. Not yet."

The uniting of Sean and his father took some unique twists and turns.

Sean was just nine at the time of his parent's divorce, and he candidly says he doesn't remember too much about his father in those first nine years.

Ironically, the year after Sean decided to attend the University of Iowa to join his father and be the Hawkeyes' punter, Snyder took the coaching job at Kansas State.

"Dad was concerned about that, but I knew it was too good of an opportunity for him to pass up," Sean said. "But he told me that he would not leave Iowa if I wanted him to stay."

Coach Snyder wanted to make sure that his son gave Iowa a chance, but after redshirting in 1988, he started the first game of the 1989 season. He didn't start again.

Sean transferred to Kansas State in 1990, with hopes of becoming the Wildcats' punter in 1991 after sitting out the NCAA-mandated year for transferring.

He not only won the punting job, he became an All-American punter, averaging 40.5 yards as a junior and a school-record 44.7 yards in his 1992 senior season.

Those numbers could have been even better. One of the hardest things Coach Snyder said he had to do was send player Snyder out on the field a dozen times on a blustery November 21 afternoon at KSU Stadium, where the wind sails along at 20 miles per hour on the calmest of days.

At the time, Sean led the nation in punting and was on track to set an NCAA record for season punting average held by former Iowa punter Reggie Roby, but after a 12-punt afternoon averaging 34.6 yards he lost that title.

"I offered to let Matt Argo punt a few times, but Sean declined, saying it was his job and he wanted to help the team," Snyder recalled. "That day cost him the national punting title. It's not like me to have those types of things bother me, but this time it did."

Sean asked for no favors from his father, and his father offered none in return.

"As a son, you know people are looking to see if you're getting special treatment, but I didn't want that and neither did he," Sean said. "Really, I think it was harder on him than it was me."

To Coach Snyder, it was a blessing. "It's one of the best things to ever happen, to be able to coach your son. But it was tough. I had to watch that I wasn't too hard on him when I'd help him with his punting. Punters are like quarterbacks in that you have to block things out of your mind and go do your job. I was one of the things he had to block out of his mind."

Though he learned of his father's retirement plans that Monday morning, Sean would still have to prepare for the game that Saturday against Missouri.

For Sean Snyder, it was the toughest week of his life.

"When the reality of his retiring hit me, it was extremely challenging," Sean said. "I would be walking down the hall and pass pictures that would bring back memories and my emotions would get the best of me. I would see a picture, and a memory would pop up. Dad and I went through so many great times together ... my emotions were uncontrollable at times."

Game day was no different. Young Snyder had his assistants handle the majority of the operations because, as Sean said, "I simply wasn't functional."

With 15 unanswered points in the fourth quarter, and with Brandon Archer's interception return of 45 yards for a touchdown solidifying the 36-28 win with 1:22 remaining, Sean Snyder breathed a huge sigh of relief.

"Nothing could have felt better than that," Sean said. "To think of dad leaving this place with a loss was just horrifying to me. The way the season had gone, it haunted me all week. The day and the win was what he deserved."

Shannon was next to hear from her father. "He called me at work and asked me to come by at lunch. I went into his office, and he got up and shut the door.

"He said, 'I'm going to retire.'"

Shannon's reply was, "You're going to do what?' Is this a good thing or a bad thing?"

Shannon said her father's reply was, "Don't know, I've never done it before."

"And that was that," Shannon said. "I had just told someone the week before that I thought he would coach until he won a national championship."

Pausing, she continued, "I think we're still in shock. I really don't think it will hit until the start of next season."

Shannon honestly believes that her dad made the decision to retire for the reasons he announced: the betterment of his family, his program, and his school.

"As boring as that sounds, it's just him," Shannon said. "What he says, he means. It's not fluff."

If one wants to draw Shannon's ire, just mention the fact that her dad was football, football, football.

"That's absolutely not true," she insists. "There might have been a time he was focused like that, but I've been back in Manhattan for over a year, and I know during that time his focus has been family, family, family."

Noting that her father calls her every single day of the week, she said, "I don't know how I could be any closer to him. There's not a single subject that I can't talk to him about. He's my confidant."

Shannon broke the myth that you couldn't pry her dad out of the Vanier Football Complex.

"On Sundays, he would break away between meetings to come to one of my daughter Sydney's flag football games," Shannon said. "You talk about two people who are close. Sydney loves her papa, and he's just that, your typical grandpa."

Meredith, Ross and Whitney also got calls that Monday morning and afternoon, prior to Snyder telling the team of his decision that night after practice.

"I just remember hearing him say that it was time and he was ready," said Meredith, who took the call from her Greenville, Texas, home. Meredith is the mother of two—Gavin and Kadin—and owns and operates Scrappin' Shack.

Meredith suffered a broken neck, her fourth, fifth and sixth cervical vertebrae were shattered, and her spinal cord was crushed in a car accident her senior year. It was in February when the family was told that she would likely never walk again, but by May she had improved to the point that she was able to graduate with her Greenville High School class, Sean wheeling her across the stage.

"It was such an emotional moment. The gym was filled and it brought everybody to their feet," Snyder said. "To do that in view of 3,000 people was a large step in overcoming an anxiety and fear. What she accomplished in that amount of time borders on miraculous."

Meredith later graduated from Kansas State University, making the trip across that stage arm-in-arm with her father.

"It was the highlight of my life," said Snyder.

Meredith admits that she's not sure what her recovery from her car accident would have been like without the support of her father, who made weekly trips to visit his daughter while she was in a hospital in Dallas.

To the rumors of being ultra uptight about football, Meredith only laughs.

"When we come to town, my two-year-old is all over his office. Dad loves the way Gavin runs up to him," Meredith said. Laughing, she added, "Dad has all those stacks of tapes in his office, tapes everywhere and I go into a panic state when Gavin looks like he's going to knock them over, but Dad tells him, 'They're just tapes, it's okay.'"

When Meredith was readying to open Scrappin' Shack, it was her father who helped her with a business plan.

"He's like he is with his players," Meredith said. "He tries to guide us to be the best we can be."

And yes, Meredith remembers the constant messages of proper decision making: "You got tired of them, but there was a message there. I wish I would have listened a little closer at times."

"I was shocked," said Ross upon learning of his father's retirement plans. "I thought he'd be coaching until he absolutely couldn't do it any more, until something physically would take him out of the game. I honestly didn't think he would retire until he got that big one, the national championship. I guess because of that, I'm a little disappointed that he's retired. I support his decision, but I wish he was still the coach. That is what he loves and does best."

Like Sean, Ross also spent time as a Wildcat player, seeing action in four games during the historic 1998 season, when he rushed the ball 14 times for a net 43 yards.

Ross, who lives in Kansas City, said, "I loved the game, I loved the Kansas State atmosphere and always wanted to be a part of it. It was a real highlight to be able to play for my dad and to see firsthand how all of the players respected him."

While not a star on the field, some of Ross' favorite memories came after practice and study hall at the Vanier Football Complex.

"I'd get out of those sessions around 10 at night and his light would be the only one on," Ross said. "I'd walk back there and have a short conversation about school and life."

Like his older step-sister, Ross had an early-life scare when colon cancer was diagnosed when he was only 21. Ross was rushed to the Mayo Clinic in Rochester, Minnesota, where a two-inch tumor was removed. He's been in a five-year remission.

"Dad made sure I was in the right hands and would be given the right treatment," Ross said.

Ross wishes he could hear a more definitive, black-and-white answer on the retirement.

Laughing, he said, "Sometimes it's hard to get much of a response out of that man. I still have questions, but there's a respect and you check that stuff at the door when you go home. He's getting questions from enough other people, he sure doesn't need it coming from his own family."

Whitney, a Kansas State student, also was asked to drop by dad's office to hear the news.

"I was shocked, very shocked," said Whitney. "There was some crying, I can tell you that. It was very emotional for me. Dad coaching at K-State is what I had grown up with all my life."

Whitney proudly admits that she's a "daddy's girl," but quickly adds, "I think all of us are daddy's girls."

The youngest of the Snyder daughters says her dad is your "typical dad" when it comes to approving boyfriends or meting out punishment.

"I have an ornery side, just like dad did when he was young, and I can be a little stubborn," Whitney said. Laughing, "There were times we would butt heads pretty good, but I always knew he only wanted what was best for me."

Whitney began riding in equestrian competitions when she was just nine, and ten years later she had developed into one of the elite riders in the nation.

While Snyder enjoyed his daughter's success, he had a sincere appreciation for her work ethic.

"Sharon would drop her off at the stables early in the morning, and we wouldn't pick her up until it was dark," Snyder said. "She worked at it like some coaches I know work at football. But I appreciated the fact that not only was she an accomplished rider, but she worked hard cleaning stables, feeding and grooming the horses and the grunt work you would think a young girl would not want to do."

Whitney says her father has always been supportive, but she's disappointed that she's yet to get him up on one of her horses. "That day will come," she promised.

As for what August and September will bring for her father, Whitney says, "I have no idea. I'm scared, myself. It will definitely be different."

While acknowledging that their father is a bit business-like, the Snyder kids still like to poke fun at some of his ways. Shannon says she caught her dad Christmas shopping in the mall this past year.

"Dad will shop, but you're not going to try on the clothes," Shannon laughed. "It's more, 'What do you want? Get it. Let's go.' He understands that we leave the tags on things so we can take them back."

As for their father being any type of handy man around the house, Sean breaks into laughter and says, "He wouldn't know which end of the hammer to hold and you can quote me on that."

And rumor has it at a recent grandchild's birthday bash at the Snyder home, Coach volunteered to hang the "Happy Birthday" sign across the doorway.

"The 'H' was crammed against the doorway, and all the other letters were bunched together to where there was only string across the rest of the doorway," Ross laughed. "The thing was supposed to be centered, but not with dad."

With each member of the family—Sean, Shannon and Meredith, the daughters of Coach and his first wife, Judy; Ross, the son of Sharon; and Whitney, Coach and Sharon's daughter—there is a unique father-child tie.

Dad Snyder remembers precious times from the kids growing up: rough-housing and playing football in the hallway with Sean; teaching Shannon to swim, catching Meredith, at age 3, as she jumped off the three-meter diving board; mowing a base-ball diamond in a vacant lot beside their home in Sherman; taking Ross fishing in a stream beneath their home in Iowa City, and sledding down that same hill during the winter; games of pool, tennis, ping pong and the gymnastics events staged in the living room of his Iowa City home.

He has fond memories of taking the three older kids—"my hotel rats"—on bowl trips with the Hawkeyes.

"Me with three kids in a hotel," Snyder said with a slight roll of the eyes. "There were some wives of assistant coaches, like Cindy Alvarez, who saved my life. I would lose one of the kids every once in a while in those resorts where we stayed, but they probably knew their way around better than I did."

To be honest, Sean, Shannon and Meredith say they were so young, they can remember little about the home life, but all admit that, yes, dad was pretty singular in focus.

That focus was football.

To a slightly lesser degree, each child has followed suit in having a strong work-ethic and a focused vision in life.

Of each child, Snyder says, "I love them to death."

In addition to having a great group of kids, Snyder is equally blessed with a won-derful wife. Sharon Snyder didn't know until the Sunday night prior to the retire-ment announcement, but provided the support her husband needed to make such a monumental decision.

Snyder said, "She was a wonderful sounding board. She listened, and just wanted to make sure that I was sure this was the right decision."

Sharon Snyder has been in the background during the last 17 years, living a semi-solo life from the opening of fall camp in August through the off-season, recruiting and spring football in April.

"Being the wife of a coach can be a lonely life," admitted Coach Snyder. "I don't know if there's a model for a perfect coach's wife, but the important thing is for her to be herself."

Along with motherly duties, Sharon busies herself with university organizations such as Friends of the Library, the Beach Museum, the University Gardens, and the equestrian board, plus Manhattan community activities such as the art's council.

In addition, she serves as hostess in the press box and organizes functions for the wives of coaches as well as the monthly family dinners at the Vanier Football Complex.

"She has done a great job of being a fulltime mother, plus staying active in the community, so she has developed her own identity," Snyder said. "Especially in our sport where you are in the public eye so much, if you get caught up in your own ego, it can drive a wedge between you. She has not allowed that to happen, and I love her for it."

FAREWELL TO THE FANS

Dear fans, friends, family and all associates with Kansas State University football:

It is often said that "The joy is in the journey." For me it has been the relationships along the way. I have been truly blessed to have had so many wonderful people in my life.

Coaching is problematic. As I've often said, if we haven't dealt with a problem yet today, hang on to your hat, one will appear shortly. For me, it has been the wonderful people, who along the way softened the burdens of the day to day issues that make this profession often times very trying.

Included in my journey has been the process of growing up and maturing and having the good fortune of sharing my life with so many who truly cared and who truly wanted to make my life better, and did.

I will always cherish and have a deep heartfelt gratitude for:

• My mother and grandparents for their sacrifices, their nurturing, their love, and their gift of values which have guided me throughout my life.

• Lafayette High School coaches Richard Shrout, Jerry Hampton and vice-principal Basil Hohen; William Jewell coaches Norris Patterson, Jim Nelson and Darryl Gourley ... for their patience and reinforcement of life's values and for truly caring for me as a person.

• Coaches Richard Roda and Jerry Brown (Gallatin High School); coaches Marv Dennis, Don Dutcher and Jerry Dougherty, and vice-principal Bartley Sims (Indio High School); coaches Ed Bain, Bob Osborne, and Jerry Sedoo (Foothills High School), who gave me opportunities and guidance and genuine friendship during my high school coaching career.

• Dr. Robert Mason, Ralph McCord, Vance Morris and Larry Kramer of Austin College for providing me with my initial fulltime college coaching experience and for their caring and lasting friendships.

• Hayden Fry and the many excellent coaches at North Texas State and the University of Iowa, who molded my philosophies and concepts about coaching at the Division I level, and who reinforced my spirit and supported me during a difficult time in my life.

• Kansas State athletic director Steve Miller for convincing me that Kansas State was right for me, for his friendship over the years and for his relentless support. It could not have been done without him.

• Current K-State athletic director Tim Weiser for trusting and supporting my judgement until the end.

• Kansas State associate athletic director Jim Epps. Were it not for his insight, I would never have come to Kansas State.

• Kansas State President Jon Wefald and vice-president Bob Krause for accepting me at Kansas State; for their patience, their friendship, and for lighting a path when darkness would set in.

• The many excellent young players who through their belief, perseverance, hard work and commitment gave us all the opportunity to experience what so many claim to be "the greatest turnaround in college football history."

• The Kansas State assistant coaches for putting up with me, for caring, for their unbelievable hard work, for being effective teachers, for their coaching expertise which always put us in a position to be successful, and for being loyal K-Staters.

• The countless loyal and caring Kansas State fans throughout the world (especially the 13,000 who were there in the beginning and those 50,000 who remained in their seats at the conclusion of our final game of 2005 to recognize me and my family) for absolutely amazing support, love and friendship through these past 17 years. There are no better fans anywhere in college football.

• Tom and Gay Ross, Max and Lynn Urick, Earl and Edna Yoder, and Ron Ameche from Iowa; Jack and Donna Vanier, Jim and Marsha Colbert, Ernie and Bonnie Barrett, Howard and Patty Sherwood and so many others from Kansas State; L.A. Nelson from North Texas State ... for their undying and sincere personal friendships, for caring in a very special way; for their generous and unselfish support and for always being there for me and my family.

• A special thanks to the Ross', the Vaniers, and the Krauses for coming to Dallas to see Meredith at the hospital shortly after her accident.

• And my family who made it all possible, who gave me strength in the darkest of times; whose love never waivered; who defined the word "patience" with me; who were always there with a gentle word, and who made unbelievable sacrifices on my behalf. You are the true loves of my life.

Sincerely,
Coach Bill Snyder

THE ALL-SNYDER TEAM

Position-by-position, here's the All-Snyder team as chosen by Coach Snyder.

OFFENSE

QB — Michael Bishop, 1997-1998 ... great competitor ... aggressive, strong runner ... passion for winning and for the game ... great self-confidence ... strong arm

RB — Darren Sproles, 2001-2004 ... humble-team player ... always 100 percent effort ... gifted feet ... passion for playing ... great person ... so explosive

RB — Eric Hickson, 1994-95; 1997-98 ... team leader ... played hard ... good balance ... competitor ... good person . . . he cared

FB — Rock Cartwright, 2001-02 ...played beyond expectations ... explosive ... ability to stay on his feet ... competitor .. undersized but highly respected by teammates

WR — Kevin Lockett, 1993-1996 ... excellent athlete ... made difficult catches look easy ... excellent leadership ... set the example on and off the field

WR — Michael Smith, 1988-1989 ...great competitor ... played hard ... loved the game ... excellent hands ... made the hard catches ... good leadership

C — Quentin Neujahr, 1990-1993 ... leadership ... intelligent player ... team player … practiced hard ... studied the game

OG — Nick Leckey, 2000-2003 ... good leader ... practiced hard ... great understanding of our offense ... set example on and off the field . . . a great person

OG — Ryan Lilja, 2002-2003 ... under-rated player ... played to his maximum capabilities through hard work and great focus on fundamentals ... team player

OT — Todd Weiner, 1996-1997 ...grew into position by gaining nearly 100 pounds ... intelligent player ... great technique ... set example on and off the field ... team player

OT — Ryan Young, 1996-1998 . . . wonderful person ... good athlete for his size ... team player .. .quiet leader ... set example on and off the field

TE — Justin Swift, 1996-1998 ... physical tight end ... good hands ... effective blocker ... team player

DEFENSE

DE — Darren Howard, 1996-1999 ... athletic ... great range ... great anticipation ... sense for the game

DE — Monty Beisel, 1997-2000 ...fundamentally strong ... extremely hard worker . . . athletic at his position

DT — Tim Colston, 1992-1995 ... studied the game ... intelligent player ... made plays mentally ... played hard ... gifted artist

DT — Mario Fatafehi, 1999-2000 ... great strength and leverage . . . played hard ... relentless pursuit ... great toughness ... had a love for the game

LB — Ben Leber, 1998-2001 ... smart player ... understood his position better than most ... fundamentally sound ... used hands well . . . excellent person

LB — Mark Simoneau, 1996-1999 ... great knowledge of the game ... played error-free ... practiced as hard as he played ... set great examples on and off the field ... loved the game . . . great role model

LB — Brooks Barta, 1989-1992 ... silent leadership ... always set the example ... always knew where to be and how best to get there ... great team player

DB — Terence Newman, 1999-2002 ... great example of the value of sheer speed ... great desire to win ... played on all units ... great improvement throughout career

DB — Chris Canty, 1994-1996 ... athletic ... great anticipation ... played both ways . . . played 119 snaps against Texas Tech

DB — Jaime Mendez, 1990-1993 ... great competitor ... team player ... active leader and worker ... set example on and off the field

DB — Lamar Chapman, 1996-1999 ... great range ... good leadership ... intelligent player

DB — Jon McGraw, 1998-01 . . . great worker ... great leader ... great person ... great improvement throughout career ... great feel for the game

SPECIALISTS

P — Sean Snyder, 1991-1992 ... team person ... hard worker ... technique sound ... did the right things on and off the field . . . great son, father and husband

PK — Martin Gramatica, 1994-95; 1997-98 ...great technique ... toughness ... great timing ... good person

PR — David Allen, 1997-2000 ... versatile ... deceptive speed ... excellent hands ... big-play maker

KR — Andre Coleman 1990-1993 ... very fluid ... deceptive speed ... big-play maker . . . versatile

HONORABLE MENTION
OFFENSE

QB — Ell Roberson, 2000-03; Jonathan Beasley, 1996-00; Chad May, 1993-94

RB — Josh Scobey, 2000-01; J.J. Smith, 1991-94; Eric Gallon, 1989-92

FB — Brian Goolsby, 1995-98

WR — Quincy Morgan, 1999-00; Darnell McDonald, 1997-98; James Terry, 2002-2003; Mitch Running, 1992-95

OL — Randall Cummins, 1998-00; Barrett Brooks, 1991-94; Kendyl Jacox, 1994-97; Andy Eby, 1999-01; Jason Johnson, 1993-96

TE — Shad Meier, 1997-00

DEFENSE

DE — Nyle Wiren, 1993-96; Chris Johnson, 1997-00

DT — Tank Reese, 2001-02; Damion McIntosh, 1996-99

LB — Josh Buhl, 2000-03; Travis Ochs, 1995-98; Jeff Kelly, 1997-98; Percell Gaskins, 1993-95; Terry Pierce, 2000-02

DB — Jarrod Cooper, 1997-00; Rashad Washington, 2000-03; Jerametrius Butler, 1998-00; Dyshod Carter, 1997-00; Joe Gordon, 1993-96

SPECIALISTS

P — James Garcia, 1995-98

PK — Jamie Rheem, 2001-04

PR — Aaron Lockett, 1998-01

KR — Terence Newman, 1999-02

BILL SNYDER COACHING HONORS

1990 Co-Big Eight Coach of the Year, Big Eight Coaches

1990 Big Eight Coach of the Year, *Associated Press*

1991 Co-Big Eight Coach of the Year, Big Eight Coaches

1991 Big Eight Coach of the Year, *Associated Press*

1991 National Coach of the Year, *ESPN*

1992 Co-Head Coach Blue-Gray Game

1993 *Kodak/AFCA* District Coach of the Year

1993 Semifinalist for Football News National Coach of the Year

1993 Finalist for *FWAA*/Bear Bryant National Coach of the Year

1993 Finalist for *Kodak/AFCA* National Coach of the Year

1993 Big Eight Coach of the Year, Big Eight

1994 National Coach of the Year, *CNN*

1995 East-West Shrine Game Coach

1995 Finalist for Football News National Coach of the Year

1995 Finalist for *FWAA*/Bear Bryant National Coach of the Year

1996 Big 12 Coach of the Year, *Houston Chronicle*

1997 Big 12 Coach of the Year, *Kansas City Star*

1998 East-West Shrine Game Coach

1998 Big 12 Coach of the Year, *Kansas City Star*

1998 Big 12 Coach of the Year, *Associated Press*

1998 Big 12 Coach of the Year, Big 12 Coaches

1998 *AFCA/GTE* Regional Coach of the Year (Region 4)

1998 Football News National Coach of the Year Award finalist

1998 Eddie Robinson Coach of the Year finalist

1998 Bobby Dodd Foundation National Coach of the Year

1998 *Associated Press* National Coach of the Year

1998 Walter Camp Foundation Coach of the Year

1998 *FWAA*/Bear Bryant National Coach of the Year

1999 *AFCA/GTE* Regional Coach of the Year (Region 4)

1999 *ESPN*/Home Depot College Football Coach of the Decade, finalist

2002 Big 12 Coach of the Year, Big 12 Coaches

2003 Big 12 Coach of the Year, *Fort Worth Star-Telegram*, ESPN.com

I'm not sure how I want to be remembered . . . perhaps as I am and as I have been: someone who truly cared about, and was extremely loyal to the people of Manhattan and Kansas State, and a person who wanted the very best for the young people he worked with as coach.

— Coach Bill Snyder